Out On A Whim

Also by Gerald Nachman

PLAYING HOUSE

Out On A Whim

SOME VERY CLOSE BRUSHES WITH LIFE

Gerald Nachman

Doubleday & Company, Inc.
Garden City, New York
1983

Library of Congress Cataloging in Publication Data

Nachman, Gerald.
Out on a whim.

I. Title.
PN6162.N28 1983 814'.54
ISBN 0-385-12340-X
Library of Congress Catalog Card Number: 82-9412

Sections of this book have previously appeared in: San Jose *Mercury,* 1962; New York *Times,* 1969; New York *Daily News,* 1973, 1974, 1975, 1976, 1977, 1978, 1979; San Francisco *Chronicle,* 1979, 1980, 1981, 1982; *Esquire,* December 1976; *Newsweek,* April 5, 1976, April 18, 1977, March 29, 1982; *Travel & Leisure,* September 1977, December 1978.

For my mother,
the best idea I've ever had

To be as short-winded as possible, various and long overdue thank-you notes to Mike O'Neill, former editor of the New York *Daily News,* where most of these pieces were allowed to run originally, for giving the column a chance; to Shew Hagerty, who edited it with a wary but appreciative eye; to Leah Garchik, for acting as chief winnower and enthusiast; to Randie and Cathy Poe, Judy Gingold, Morrie Bobrow, Mary McGeachy, Mike Johnson, David Rubin, Tina Press, Rodi Shemeta Ludlum, Steve Rubenstein, Laura Merlo, Asher Rubin, Bob MacKenzie, Casey MacKenzie, Maggie Gerson and Bill German, for making me want to please them; to Linda Festa, for always laughing in the right places; and, first and last, to the late Robert Benchley, who still sets an impossible but inspiring pace.

Contents

Introduction

(Or, A Note on the Type in This Book)

Much as I hate to disturb a noble old literary tradition, this book needs no introduction. There is grave doubt in some circles whether it is even a book. What it is—and I want to be quite frank and up-front about this—is a lot of random, unrelated columns. Sooner or later, you were bound to find it out on your own.

The real purpose of introducing a collection of assorted columns is to pull the wool (cloth, in this case) over the eyes of unsuspecting readers by pretending that the pieces within have a common thread running through them; I'm afraid nothing could be further from the truth.

The sorry fact of the case is that *none* of these columns and articles bears even the remotest relationship to any other, except of course that they were all written by the same fine young chap. Of course, that's the idea of a collection. Granted, it isn't much of an idea, but it's the best I've got.

Instead, let's look on the positive side and point out that, in a sense, it's actually a *plus* that each and every one of these little gems is so very different from the others. Just like snowflakes; or perhaps thumbprints.

This is what distinguishes a collection from the ordinary novel or history of Western Man, where everything has to relate to everything else and must be neatly tied up at the end, leaving the reader satisfied and feeling quite pleased with himself at having finally finished a real book.

In a batch of willy-nilly pieces such as this, however, the reader need never worry about keeping all the characters straight in his head or remembering whether the Age of Reason comes before or after the Age of Consent.

It's a terrific bonus that nothing in these pages follows in any order whatever. I even recommend that the book (for lack of a better term) be read from the middle, working carefully forward and backward at the same time, a technique that should make it seem as little like reading as possible, almost like scanning a menu.

By reading the pieces in this helter-skelter fashion, you'll never know exactly how much more there is left to plow through, which ought to brighten your mood considerably. The reader is encouraged to throw caution to the winds and start the book anyplace that appeals to him—with, naturally, the implicit understanding that he will return at some early date and read the rest of it.

To do otherwise is not merely rude but breaks a gentleman's agreement with the author (I'm fairly tolerant but I do have some standards). Skimming an occasional paragraph is understandable, but the wholesale skipping of twenty-five or more pages at a clip is frowned on in even the most lenient literary circles.

Another advantage not to be sneezed at in a hodgepodge like this is that such a collection, by its very nature, isn't likely to be hotly discussed at dinner parties. Thus the reader is under no obligation to (a) recall anything he reads in here ever again or (b) form a strong well-reasoned opinion of it. In brief, this book, aside from being a wise choice for either the shut-in or the gadabout, requires no retentive memory at all.

What's more, there's not a single fact in it. I've been over each column several times, along with my researcher, and we've done our best to delete anything that even approximates a fact. Now and then, a date or the name of a treaty may have snuck past us if we were looking the other way or fooling around on the couch. But I can virtually guarantee that the book you hold is 99 percent fact-free.

Some serious readers of the column are under a mistaken impression that I do a certain amount of what they call "research" prior to writing. If someone disagrees with something I've said, he or she will send an outraged letter demanding to know where I get my "facts." So far as I know, I have no facts. All my research is done after the columns are safely written and have gone to press. I'm able to verify this.

When I began as a boy reporter, once in a while I was forced to use a few facts, but it never quite worked out. All the really best columnists try to keep their facts to a minimum, so that nothing comes between the writer's ego and the reader; it's a basic rule of journalism. Political pundits and humor columnists are the most scrupulous of all about this.

Just as there are no real facts to fret about, there are also no lengthy descriptive passages, which in even the very finest novels have a way of holding things up. Just when you can't wait to see whether Daisy Miller is going to run off with Count Vronsky the author will step in and do thirty minutes on how her cottage looks with the sunlight slanting on it in late October. This is always quite nicely rendered, and I wish there had been a way to work it into some columns, but I can promise that you won't find a single description of a cottage in the autumn twilight. Maybe next time.

Let me confess, however, that I've knuckled under to outside pressures and peppered the book with as much sex as I have at my command. *You* may not be shocked, but it's the best I could do. You may also be disappointed to find no violence or car chases at all. In the first draft, I attempted a gruesome scene in which several young nurses were left squirming on butcher blocks, but I took it out at the last minute, feeling that it slowed down the narrative.

As long as I've brought it up, I also probably should admit that there's no actual narrative *in* the book, per se, so there's nothing to be speeded up—yet another big plus. This daring literary technique is only one of several such innovations in the collection. Another typical inventive touch is that the book is not couched in the Third Person Famous, as in the case of Norman Mailer or Gay Talese. I'm a Capricorn myself, but you won't find me flaunting it all over the place, like Mr. Aquarius there, and nowhere inside do I refer to myself as "Gay Talese," sorely tempted though I was. This collection is nothing if not modest and unassuming.

Another positive (and I like to think devilishly clever) device is that I've chosen not to mix fact and fiction into a boldly imaginative "faction"-al goulash. This took some restraint, but I finally decided against throwing in, just for the hell of it, Harry Thaw, Babe Ruth, Diamond Lil, Bronko Nagurski, Leo Tolstoy, Marilyn Monroe, James McNeil Whistler, F. Scott Fitzgerald, Ty Cobb, Isadora Duncan, Enrico Fermi, Grace Coolidge and Jimmy Durante.

Many of these famous figures cried out to be included, but I stuck to my guns. (As I told Billy the Kid, "Look, pal, I'm the hero of this thing. If you want to be a mythic character, go find your own publisher.")

Many of the above people played a crucial part in my growing up, and I was anxious to use them in some way (or at least their photographs), but in the end I felt that combining the traits of, say, Samuel Gompers and Uncle Remus might lead the reader to expect more of the book than even I could quite deliver. If you should find somebody like Calamity Jane or Billy Sunday wandering aimlessly through these pages, it's entirely coincidental and not to boost sales.

One last confession: This book is completely autobiographical. The central character, though thinly disguised as "I" or "Nachman," is based entirely on the author (and a pretty good likeness it is, too); certain liberties were taken with the jacket picture, however. The jacket is mine but the handkerchief belongs to the photographer.

Gerald Nachman

The Dirty Parts

DO YOU ENJOY SEXUAL QUERIES?

SOMEONE HAS TAKEN a survey of male sexual attitudes but neglected to ask for mine, assuming I don't have any, so I've taken my own little poll—the Nachman Survey of Sexuality & Surrounding Countryside—with the following smarmy results:

—The average male is "turned off" by a woman who asks him to make the bed after making love.

—More men enjoy sex nude than fully clothed, contrary to prevailing female beliefs.

—Some 78 percent of men interviewed dislike women who indulge in sex while reading *The Hite Report.*

—Of men between the ages of 14 and 89, 64.3 percent are not interested in foreplay but are too shy to tell their partners.

—Twice as many men would as soon read the paper as hold hands.

—Some 47 percent of men questioned enjoy contemplating sex more than sex itself.

—Nearly 16 percent of all husbands do not know what sex is, but two thirds indicated an interest in "trying anything once."

—Of the men interviewed, 99.7 percent over the age of 40 stated that their primary interest in women under 23 was their intelligence.

—Exactly half the men queried had "no idea" how to please a woman aside from buying expensive jewelry and furs. Said one 42-year-old attorney: "These dames are never satisfied."

—At least 77.5 percent of all men admitted to having fantasies involving two or more women, and 96 percent confessed to having recurrent fantasies involving one woman or less.

—Of the men who had not "been with" a woman until the age

of 21, 78 percent found the experience "weird" and "dehumanizing."

–Some 64 percent of men surveyed were in favor of women wearing lipstick and makeup, but 41.1 percent professed to being "disgusted" by body hair, especially handlebar mustaches, beards and muttonchops.

–Of the men questioned, 48.4 percent said they had "little or no" interest in "fondling" or "talking" before dinner; 63 percent said they had been introduced to "hugging" by their wives.

–Four fifths of all husbands interviewed admitted to a lack of understanding of the woman's role in the sex act, but all except five said they were "delighted" to hear she had one. As one Minnesota stockbroker put it: "The more the merrier."

–57.2 percent of the men had no knowledge that the Sex Act of 1981 had been ratified.

–Some 33 percent of the men studied look forward to having sex with "as many women as possible," but 91.8 percent told interviewers they would settle for one a year. (Among female pollsters, 74 percent reported being mauled by interviewees.)

–The survey found 46.5 percent of all men believe that "how a woman looks in her nightie" plays a significant part in sexual compatibility. In 75 percent of the cases, flannel long johns were cited as a leading cause of male frigidity.

–An overwhelming number of men (83 percent) say they prefer sex in the dark but most were not against using 25-watt bulbs "for variety"; 91 percent had never made love before sundown, regarding it as either "nasty" (51 percent) or "unmasculine" (38.9 percent). Another 14 percent said they had experimented with "daylight sex" once or twice but found the experience "somehow shady" or "too Italian."

–97.4 percent of the men interviewed claim to indulge in sex "fairly regularly" (i.e., between fifteen and twenty times a week).

–Most men studied had "no idea" what they like best about sex, but 79.6 percent mentioned "talking it over later with the boys" (or "replay").

–At least 94.5 percent of the men surveyed said they are "stimulated" by women in tight clothing; some 46 percent believe that if the woman is "pretty" it "definitely helps."

–Of the men who have visited a prostitute, or "floozie," two thirds were "depressed" by the sparseness of the woman's room and general lack of "tasteful furnishings." Men who did not return gave as their main reason the fact that the hooker "would not get under the covers."

–Of the men who admitted to extramarital relationships, 18 percent revealed the affairs ended in "outright sex"; the remaining 82 percent of the liaisons culminated in espresso and chocolate mousse.

–Although women usually mention men's "eyes" or "hands" as important sexual attractions, 93 percent of the men questioned singled out a woman's "entire body" as ranking high on the list of "desirable physical traits." "Eyes" came in next, followed by "toes," and "hands" placed twenty-third, well below "arms."

GROUP SEX LEFT ME COLD

THERE SEEMS TO BE a sudden trend away from group sex and a return to those old-time "one-to-one relationships," which were good enough for Grandma and Grandpa.

To be frank, all this group sex was starting to grind me down. When it began, I was six feet tall and now I'm down to five-nine in my stocking feet (or five-ten in Muk-Luks).

Lately, my work has suffered, for I've been coming in around noon. It's tough to tear yourself away from the group and, of course, not everyone wants to leave at once. In my gang, there has to be at least a two-thirds majority in favor of going home. This causes plenty of bickering between couples, believe me.

There's always a guy who says, "Hey, I just got here!" or some gal who doesn't want to leave no matter how late it is. The wives are forever saying, "Honey, let's just stay another few minutes."

At first, I didn't mind group sex. What I liked was the anonymity. You could lose yourself in the crowd and there wasn't much chance of bumping into someone in your family. It was a lot like New York.

After a while, it got to be too impersonal for me. I'm fine in a group of, say ten or twelve, but more than a dozen or so strangers causes me to go over in a corner and pout. What I like best is having only a few couples in at a time—that way, you really get to know each other. In a big crowd, everyone just starts talking at once.

The first problem we had in group sex out where I live was trying to decide whose home to meet at. Nothing is more inhibiting in group sex than a bunch of rowdy kids and strange dogs galloping all over the place.

We couldn't find anyone who had a big enough living room. At the get-acquainted dance, we all agreed that if you're going to indulge in group sex, it's silly to be cramped in someone's studio apartment. As my mailman said, "Let's do this thing right or not at all."

That meant finding someone nearby with a roomy place who didn't mind a few cigar butts and coffee stains. Oddly enough, more cigar smoking and coffee drinking goes on in group sex sessions than you read about; it's rarely reported in the press.

By the way, it's tough to find somebody who'll volunteer to get up from your group and plug in the coffee. People always want to start on the sexy stuff right away; nobody's willing to put on the coffee or throw together a few sandwiches.

Then there's the wear and tear on the carpet. You can't just roll up a rug and let people sit on a cold floor. We tried it, but everyone squawked about the splinters and complained that the hard wooden floor was causing their back to kick up.

You have an idea what multiple sex is like if you've ever eaten in a Japanese restaurant with your legs folded under you and no back support. Group sex isn't quite as painful as a four-course Japanese meal (at least there aren't any paper slippers to put on) but it's bad enough!

Finally, there's the problem (rarely encountered in one-on-one sex) of when to start the actual "activity period," as it's termed. We tried a kitchen timer, but it took some of the spontaneity out of things. Then we hit on the idea of having one person stand up on a couch and shout, "Ready! Get set! *Go!*"

Our only trouble here was that many folks didn't know exactly what to do at the signal to Go. To get people over that awkward moment, we had everyone turn to the person on his or her right and shake hands. It broke the ice right away.

INSPECTOR MAIGRET ALWAYS GETS HIS WOMAN

GOSSIP COLUMNIST Walter Scott confirms a report that mystery writer Georges Simenon had love affairs with 10,000 women after the age of 13—in addition to 400 books, two wives and several short stories.

It is unseemly of me to ask for more details, but I demand to know how Simenon arrived at that figure of 10,000. I imagine that after six or seven thousand affairs you would tend to lose count, so we must assume M. Simenon kept a score pad by his bedside.

Ten thousand lovers in 61 years breaks down to 163.9 women per year, according to my pocket calculator, or roughly one love affair every other day. This is pretty impressive, even by French standards. Simenon was the McDonald's of romance.

Frank Harris, if I recall, grossed something like 10,000 affairs each year, and Casanova simply ran out of girls. These figures, by the way, are not thrown about recklessly; they have been confirmed by the International Institute for Romantic Dalliances, Flings, Liaisons and One-Night Stands, located in Zurich.

Simenon's revelation appeared in a Zurich paper, *Die Tat,* instantly depressing men around the world—writers especially. Casual remarks like this only further the myth that writers are sexual acrobats, which slows up the creative process more than usual.

The day I read that Simenon had made love to 10,000 women, I got very little work done. Not only was I discouraged by the man's incredible luck, I was even more disturbed to hear he had also managed to turn out 400 mysteries while skipping from boudoir to boudoir.

Even if Simenon had had only 2,500 love affairs in his lifetime and written but fifty books, I'd be overwhelmed with envy. Imagine how many novels he could have finished if he'd been monogamous all those years. Simenon easily might have written 10,000 mysteries and *still* gone to bed with 400 women, nothing to sneeze at either.

Probably Georges had to make a difficult choice early in his career—whether to chase every skirt in Europe or buckle down to work. Of course, he got a nice early start at 13 and for all we know already had polished off 9,000 affairs by the time he was 20.

Or perhaps he had ten or fifteen amours going simultaneously. He even may have hopped into the sack with a dozen women a night, simply to keep his average intact.

We really need more details before this 10,000 total can be verified. I'm not willing to let a figure like that just lie there, unchecked and pulsating. I want an accurate accounting by some reputable firm, such as Price Waterhouse. The combination of male chauvinism and French libido can lead to statistics like 10,000 women in no time.

I'd also like to learn what Simenon's best year was, and his worst. In 1947, say, he may have made love to 3,745 women and then had five years in which he did little more than get slapped 18,000 times.

This brings up the question of how many times Simenon "struck out," as they say in France. For every affair, after all, surely he had two or three that ended with a peck on the cheek at the front door. (Knowing men, I suspect he included these as "love affairs," hoping to pad his grand total a bit.)

Of course, a man with Simenon's experience would be able to sense within two or three seconds how well he was going to do. If you're averaging one new affair every two days, you can't waste a lot of time with women who only want to be "good friends."

It must have taken nerve for a girl to tell a rogue like Simenon: "Gee, Georges, you're a sweet guy but I just don't—well, think of you *that* way. Anytime you care to have lunch, though . . ." A man with his reputation, I suspect, is not interested in just dancing close.

According to *The Book of Lists,* Brigitte Bardot had 4,980 lovers between the ages of 20 and 40, making her a shoo-in to overtake Simenon by the time she's 61. Brigitte has 17 years left to add those necessary 5,021 lovers. Neither of them is likely to surpass King Ibn Saud, however, who is said to have had sexual relations with three women a night from the time he was 11 until his death at 76, or a total of 66,795 relationships (not all of them, I suspect, meaningful).

You wonder what sort of a line Simenon used. All the gossip item reveals is a Simenon quote: "I contend that one knows a woman only after he has slept with her, and I wanted to know women." It sounds pretty corny to me, but it's certainly worth a try.

INSIDE THE PRIM PORN RACKET

DESPITE RECENT CRACKDOWNS on pornography, blatant examples of it thrive openly, eluding police, politicians and even the public, which chooses to look the other way.

This leaves only me and my staff to blow the whistle on "Our Hidden Pornographers" (last in a series of one article).

It's easy enough to lock up peep-show operators, smut peddlers and massage parlor merchants, but what concerns me are the more obvious obscenities now flooding the public—things like *Seventeen* magazine, the yoga lady on TV and slithery girls' legs on pantyhose packages.

Such items are displayed prominently in supermarkets across the country, within easy reach of not only the children, but the fathers. Speaking of which, what is to be done about underage purveyors of cheap thrills?

Underwear sections of department store fashion brochures, slyly slipped into family newspapers on Sunday, are a sea of brazen hussies in corsets, see-through bras and bathrobes, corrupting the morals of men found slavering in the kitchen over ads for "Warner's Better Bottoms."

Hustler has had it. What now trouble Cincinnati district attorneys are *Cosmopolitan,* with its lurid covers of flaming women and randy headlines on how to please your man in a hammock, and *Mademoiselle*'s College Issue, apple-core pornography sold under the counter to men who haven't been near a campus since 1954.

Those who have peeped inside these "back to school" annuals are well aware of the rampant lust within, as innocent co-eds cavort next to ivied walls in pleated skirts, ribbed sweaters, filmy blouses and mesh T-shirts. Where are these girls' parents?

Marilyn Chambers and Seka are languishing in limbo, unlike such vixens glimpsed on "Wide World of Sports" as Nellie Kim executing a shameless double back flip on the side horse or scantily clad figure skaters making indecent leaps and whirls. Then, too, there are those scarlet sunburned foxes who splash through *Sports Illustrated*'s summer swimwear issue.

Most salacious of all, perhaps, is that crudely suggestive babe in red tights on PBS's yoga show, plus her graphic cohorts on the women's pages—the exercise girls who flail about wildly, leaving little to readers' imaginations.

It's no secret that "Charlie's Angels" is pretty hot stuff, but Shelley Hack is an old *Esquire* cartoon compared to some of the more lascivious network correspondents (Linda Ellerbee, Charlayne Hunter-Gault, Lynn Sherr) with their come-hither looks and saucy voice-overs.

TV is a veritable slag heap of hidden porn, from gamy shows like "Family Feud" to commercials that make your eyes pop—those vamps in the Underalls ad or that snapping-eyed seductress who licks Pillsbury frosting off her finger and winks.

Wherever you go, there is veiled pornography waiting to be

unveiled. Doesn't the post office subscribe to those *McCall's* sewing catalogues? Don't federal agents in Wichita read *Apartment 3-G* or *Backstage?* Isn't anyone in Memphis aware of what goes on at the ballet, night after night, between Nureyev and his partners? The simulated sex fairly sizzles in *Petrouchka.*

Written obscenity is wide open in the back pages of *The New York Review of Books,* whose personal ads are rife with such raw, unbridled passion as: "Warm, sensuous 'been around' lady in late 40s seeks man who knows a 'good woman' when he meets her, to share long walks in country and in-depth fireside talks."

All these classifieds can curl your hair, all right: "Submissive male Mahler-lover with interest in Saul Bellow and batik wants to 'get it on' with similar femme who realizes a deep relationship need not be binding."

Friends, there is no end to the slime that is all around us, if only the cops and the public will open their eyes—and I haven't even bothered to mention the Junior Miss America Pageant. Disgusting.

CAN THIS MARRIAGE BE RUINED?

AT A DINNER party the other night, a gossipy lady leaned over her mushroom soup and asked if I'd heard about Ned and Norma Darling.

"No—what?" I asked.

"Sh-h-h-h!" she hushed. "Nobody's supposed to know yet, but I hear the Darlings have just renewed their marital vows."

"You're kidding!" I said, dropping a butter knife. "You mean they're still—"

"Yep," she said. "Wedsville. It isn't official that they've decided not to split, so don't tell anyone, but I have it on very good authority that Ned and Norma are remaining married."

"I'll be darned," I said, "and they always *seemed* like such a bad match. I can't believe that, after twenty-five years, the Darlings are not about to divorce. I think that's the fifth couple I've heard about this month that's still together. It's almost an epidemic!"

"It seemed to happen just like that," said the woman. "One day they were celebrating their silver anniversary and the next day they decided to keep living as man and wife. It was a real shock to everybody."

"Well, I'm not too surprised," I said. "Ned and Norma have been getting along for years and years. I hate to say so, but I saw it all coming."

"Gee, I must be blind," said the lady at the party. "The Darlings appeared to be ideally unsuited for each other."

"Their happiness was always apparent to me," I said. "The way they'd sneak off on weekends together and hold hands in public. You can't keep on like that and expect things to go wrong. Sooner or later, it was inevitable that something had to give, and in this case it was misery."

I whispered to her, "Of course, I'd heard all the rumors for years, so I was prepared for something like this."

"What sort of rumors?" she asked me, her eyes widening.

"Oh, the usual things: You know–Ned fooling around in the kitchen, helping out, and Norma understanding him. Brag, brag, brag. They had bliss written all over them."

"They have two kids, too, you know," said the woman. "That's the nicest part."

"I always worry about the kids in a situation like this," I remarked. "Growing up in such happy surroundings can give children a distorted view of what marriage is like. They may suffer later on."

"Oh, I think kids now are able to understand," she said. "These days, a lot of parents are still together. It's a fact of life."

"I suppose so," I said.

"Norma told me she just sat down and leveled with Ned, Jr., who's thirteen. She told him that his dad and her had been happily wed for quite a while but it didn't mean they didn't love him any less, and that plenty of people get married nowadays–it's nothing bad or unusual."

"I guess the small ones are very confused," I said.

"It's difficult for little Nan to understand," the lady added. "She sees all of her school chums from broken homes and they kid her about her folks staying together so long."

"You know," I said, "it's so hard for me to think of the Darlings, of all people, not splitting up. Nobody else is involved, obviously."

"No, I'm afraid not," she said, clucking her tongue. "Ned's as faithful as they come and Norma never gets fed up. It's so much better they stay together than live apart unhappily."

"How did you first hear about it?" I asked.

"Oh, gosh, news of the Darlings' twenty-fifth anniversary is all over. Nobody at my bridge club can talk of anything but their renewed vows."

"You know," I said, "I always thought *she* was very nice, and he struck me as a real decent sort too, so I guess it was unavoidable. Everyone said Norma was crazy not to marry Ned, and vice versa."

"I just never realized their commitment was so serious," she said.

"When a couple cuddles publicly, it's a good sign that things are going ecstatically at home," I commented sagely.

"I never paid much attention to it," the woman said. "You see a lot of very happy people nowadays who are married. It doesn't mean a thing."

ALL ABOARD FOR FANTASYLAND!

THERE ARE SO many sex fantasy books–*Fantasex* just arrived hot on the heels of *To Turn You On* and *Garden of Delights*

—that the average person has begun to fret that even his *fantasy* sex life could be a lot better.

Not only are many of us missing out on a whole brave new world of erotica, we're scarcely capable of a few spicy fantasies. Much of the stuff I dream up wouldn't be ribald enough to make "Mr. Rogers' Neighborhood."

My little reveries are so paltry I'm not even sure if they qualify as full-fledged fantasies by modern standards. The reason I gave up going to pornographic films, in fact, is that they were stealing all my best ideas. I went stale very quickly, I'm afraid.

It's tough to think up sex fantasies these days that would cause so much as a raised eyebrow at a cocktail party in Toledo. Recently, somebody told me about one of his recurring fantasies—something involving Jane Pauley and a cheese soufflé—and I was instantly bored.

"Aw, I had that fantasy years ago," I yawned. "Can't you do better than that?" I think I hurt his feelings; it was one of his very best fantasies, maybe his only one. The moral here is: If you plan to discuss your sexual fantasies openly, better try them out first in Philadelphia.

Not that I seriously believe that all of these lascivious daydreams occur regularly in the suburbs, as these books would have us think. They certainly don't go on in the cities.

Well, there *is* this one little fantasy I once had: I'm home mowing the lawn, see, and a cute lady next door comes over and invites me to a neighborhood orgy that night after supper.

As usual, the fantasy ended right there, because I had to be at a meeting that started at 7 P.M. and the orgy was scheduled to begin promptly at 7:30, so there was no way I could get there on time (late arrivals would not be seated until after the first number). It was just my luck that both the fantasy and my meeting were on a Wednesday night, but this is what dooms all of my best sex fantasies—reality intrudes before they really have a chance to get moving.

If I conjure up a sensuous scene in which fifteen *Penthouse* Pets are due at my apartment for a photo session, I start wondering where I could borrow the right kind of camera (none of the girls will be impressed by an Instamatic).

Most of the truly wild ideas mentioned in these fantasy manuals require too much work ahead of time. In one fantasy, you have to be sure to have beluga caviar in the house, and the very first fantasy in *Fantasex* mentions "a wooded glen." Well, I don't know of any wooded glens, none I can lay my hands on in an emergency; if I had access to a wooded glen, the rest would be a snap.

One fantasy involves a slave auction and another talks about sheiks. I know it sounds square, but slave markets and harems are not my idea of a hot time. I wonder what a sheik with slave girls fantasizes about? (His wife probably.)

My one real fantasy lately is to write a book about sexual fantasies. It's the only way I'll ever get around to concocting some really erotic scenes. I keep putting it off. But here's the best part: After my book becomes a best seller, see, I make the talk-show rounds plugging it, where I meet this gorgeous author of *another* sex fantasy book, and—well, need I go on?

I HADN'T ANYONE TILL ME

IT HAD BEEN some time since I last bumped into Elsie and Fenton Trendy, my faddish friends, and I learned why when I caught sight of Elsie dining at an intimate French restaurant—alone.

"I'm really into solitude," she explained. "Fenton and I decided that aloneness is where it's at now, so we split last fall. I'm very active, though, as head of our local Solo Lib group."

"Solo Lib?" I asked. "What's that?"

"We fight discrimination against single people, which pervades every sector of American society. Affirmative action for the unmarried is long overdue in this country. It's only lately that the issue surfaced in Miami."

"Not Anita Bryant again," I said.

"No—Mickey Rooney along with Liz Taylor and Artie Shaw. They feel it's unnatural not to be married and want to ban single people from teaching in the schools. They claim it converts impressionable kids to solo lifestyles."

The group hopes to outlaw singles bars from opening up in the suburbs, also apartment complexes that harbor unwed stewardesses, secretaries, stockbrokers and other "unhealthy influences on young impressionable minds."

Fenton, Elsie's ex, helped block-bust a community in Ohio where single people are openly harassed. Couples hurl rocks at anybody caught walking alone on the street and yell insults at people reading on park benches or thinking to themselves in public.

Elsie told me she decided, after seventeen years, to come out of the closet. "I'd been a latent loner all along," she said. "A lot of married people are single underneath, and many even have kids. It's no guarantee of anything."

"I had no idea that solitude was so rampant nowadays," I said.

"Oh, my, spinsterhood is very In. Marriage, of course, has been Out for years, but now even living with somebody is terribly passé."

"Are you allowed to have a dog or a turtle or anything?" I asked.

"Well, it's frowned upon," Elsie said. "Pets are considered company, and so are plants. A nice fern is more responsive than many men I've met."

"Touché," I said. "Was the hermit experience hard at first?"

"It wasn't easy to admit how much I loved being with myself, so I went to a halfway house for couples trying to get off the gregarious kick—people from communes and big families who are desperate to curl up with a good book by themselves but just lack the guts."

Elsie went on, "All of which breeds what we call the 'sneak single,' someone who goes away on vacation alone and then feels guilty."

According to Elsie Trendy, singles are being denied many basic human rights granted to couples. "We're now fighting the restaurant owners of America to stop seating single people at counters."

Solo Lib, said Elsie, is also working quietly behind the scenes to elect more single people to office. "With Jerry Brown and Ed Koch two of the nation's highest-ranking bachelors, we may be able to turn things around for the unmarried minority."

Part of the movement is dedicated to inaugurating courses in "Single Studies," so the next generation won't grow up thinking that every famous person in history was married.

"Did you know that James Buchanan was single?" Elsie asked me.

"I'll be darned," I said. "I just had no idea."

"Sure, and so was Emily Dickinson, Leonardo da Vinci, Florence Nightingale, Jane Austen, Elizabeth I, Hitler–and, oh, there are hundreds more, individuals who chose the single lifestyle and struggled against horrible pressure to marry. I'll bet you didn't realize Rasputin was single."

"Never thought about it, but some of my best friends are–oops, sorry . . ."

"Oh, I've heard all the clichés by now: 'Single people are terrific dancers,' 'Singles are pushy and tight with money,' 'All single people are big drinkers,' 'Singles love flashy clothes and drive big cars' . . ."

"I'll try to be more tolerant of unmarried folks from now on," I promised. "I'm sure they're every bit as capable in their jobs as married people, and probably just as nice when you get to know them."

Then I whispered, "But tell me just one thing: Is it true what they say about single girls?"

"What's that?" asked Elsie.

"I hear they're great wives."

Digestive Tracts

SORRY PICKLES

FOOD EXPERT James Beard has expressed his alarm over the increasing preponderance of orange slices on plates whenever he sits down to eat, but he failed to mention the doubly disturbing omnipresent sliced pickle.

It has never been clearly determined whether the purpose of pickle slices is to be eaten or to be looked at, but the pickle industry has definitely got the point across that sliced pickles are a force to be reckoned with, if not necessarily munched.

I can't believe that pickles just appear spontaneously on plates in restaurants all over America. There seems to be some plan behind it, plenty of real thought and dedication.

Wherever you eat, from roadside diners to chic French cafés, you're going to encounter unwanted pickles in one form or another. I notice people who love dill pickles refuse to touch pickle slices on their plates (and reject mine with a shudder).

This must be because pickle slices are of an inferior cut, nothing at all like the kind from barrels that people purchase wrapped in waxed paper. The pickles that arrive, unbidden, alongside your egg salad sandwich, or inside your hamburger, are warm and limp and fail both as decor and as cuisine.

Originally, I suspect, the idea was to make the dish more appetizing, but something has been lost along the way. Two worn-out pickle slices on the edge of a plate are truly a dreary sight and render everything nearby inedible. If the sight doesn't get you, the smell will.

Pickle manufacturers ought to take a study to learn the amount of pickles that are returned each day to restaurant kitchens, uneaten and untouched.

What becomes of all those zillions of pickles that get shoved aside? Do they become fertilizer or does the pickle you don't eat today turn up tomorrow on somebody else's plate? There must be an awful worldwide waste of sliced pickles.

Some dishes might conceivably call for a pickle, but you find them alongside food that has nothing to do with pickles. In fact, the plates often are lined up out in the kitchen with the pickles already sitting on them, where they've been for days.

It's possible to order a steak sandwich and find a pickle slice on the side, yet nobody I know eats pickles with steak. Likewise, there's no need for a pickle to accompany an omelette, or a green salad. For all I know, they now serve pickles with cheesecake.

Some high-ranking chefs ought to devise a list of dishes that call for pickles on the side. I can't think of any offhand, but there may be two or three. If there are none, let us face that fact and forever banish pickle slices. They take up valuable space on people's plates.

It's impossible to avoid a pickle with a hamburger or a hot dog unless you specify, in a strong voice, "Hold the pickle!" I don't even bother to say "Hold the pickle" anymore, because it doesn't seem worth holding; also, it doesn't work—they'll find some way to slip it in there anyway. If you say "No pickle, please," it sounds almost rude and vaguely un-American.

A pickle that has been lodged in a hamburger and allowed to sit there for any time will quickly contaminate the entire patty, infect the bun itself and give your nice chaste rare burger a sickly picklish taste. If I want a pickled hamburger, I'll order one.

In real life, nobody puts a pickle on top of his sandwich with a toothpick through it. Or if he does, the pickle is right out of a jar, cold and crunchy and wet. It is meant to be consumed and isn't simply along for the ride.

I've been ignoring, hiding and discarding pickle slices ever since I was a boy. In my time, I've probably dumped upwards of 50,000 slices. It's not a record I'm proud of—in fact, I feel a little bit guilty. There must be people in poor countries who would give a lot for a sliced pickle or two, although I doubt it; they probably have pickles of their own they'd like to trade in for something else.

I'm not a pickle fancier to start with—and a bowl of soggy dills floating in cloudy brine makes me think twice about ordering any food—but even hard-core dill-pickle eaters overlook the mushy fourth-rate pretenders, those pathetic corrugated sliced-up versions.

Often, alongside the pickle, there's also a pair of decomposing carrot slices that have lost their curl, and perhaps a drab olive without its sheen, trying their darnedest to look hale and hearty while lying exhausted atop a wilted lettuce leaf—all of it set off by the chief over-the-hill garnish, a dispirited sprig of parsley.

A WATERY GRAVE

IN A RECENT *Reader's Digest,* I pointedly ignored a chilling piece entitled "How Safe Is *Your* Drinking Water?"

I can well imagine what the answer is going to be, which is why I didn't go any further. Titles like that are enough to put me off water forever—if I wasn't already off the stuff anyway. Luckily, I don't drink my water straight, but it would be nice to know that, if I ever did want a glass, it would be relatively free of mosquitoes.

Now that the drinking supply may be polluted, there's not much left for us to worry about. This means we can all relax. If the water department plans to liquidate everyone, I'm ready to go quietly; I've got that resigned death-row attitude you hear about. I almost feel better now, knowing there's no way out anymore.

I've grown pretty reckless lately about being surrounded at every turn by doom of one sort or another. Much as I dislike saying it, I'm afraid we're about to be done in by Mother Nature herself—or "Smother Nature," as I now call the old biddy.

It's a load off my shoulders to know that, if fat and tobacco and alcohol and my local neighborhood gunman don't get me first, there are always pesticides, beef, air, milk, eggs, additives, coffee,

Coke, spray cans, exhaust fumes, tension, caffeine and Old Man River.

Back in my day, boys and girls, there was only nuclear war to fear; it shows you how far behind the times we were—and we thought our bomb shelters were pretty hot stuff. The H-bomb is plenty scary, all right, but keeling over from a glass of water is ten times as ghastly.

Well, it's a slower death, for one thing, and there's no ten-minute warning siren. One moment, you're walking around in the yard with a cool glass of iced tea in your hand and the next moment you're flat on the grass.

When the coroner comes over for a look, he'll be stumped: "Hmmm . . . Well, he's dead, that's for sure, but it could be almost anything—the water, the tea, the ice cubes, the sugar, the lemon. Guess I'll have to send a sample down to Water Pathology."

In brief, I'm not going to let any water scare frighten me. Right now, I'm too busy worrying about being wiped out by some hothead kid up the street with a do-it-yourself missile whose folks won't let him use the car. ("O.K., Pop—hand over those keys to the Chevy or I'm taking the whole city with me!")

I simply realize that, whenever we sit down to dinner, each dish before me is capable of murder. Now the only difference is, as you lie there gasping for air, you can't even ask for a sip of water. You must remember to say: "Quick—get me a bottle of Alhambra!"

I just snuck a peek at the *Digest* piece (well, you can't get *too* complacent) and it says the real villain lurking in the water supply may be the chlorine itself. Observes the writer: There may be "potentially cancer-causing agents *in the treatment plant itself.*" I can't recall ever being quite so shaken by a set of italics.

I've always thought water tastes kind of funny, anyway, which is why I lay off it as much as possible—though, of course, *not* drinking water is equally hazardous to your health. Bottled water isn't really the answer either. God only knows what those blue-green bottles are made out of.

CRANBERRY SAUCE FOR THE GANDER

WOMEN HAVE SO totally taken over the holiday season that the only thing men are allowed to do now is pull out the chairs and (as a sop to their tender egos) carve the turkey.

In recent years, however, with the rise of feminism and the decline of masochism, more women are hacking up turkeys than ever before in history, and more men are cooking them too long (figures courtesy of the National Groaning Board).

Many holiday suicides you read about are the result of husbands who feel ignored and left out of the holiday decision-making process. They have a home to go to, but no vote; at Christmastime, men are disenfranchised, overnight orphans.

Issues such as Whose Turn Is It for Christmas This Time? and What Should We Do About New Year's? are solved by women meeting in smoke-filled back rooms in early November. If you wonder how most Christmas trees get decorated, the answer is: plain old machine politics at its most naked and ruthless.

Men, for instance, are never consulted as to Who's Bringing Dessert? Sometime, I think it would be nice if *I* could bring the dessert, or maybe even be entrusted with a salad mold. I have some very definite ideas on salad molds that have never been given a real chance.

Husbands are not taken seriously in December. If a man attempts to offer a solution to a thorny holiday problem—e.g., If We Go to Your Mother's on Thanksgiving, What Happens Christmas? —he is told to run along and play.

"Why don't we just all go out somewhere?" I once suggested, an idea that was quickly and routinely ruled out of order. "Oh, don't listen to him—he's just teasing" was the response to what I regarded as a sincere alternative plan.

Just to be tactful, of course, the woman will pretend to ask a man's opinion but in fact it's never a legitimate consultation—

simply her way of feeling out his general mood so as to know exactly how to proceed next.

"Don't you think we ought to buy our tree early this year?" is not a request for an honest viewpoint but for a unanimous rubber-stamp Yes. Of course, if holidays were left up to men, they wouldn't ever quite get celebrated; Thanksgiving would be held around December 14.

Historically, men are supposed to go to a movie on days when the feast is being prepared, to keep from getting underfoot, but it never works out in reality because women *like* men underfoot—the more the merrier. Men are necessary to get down the wine goblets from the top shelf, to decide if the gravy needs more salt and to applaud from time to time.

A woman may snap, "I wish you'd read your book somewhere else while I'm trying to arrange these flowers," but if you try to read somewhere else, she'll always find you and give you a little poke to make sure you're paying attention.

During this period, wives treat husbands like kids on vacation, looking for small, time-consuming tasks they can handle without making a mess. They'll sigh, "If you're just going to *sit* there, I guess you could chop the walnuts," only to snatch the bowl away as soon as you've chopped one walnut.

"Oh, here—let *me* do it!—you're taking too long," the woman will frown. Or "You're holding the chopper all wrong." Or "You're getting walnut shells all over my nice waxed floor."

If you make even the slightest move in the direction of a doorway, that is the very moment a woman will decide she desperately needs you to do something. If you protest, "But I thought I was in the way," she'll say, "Well, I *might* need you—don't go too far."

So that a man can't relax completely, a woman will devise various make-work mini-chores to keep him in the vicinity, such as asking him to twist the top off the olive jar and empty the ice trays, or sticking a wooden spoon in his hand and saying, "Here—stir this while I finish drying my hair." (If a man tries to take charge of much more than a wooden spoon, however, he'll quickly be shoved aside and told to get lost.)

It's also against all rules of holiday etiquette for husbands to say anything containing even the mildest hint of criticism, such as "Isn't your fire up too high under the yams?," or "I wouldn't start that stuffing just yet." A man's place is in the closet.

MY BLACK BELT IN EATING

AS THE LEADING picky eater of Western Society over the age of six, an invitation to partake of an authentic Japanese-style dinner at somebody's home was not met by me with the expected gasps of delight.

It was met, instead, by much sulking and whining. I was not impressed by the word "authentic." When it comes to exotic cuisine, my rule of thumb is: The less authentic the better. Upon hearing that our hostess was Japanese, my normal authentic fears were tripled.

I hope the Japanese people won't think I'm picking on them, but for years I've had nothing but trouble with their meals. At first, I assumed the problem was all mine, but lately I've begun to suspect that perhaps Japanese culture is partly to blame. As cultures go, it's extremely pretty—until they get to the food part. Here is where Japanese culture and I go our separate ways.

Three times I've been dragged off to Japanese restaurants and each time I ate nothing and was a swell sport about it. Now I reply that I'm under strict doctor's orders not to get near raw food under any conditions, no matter how quaint.

I am inherently suspicious of any custom that forces you to remove your shoes and sit cross-legged at a sawed-off table. This is no way to eat a major meal, or even to sit down.

The obvious purpose is to divert you from the food by putting you at a terrible physical disadvantage. You feel foolish in stocking feet and you can't budge from your lotus position to stand up. Even if you do struggle to your feet, you can't leave because they have your shoes.

To me, this has all the earmarks of a trap—or, at the very least, a style of cuisine that shows very little confidence in the cook.

Apparently this is how the Japanese have overtaken us in science and industry. It's not because of their vaunted attention to detail and hustle. Rather, they have succeeded economically because of their attention to strange vegetables served at tiny tables.

Here's how it works: A big electronics executive from, say, Chicago will be taken to dine at a fancy place in Tokyo. While the man is folded in half on the floor, praying for something recognizable to eat, the Japanese exec whips out a contract and the starving American signs over his company for a song—or in this case, a bowl of rice.

The invitation to me arrived via a go-between, a typically sneaky way of getting me to an Asian dinner.

When I protested, saying I don't eat Japanese food in months ending in R (or Y, H or L), our mutual friend said, "Look—don't worry. They'll be serving essentially beef and vegetables." His use of "essentially" bothered me for weeks. If you don't know about curry or chutney, Indian food is essentially leg of lamb.

To me, Japanese food is essentially sushi. I'm always promised, "You don't have to eat the raw fish," but raw fish is just for openers. Even if you manage to wriggle away from the fish course, you still must cope with clam broth (with a darling little clam staring up at you through the soup), or sliced turnip salad, or an almost perverse emphasis on bean curd.

If somebody—Prime Minister Nakasoñe, say—would simply sit down and calm our fears by explaining to people what bean curd is (are?), millions of Americans would feel safer around Japanese food. On the other hand, they might throw up.

The very words "bean curd" do not have an especially inviting sound. My basic premise involving anything like bean curd is that if it really were such an irresistible item, 7-Eleven would carry it.

After losing my shoes, I spent the next hour trying to find a position that wouldn't expose my feet. Tucking them under the couch is one way; however, you can trip getting up. Women simply sit on their feet, but my knees only bend when I'm walking.

The meal itself was fairly edible, considering that it was all digested while huddled on a rug playing footsie with strange men under a table made for midgets—and skinny midgets at that.

Somehow, by foraging through the skillet, I made a meal of water chestnuts, scallions and what few slivers of meat I could stab with one chopstick. When my back collapsed, I had finished eating. As a reward, we were all allowed to leave the dining-room floor and go into the living room for ice cream and chairs.

Later, in a car on the way home I pulled out an emergency cookie I had smuggled along just in case. It was instantly pounced upon by the very people who only an hour before had said how yummy everything was.

As exotic food goes, perhaps, but there is an ancient Occidental saying I'm reminded of: "One cookie is worth a thousand bean curds."

MEATLOAF FOR BREAKFAST

DETERMINING INEDIBLE SUBSTANCES in our refrigerator is entirely a matter of counting the rings. It is not a healthy idea to guess, for instance, how old a piece of cheese might be.

At this very moment, we have a hunk of petrified cheddar cheese in the butter holder that was purchased at the time of the Spanish Inquisition. A bite was taken out of it sometime during the reign of Queen Victoria, and then it was wrapped up again. It has gone untouched since.

There are certain regions of the refrigerator I would not ask an experienced hunter to venture into alone. Some of the items we have managed to capture in bowls and jars may turn out to be lethal.

For several months now, I have hesitated uncapping a jar of yellow matter with lumps in it, and I have no intention of doing so without a large paper bag open and ready. It looks to me to resemble chicken soup, but it may turn out to be petrified cranberry sauce.

If a complete survey was ever taken of the inside of this refrigerator, almost anything from a small ball of tuna fish we're saving for the poor to a pair of slightly used cabbages would be uncovered.

A quick inventory of the refrigerator reveals the following "substances" which may be in any state now, from semi-liquid to penicillin: one jar of chicken gravy, one jar of turkey gravy, one jar of beef gravy, one smaller jar of chicken gravy. (The big day is almost here when both jars of chicken gravy will be joined in a grand alliance.)

Also to be tallied are some bundles of meat, of which one is edible and the others are there to keep them company.

We also stock five or six unopened cans of fruit juice to be opened only in the event of nuclear attack when all drinking water is contaminated. Otherwise, the cans stay closed.

Way in the back you will find a small plate of mashed potatoes which are second in seniority only to the lemon used every summer for iced tea. It would be downright cruel to throw away the mashed potatoes without first getting rid of the lemon.

Those cold mashed potatoes have become—well, a part of the family. And we are not the sort of people who keep mashed potatoes around until they outlive their usefulness and then say, "All right, mashed potatoes, out you go!" No, indeed, we keep our mashed potatoes around for sentimental reasons. And besides, you never know when mashed potatoes may be hard to get.

The meatloaf is an old friend too. He's been with us now for six weeks, and darned if we haven't become attached to the little fellow.

Canned milk is also an important member of our museum of natural history. We do not believe in throwing away a can of cream until it refuses to pour and must be chipped away with a small mallet.

The refrigerator freezing unit has replaced the hall closet. In the rear, we store wooden hangers, galoshes, leftover rolls of wallpaper, and umbrellas, but that will never be fully known until future civilizations dig their way through to the back.

What they will never realize is that we only stored all this food. We rarely eat anything from the refrigerator. It is only there to impress the company. It stays until either the Goodwill takes it away or we move out.

If we ever ate anything in the refrigerator, I'm afraid it would upset the delicate balance of nature we have established. One of these days, a leftover is going to stay in there so long it will sprout legs, walk into the dining room and eat *us* up.

THE TURKEY'S CHANGING ROLL IN SOCIETY

IF EVERYBODY WILL come to order, I'd like to announce the founding of the American Anti-Turkey Roll League, whose members are dedicated to wiping out the turkey roll plague by 1985. It can be done but we must make it a national priority.

Turkey roll is destroying our national purpose, weakening the fiber of the young and making it impossible to bite into a club sandwich anymore with confidence and purpose. The dread turkey roll is everywhere.

Even as I write, turkeys are being rolled and packaged and sliced up by once respectable restaurants that pass it off as actual turkey when in fact it is 10 percent turkey and 90 percent roll.

There is no such bird as a turkey roll, not even in Lewis Carroll. Farmers have tried to breed one, but it won't fly or even walk. All that this fowl substance does is roll around on the floor; it has no wings, feathers or claws, let alone succulent thighs and breasts. The turkey roll is not related to a turkey but is a distant cousin of rolled veal, the pork roll and rolled socks.

The turkey roll has made dining out an even more precarious and potentially hazardous experience than it is already. At the healthiest-looking deli or lunch counter, known to have the highest standards of honesty, you may encounter a balled-up turkey.

At one formerly upstanding luncheonette recently, I ordered a "turkey sandwich," but to be on the safe side I asked the waitress bluntly: "Miss, just to make sure we're discussing the same thing, let's define our terms. This is fresh turkey, am I correct?" She smiled and said, "Oh, yes, sir! We cook it here every day."

When she slid the plate in front of me, I quickly spotted a turkey-roll sandwich. You can tell one right away, because a slice of turkey roll is round and shiny and generously mottled with gelatin as opposed to the authentic fresh-carved kind, which is ragged, grainy and—well, real. Turkey roll slides around on your bread and feels like fresh breast of snake, which it well may be.

I nibbled at it, pretending it was real turkey, but there's no doubt when you've got turkey roll on your hands. It has no white or dark meat; it is all grayish and there is nothing remotely turkey-like about it. It might as well be veal or lamb or papier-mâché, except papier-mâché is tastier.

Another time, I ordered a "turkey sandwich" at Denny's and it was so obviously a turkey roll that the waitress finally fessed up. Most waitresses, chefs and owners who are part of the nationwide turkey-roll ring, won't blink an eye if you accuse them of harboring ersatz turkey in the back room.

Do not cringe or back down. Instead, gently slip the offending slice of turkey into a long envelope and send the specimen to the FBI in Washington, D.C., to have the thing analyzed by trained laboratory experts.

They have scientists there to detect turkey roll, no matter how cleverly disguised, and will let you know if you've got a piece of fraudulent turkey, which ought to be against the law to ship across state lines.

Once you've notified the FBI, your duty as a member of the American Anti-Turkey Roll League is (1) to confront the restaurant owner with the fact that he is involved in the international turkey-roll conspiracy and (2) to write your local congressman, SPCA and the nearest restaurant critic. Tell them what's going on and give the name of the place peddling illicit turkeys.

Meanwhile, real turkeys are suffering a horrible disgrace. Thanksgiving is humiliating enough, but consider what's happening to the image of the good, old-fashioned, God-fearing turkey, a noble and traditionally digestible bird.

Turkey is about the last meat left that is good for you. It is thinning and doesn't cause anything. Turkey roll, on the other hand, causes death if eaten regularly over long periods, such as a week.

We must put an end to this reckless rolling of turkeys. One way is to write in the word "roll" on menus after the phrase "fresh breast of turkey." Otherwise, we soon may be confronting such delicacies as sirloin steak roll, deviled egg roll, ham and Swiss cheese roll, lobster Newburg roll, calf's liver and bacon roll, mashed potato roll, Dover sole roll and ham and eggs roll.

It won't be an easy fight. The U.S. Turkey Roll Foundation claims that its product is no different, really, than regulation turkey roasted in an oven and carved by hand. A turkey roll, you'll notice, is never sliced before your eyes. It is carved somewhere else, probably in Detroit at some turkey-rolling plant. Or maybe it comes already serrated for easy peeling along the dotted lines.

So we've got to get this stuff out of here. *Now.* Time grows short. This nation cannot exist any longer half turkey and half roll.

JELLIED GRAPES OF WRATH

YOU'D THINK THAT despite the economic and energy crunch, the least we could demand in this country is a little better jelly. Well, not better jelly, really, so much as a heck of a lot less *grape* jelly.

Maybe I'm all alone in my feeling about grape jelly—that it's an abhorrent slimy substance—but is it possible all of America is that crazy for grape jelly? No, I suspect it's just a typical case of citizen apathy.

Probably nobody thinks grape jelly is serious enough to gripe about, yet everyone knows perfectly well that any breakfast succeeds or fails largely on the basis of what kind of jelly is available. Is this such a radical idea? And is it also radical to ask just who decided that, in coffee shops and restaurants all over the United States, the standard jelly would be grape? (I'm ruling out that glutinous orange library paste, known to some as marmalade, which is purposely made gooey so you'll learn to appreciate grape jelly.)

Many people in America must grow up knowing no other jelly but grape. You don't encounter it in such massive doses in Europe, where grapes are ground into wine, the only reasonable place for them.

Once, on a cross-country drive from California, I noticed that the farther east I got, the more grape jelly I got. Around Kentucky, I began running into grape jelly in serious amounts, and by the time I reached Reading, Pa., it had taken over completely. Apparently, I was in the Grape Jelly Belt.

Occasionally, to test a restaurant's ingenuity and to assert my own individuality, I'll recklessly inquire into the possibility of a choice of jelly besides grape. The waitress, if she doesn't laugh, cocks an eyebrow and calls the manager. Often, just to be ornery, I order "mixed fruit." Not that I'm at all enamored of mixed fruit, whatever that means, but it beats grape jelly—*anything* beats grape jelly.

What's all too apparent to me is that jelly just isn't taken seriously enough in America. If it was, it would come in bowls and you wouldn't have to jimmy it open from its doll-size plastic packet.

The tragic result of being forced to confront grape jelly morning after morning is that, eventually, you just give up and, what's really depressing, start eating it without even thinking. Just a few weeks ago, I actually found myself asking for "a little more grape jelly, please."

WHAT'S YOUR POISSON?

IT HAS TAKEN me forty years to face up to the fact that I don't like fish, an unpopular position not arrived at hastily. I've finally reached an age when I don't have to fake an interest in fish anymore.

Oh, I enjoy fish enough if they're swimming around underwater, where they belong and can't get at me, but they don't quite measure up as legit food. This is sure to raise the hackles of fish lovers and, indeed, even the fish themselves–assuming the hackles haven't been cut off and served as an appetizer.

Fish, in food form, tastes either (a) fishy or (b) not at all. There is no in-between and almost no variety, with the exception of tuna, which I don't regard as a true fish. It has too much substance and good red meat; tuna must be some kind of underwater cow.

I don't know how people ever got into this habit of eating fish–or "seafood," as it is more appetizingly termed. In theory, seafood sounds delicious, but once it lands on my plate in some slippery white tangible form, I'm ready to throw it back.

I want to tell the waiter I didn't think he would actually *bring* me the fish, that I was just showing off by ordering halibut and what I'd really rather have is a nice juicy slab of prime rib.

When people say, "Hey, I'm in the mood for some seafood!" I usually reply, "That's a good idea," when it's not a good idea at all. I simply fail to think it through, forgetting that sooner or later I must choose from a roster of suspicious-sounding items called petrale, mussels, scallops and pike. Imagine–*pike!*

It's not until the scallops are right there in front of me, trying to pass themselves off as dinner, that I discover again how much I abhor fish, especially round ones. I'd come to my senses much faster if people would say, "Hey, I'm in the mood for calamari!" or "How about some turbot?"

Right away, I'd snap, "Hold on just one minute, pal!" and that would be the end of that. Even those few types of seafood I can digest—crab, swordfish, salmon, halibut—I don't really much like. Given a choice of honest food, I'd never order sole on purpose, but people shame you into eating fish.

I hate myself for knuckling under to outside pressure and ordering sole when I should be man enough to say, "I'll have the chicken."

Nobody exactly forces you to eat fish, but if you even faintly suggest the possibility of broiled chicken, everyone looks at you crossly and says: "What? You mean we drove all the way out here to the Old Grotto and you're going to eat chicken? Why, that's crazy!" I suspect they're just jealous.

Very few people today have the guts to walk into a place called Fisherman's Cove and order leg of lamb. "You can eat lamb anytime at home," fish fanatics say. "Why not try the scallops? They're excellent." (Scallops are *not* excellent and never were. Nobody even knows what a scallop looks like in real life, without the parsley.)

I don't need to be reminded that there are thousands of thriving seafood restaurants serving famed fish dishes—I'm still not convinced. If you went up and spoke to people who frequent such places, you'd find that almost none of them are there for the seafood itself.

At least 75 percent have come for the tartar sauce, the melted butter, the French bread, the cole slaw or the decor. The fish is just something you have to put up with if you want the other stuff. Most people leave a third of their fish on the plate.

Rarely does anyone rave about the entrée. Instead, you hear: "Ya know, this place has the most marvelous french fries!" Or "I really come here for their great clam chowder." Or even "I just love looking at all the boats." (A sirloin does not require any boats.)

I also have a hunch, deeply felt, that there is only one actual major fish, which chefs then slice up into various shapes and give cute names to, like mahimahi, red snapper, sand dabs and hangtown fry.

Whenever I try to learn what anyone's fish tastes like, the best they can report is: "Um, well, it tastes like a whitefish of some kind, but it's not bad." Obviously, all they're eating is this vague white fish that has been slickly done up with garlic butter or cocktail sauce.

Lately, seafood has had a great press, just because it's thinning and good for you. Everyone nowadays is pretty annoyed at roast beef. Meat can lead to an early death. This may be, but you always know where you stand with beef, whereas fish is the most devious of all foods.

It has no taste anyone can identify; it goes under hundreds of mysterious assumed names; and, of course, it smells funny. Not only that, but at least a prime rib has all the bones right out there in plain sight.

GREECE SPOTS

"LET'S GO TO the Greek place!" someone suggested for lunch last week. Naturally I demurred, as I've done for years. People keep trying to drag me to the Greek place, and I keep suggesting we try it another day.

That day has never arrived, but it hasn't been easy. I have nothing specific against Athenian cuisine–it's just a generic term I cooked up for lunchtime exotica.

If it's not the Greek place, it's the new Filipino place (there is always a new Filipino place and there always will be) or perhaps a Taiwanese place. Thai places are coming along at an incredible clip and seem determined to knock out not only Chinese but Greek and Filipino places.

If they don't get you one way, they'll get you another, but I've had more experience in the foreign lunch racket than the Thais and I expect to survive their threat, too.

Left alone, I head for the German place (a Hofbrau, actually) or what I think of as my favorite non-Greek place (Joe's). Somehow, it never seems quite the right time to try the Greek place, though it's become almost unavoidable.

Even when I meet someone for lunch in another city, they always say, as we're coming down in the elevator: "Say, there's a wonderful little Greek place around the corner–how does that sound?" It's always a favorite spot, maybe even a hangout, so I hate to say no, but somehow I get up the courage to ask, casually: "Um, is there anywhere else we could try? I'm really not in the mood today for Greek food."

This is a gross distortion, of course. It would be closer to the truth to say that I am never in the mood for Greek food. Sometimes, for emphasis, I'll add, "My stomach's been acting up lately."

A polite no-thanks never does it, though, because in each and every case, *this* little Greek Place is the Greek Place of All Time, the greatest little Greek Place that ever was.

There's one in every town, if not neighborhood. I think maybe they're secretly franchised. They all look the same, I know that. Even the menus are identical–blue printing, four dishes, dog-eared and slightly splattered with particles of what I take to be their marvelous moussaka.

Greek places are, by definition, marvelous–or so they're invariably touted. This only increases my innate deep-seated suspicions. Maybe if people said, "Hey, there's a so-so little Greek place around the corner," I'd be more inclined to give it a try.

In an attempt to lean on me a little, they'll add, "They do a *wonderful* version of moussaka." Well, that does it. I don't even like the regular version of moussaka. Everything in a Greek restaurant is a version of moussaka. Actually, any dish I don't like reminds me of moussaka.

I'm sure moussaka is delicious; I just don't want any. I used to feel guilty about it, fearing that people would think I'm anti-Greek or something. Then someone pointed out that when you're over 40, you have a perfect right to turn up your nose at moussaka. It's one of the few perks of aging.

I think I've paid my dues, foreign-food-wise, and there's no longer any reason why I should be forced to eat moussaka–or even "try it," as all moussaka lovers insist. I've tried it, really I have, but nobody will believe me. All they'll say is, "Well, try *this* kind."

Then they'll smile (thinking they've got me where they want me now) and ask, "Do you like eggplant?" "No, I do not like eggplant," I'll reply firmly. At this, their faces drop slightly but they're not about to give up. In a confiding tone, they say: "Well, this doesn't taste that much like eggplant."

It's what they always claim—the last resort of the diehard try-it-you'll-like-it crowd. Insist you don't like a dish and they'll insist that, in fact, it really tastes like something else, usually chicken, but they'll tell you anything you want to hear. Greek-place lovers are ruthless.

As a last-ditch try, they say, "Oh, I'm sure they'll have *something* you can eat." This makes me feel like I'm eight years old—and that, once we sit down, one of the women will ask the waiter discreetly if he can bring me a bowl of Cheerios and a balloon.

Political Overtones

THE PEOPLE, YES (67%); NO (33%)

ACCORDING TO THE Harris Survey, more people feel disenchanted and alienated by government now than ever before in history—or at least since 1966, when the survey began.

If there had been a Louis Harris in 1776, what would people have told pollsters who asked them how they felt about the drafting of a Declaration of Independence? Luckily, if rather belatedly, the results of an old Franklin Poll taken for the *Saturday Evening Post* in June of 1776—while the Continental Congress was meeting in Philadelphia—have just been revealed.

Here's what Ben Franklin's poll takers found, as reported:

"Americans in nine of the thirteen Colonies expressed overwhelming dismay with the way Congress is dissolving political bonds with England, according to a new Franklin Poll released this week. A whopping 79 percent of those polled answered 'Yes' when asked:

" 'Do you think that all men are created equal and endowed by their Creator with certain unalienable Rights, that among these are Life, Liberty and the Pursuit of Happiness?' (The remaining 21 percent were 'Unsure' if such truths are self-evident.)

"Citizens from Boston to Baltimore told the poll that, while they felt some kind of Declaration was called for, 57 percent were 'turned off' by their Representatives in Philadelphia; 44 percent agreed that Congress is 'dawdling' and 'wasting time on the exact phrasing of the documents.'

"A typical statement of disaffection was summed up by a Lenox, Mass., apprentice cabinetmaker, who said, 'If you ask me, those so-called "Founding Fathers" down there in Philly are selling us a bill of goods and lining their own pockets.'

"His frustration with the political process was reflected in the

81 percent of those surveyed who say they feel 'left out of the democratic process.' In the words of a Bull Run, Pa., silver engraver, 'This Jefferson guy, especially, seems to be getting an awful lot of personal publicity out of the whole thing.'

"Like 64 percent of those questioned, he believes there is 'too much secrecy in government' and that the sessions at Independence Hall should be open to the public.

"Frustration has leaped to a new high of 79 percent among both affluent merchants earning more than $1,500 a year and the nation's no-collar workers—blacksmiths, tinkers, chimneysweeps, etc. Each group responded 'Yes' by a four to one majority when asked if they 'distrust all politicians'; 47 percent of this segment also agreed that 'a new morality is needed in Philadelphia.'

"The Colonies' anxieties were mirrored by a Tarrytown, N.Y., cooper, who said, 'Let's sign the doggone declaration and get this 'independence' thing settled once and for all so we can get on with the rest of the country's business.'

"Along with 48 percent of his fellow countrymen, he claimed that 'high taxes and inflation' are his No. 1 concern.

"Some 68 percent of those polled by Franklin—an increase of 66 percent since the last survey, taken twenty-five years ago—responded 'No' to the question, 'Do people running the Colonies care what happens to you?'

"An all-time low of 12 percent told the survey they were 'satisfied' with the Colonies as they are and see no reason to put England through a revolution that could tear the Mother Country apart. Nearly all, or 93 percent, agreed that the King's ability to govern America might be seriously impaired if a Declaration of Independence is signed.

"A steady 62 percent of the population continues to blame the press—specifically the *Federalist Papers* and other members of the so-called 'Eastern liberal establishment hand-press'—for 'blowing up out of all proportion minor differences with the British Crown.'

"One woman, a Salem, Mass., deacon's wife, remarked: 'All we read day after day is "freedom" this and "liberty" that, and—well, frankly I'm pretty fed up with it. Why can't the press ever print anything *nice* about King George? The man has been through enough. I say we ought to sever our ties with the King or get off his back.'"

PRESIDENTS MAKE STRANGE BEDFELLOWS

NOW THAT WE know the sleeping arrangements of the Nixons, Fords and Carters, there's been a great clamor to discover the boudoir habits of the other Presidents and First Ladies:

Mr. and Mrs. John Quincy Adams did not sleep in the same room, although they did sleep in the same bed, which was cut in half and put in their separate bedrooms; they did, however, turn in at the same time—11:20 P.M. Mrs. Adams snored lightly.

President and Mrs. Herbert Hoover rarely slept at all.

Benjamin Harrison and his wife slept on the floor, but shared the same pair of pajamas.

Harry and Bess Truman slept curled up at opposite ends of the bed to avoid bumping heads. Mr. Truman often took early-morning walks around the bedroom, followed by reporters.

Warren G. Harding hogged all the covers.

George Washington, who was famous for sleeping around, went to bed at different times each night to fake out Martha.

Mr. and Mrs. Calvin Coolidge slept in bunk beds, he on the bottom and she on the top. This was because Coolidge was a short man and it was easier for him to climb into the lower berth (since he was President, he got first choice); also, in case of war, he could leap out of bed quicker on the bottom bunk.

President and Mrs. Franklin Pierce had trouble sleeping. They tossed and turned—she tossed and he turned.

Theodore Roosevelt slept with all his clothes on, as Mrs. Roosevelt was a rather prudish woman.

Woodrow Wilson liked the bedroom window open; Edith Wilson wanted it closed. He lost by a very close Senate vote.

Mr. and Mrs. William Henry Harrison slept standing up, to save on sheets.

Grover Cleveland liked to cuddle.

The Zachary Taylors slept with a dog in the middle.

William Howard Taft slept with three pillows, and occasionally with Mrs. Taft.

Chester Alan Arthur ate cookies in bed; his wife dined alone.

President Lincoln slept standing up, which was his wife's preference. Mary Todd was a difficult woman who often got her way, and Mr. Lincoln was too nice to say he'd rather sleep lying down.

Andrew Jackson refused to go to bed without his stuffed bear. Rachel Jackson, to comply, dressed up in a panda suit.

FDR slept with a cigarette holder clamped rakishly in his teeth. Eleanor Roosevelt ground her teeth.

William McKinley and Mrs. McKinley slept together, but she preferred to sleep under the bed.

James and Mrs. Polk liked breakfast in bed—but in different towns. (Mrs. Polk ate her eggs poached and the President liked his over easy with a nice brown edge.)

Thomas Jefferson slept with a night light; Mrs. J wore a sleep mask.

Lyndon Johnson slept in a ten-gallon hat; Lady Bird did not.

Rutherford B. Hayes slept with his beard outside the covers, as did Mrs. Hayes.

Ulysses S. Grant kept his beard under the covers during most of his scandal-ridden administration.

Martin Van Buren slept fitfully; his wife slept on a board.

Millard Fillmore was always sleepy and wore slippers and a robe in the Oval Office.

The John F. Kennedys often slept on their sides.

Andrew Johnson, too short for the Lincoln Bed, slept in a bathtub during the closing, chaotic days of his administration.

Mr. and Mrs. John Adams tried to sleep together, but Abigail kept falling off the edge.

James Monroe had bad dreams that led to the Monroe Doctrine.

President Madison and his wife Dolley both slept in their socks.

James Buchanan, our only bachelor President, hated sleeping alone, so to maintain the public pretense of being married he frequently slept with the Vice-President or Speaker Pro Tem.

Ronald Reagan slept soundly; his wife, Nancy, looked on admiringly.

HELP STAMP OUT LETTERS

SO MANY PEOPLE find it hard to grasp the reason for the new 20-cent price of a first-class stamp that I want to break down the cost in easy-to-understand terms.

Of that 20 cents, 7.8 cents goes to delivering the mail late. Years ago, when mail was simply delivered on time, it cost the post office almost nothing. Today, however, with the high price of detaining a letter, the cost has skyrocketed.

In 1975, the Postal Service installed expensive modern equipment that can delay a letter up to six times as long as old-fashioned hand-delayed mail. Each letter goes into a mail-dawdling machine that holds it motionless for several days. Three years ago, it took ten people the same amount of time to delay a letter.

About 2.2 cents of this 20-cent rate goes into crushing envelopes, magazines and packages. Efficient magazine manglers, run by computer, can now wrinkle, twist and rip 750 pieces of mail every minute, including all letters marked "hand cancel."

Lyle C. Understaff, chief of the Postal Service mail-mangling division, explains: "In the old days, we had to hire experts to crush letters, other specialists to crumple magazines and yet a third group of people to jump up and down on packages. Now, one $2 million machine can do it all!"

I told Understaff I always thought my letters and magazines were crushed by mail carriers wedging them into tiny mailboxes and narrow slots, but he shook his head. "We've come quite a way since those horse-and-buggy days. That took the carriers too long and left them with rough, red hands. These automatic crushers are real time-savers."

He pointed out that 3.7 cents of the 20-cent stamp goes for complex letter-losing equipment, which has replaced the occasional lazy or crazy postman who used to dump all the mail in a garage.

Of the 20 cents, said Understaff, 1.6 cents goes into fewer mailbox pickups per day. It's very costly, he emphasized, to print up—and install—new signs for mailboxes telling you that pickup times have been reduced.

Two cents of the higher cost of stamps will go toward slowing down so-called "special delivery" service.

"Converting to slower special delivery was quite expensive," said Understaff, explaining that the purpose is to get more people to use "air express," which costs $8 but gets your letter there as quickly as special delivery used to.

I asked him how he managed to slow down special delivery so efficiently. He said it had meant buying a lot of old banana boats, bicycles and horses. "Those express ponies don't come cheap anymore," he added.

Understaff told me that 1.3 cents of every new stamp will be used to improve junk mail service, which supports the entire postal system.

"Junk mail always arrives on time, crisp and neat, because it's bundled beforehand by companies. We'd like to get more people to send their letters in bulks of 500 or 1,000. It's cheaper and faster for everyone."

He added, "We're trying to phase out all first-class delivery by making it so poky and exorbitant that the public will be discouraged from writing letters."

Finally, the last 1.4 cents of first-class service has been earmarked for designing and printing new 20-cent stamps. "If we didn't have to keep designing more expensive stamps," Understaff concluded, "we could probably hold the price down."

CAUTION: HUNTERS CROSSING

AFTER A CONTROVERSIAL television airing of all sides in the hunting controversy, somebody finally thought to consult the animals themselves at a seminar held last week at Hunter College.

Present at the meeting were various spokesbeasts—eminent stags in the field, elk, ducks, geese, foxes, quail, rabbits, pheasant, etc. As moderator, game warden Dusty Trail (Mark's son) began by asking a prominent six-point buck what he thinks of the argument that hunting is a sport.

"Well, it's not a favorite sport of the animals I run with," he said. "We much prefer to watch boxing, auto racing, dueling, harmless pursuits like that. Our statistics show that, in hunting, animals are just not your big winners. We don't seem to have the hang of it yet; no coordination, I guess."

An antelope added, "Fleet of foot as some of us are, you got to hustle some to beat a bullet going 750 miles an hour."

Remarked a mallard, "Hunting is a fun pastime if you're the suicidal type. Me, I try to lay low during duck season—whenever the hell it is. God knows they don't tell us."

Trail asked the group how it felt about the theory that hunting is necessary to "thin certain species" and is merely man's way of giving Mother Nature a helping hand.

"If I had my druthers," clucked a pheasant, "I'd choose Mother Nature any day; she plays a cleaner game. I'll take my chances being hit by lightning, forest fire, starvation or disease as against a .38 shell. I like the odds better."

A moose stood up and said, "What kills me is, so many hunters are such lousy shots they plug almost as many hunters as game. Last year, thirty hunters shot themselves." The crowd roared.

"Good for them!" shouted an outspoken possum. "There are too many hunters as it is. It's an act of conservation—mercy even

—to thin their ranks each season. Otherwise these poor hunters will overpopulate our woods."

Trail said that most hunters are decent people who know how to handle their guns and don't go around shooting up mailboxes, as depicted. "I'm not much relieved to hear their aim is improving," said a fox with a cane. "I can't decide if I'd rather be maimed or mounted."

When Trail asked for ideas, a forest ranger, who had just been wounded when a hunter mistook him for a grizzly in a Smokey the Bear hat, offered a compromise: "I say we allow hunters to go on safaris through darkest Montana, replacing helpless native wildlife with rhinos, grizzlies and tigers."

He explained, "It'll make a more even match and will satisfy both the hunters' need to hunt and American animals' need to stay alive." A lion in the audience got up on his hind legs and seconded the motion.

"Last fall," he said, "I bagged two rich stockbrokers from Chicago and both are now stuffed in my den in Kenya. The wife says it's just a silly macho exercise on my part but to me it's a harmless escape. I just love the outdoors."

A black panther in back yelled, "Right on!" but insisted he never mauls a hunter just for a trophy. "It's the meat I'm after; otherwise, I wouldn't even bother."

Both wild cats are now working toward establishing a game preserve in upstate New York where deer and other quarry can stalk urban hunters, exotic creatures dressed in such colorful plumage as blazing orange vests and red earflaps. They have imposed a strict limit, however, of only fourteen hunters per season; all women, children and men under 5′6″ are illegal.

O.K., SARTRE—START TALKING!

Find out who Sartre is. –J. Edgar Hoover directive during 1964 inquiry into the Kennedy assassination

To: J. Edgar Hoover, Director, FBI, FBI Bldg., Washington, D.C.

From: Agent C. J. McEvoy, Head, Foreign Operatives Division.

Dear Chief: Got your memo on "Sartre" matter and am now on the case to uncover identity of man known only in our files as "Jean-Paul Sartre, author." Quick check with all bureaus turns up no such person, though am told that one "Paul J. Sarter" resides in Atlanta.

On further investigation, we found Sarter is a TV repairman. No relation to individual referred to in your directive of 6/5/64. Trail now cold. Have no leads except rumor that someone with similar name said to live in France and write under name "J. P. Sartre." He may be man we're searching for. Have notified all European units to be on lookout for person calling self "Sartre."

Dear Chief: Am in close touch with underworld informants overseas who believe man identified as "J. P. Sartre" could be using alias.

According to Dallas police, nobody called "Sartre" has any known connections with either Oswald or Ruby, but Ruby had wide circle of acquaintances in and around Dallas-Fort Worth. Various strange types were regular customers at his Carousel Club. Ruby may have known Sartre casually.

Chief: Sorry to be slow getting back to you re Sartre query. Am pressing search on two continents as fast as possible. Dallas police say man named "John Paul Sartt" was hanger-on at bookstore near Dealey Plaza. Sartt claims he's not the writer, but advises we read Sartre's *Age of Reason* and *No Exit* for clues to modern man's malaise.

Chief: Paris police have cabled mug shot of man known in and around France as "Jean-Paul Sartre" along with dope sheet that lists him as "local freethinker and free-lance philosopher known to frequent literary salons." Paris op says Sartre reputed to be leader in French intelligence circles, full of radical ideas.

Chief: Sartre trail warming up. Paris police flash word that Jean-Paul is weirdo co-founder of so-called "existential school of philosophy." Paris phone directory lists no such school. Am checking academies in nearby provinces. Feel we're closing in on him.

Chief: Got new poop on Sartre: Homely man of medium stature, combs hair flat, heavy smoker, wears thick glasses and has major distinguishing characteristic—a wandering left eye. Known to talk at length, has written play about flies. Is often seen on arm of handsome French woman, S. de Beauvoir, but not sure if they married or just live together. Woman also extremely big thinker. Sartre occasionally seen with other women.

Chief: Far-out notions of Sartre may be dangerous. Proceed with caution. Watch for theory on "being and nothingness" and any possible connection to assassination. Warren Commission failed to interview Sartre, even though he was once in New Orleans and may have met Clay Shaw and Al Hirt. On two separate occasions, says New Orleans bureau, man of Sartre's general description visited Dixieland joints.

Chief: N.Y. bureau informs us Sartre turned down Nobel Prize. Friends say he's an outsider, loner, seems detached from society, continues to pursue interest in "existentialism," a godless philosophy in which existence precedes essence, essence being the possibility of being, existence the actuality. Sartre claims there is no reality except in action. Please advise what action to take, if any.

Chief: Questioned Sartre last night for two hours but unable to break him. Seems to have answers for everything. He talked mostly of "living in a void," "being adrift." Not sure what it all means but suspect Sartre knows more than he's telling us.

Chief: Have closed folder on Sartre, as ordered. What do you have on man called "Descartes"?

DRUNK ON THE JOB

I KEEP HEARING a lot about "workaholics," those people who are such falling-down labor lushes that they make life miserable for everyone around them.

One of the more acute cases of workaholism is Governor Brown of California, who, like most chronic workaholics, is fond of calling up aides at 3 A.M. with all sorts of exciting ideas and executive proposals.

Such a person, were he not governor of the largest state, might quickly be termed a common pain in the neck, but workaholics always seem to be celebrities who somehow can get away with pestering people at three in the morning.

Personally, I can't imagine an idea so terrific that it won't keep until 9 A.M.—with such obvious exceptions as (a) going out for pizza or (b) bringing some girls in for a small orgy, or even a small pizza.

I guess you can't very well tell a workaholic on an all-night binge to wait until after breakfast, but these profiles never explain how people on the other end of the line react when Jerry Brown, say, wakes them up at 3 A.M.

I must say, if Brown called me up at that hour with a hot

new plan for trimming the budget, I'd be hard put to be polite, let alone display much enthusiasm.

Governor Brown (barking into phone): Hello? Hello? Are you there, Nachman? Look, I've just come up with some additions to that malpractice bill we sent to the legislature and I want to get your thoughts on it. I know it's late, but–

Me: Sorry, Governor, my clock says 3:15 A.M. I don't know about you, but I've got to be at work in the morning.

One advantage of being a round-the-clock taskmaster governor is that *you* can crawl into bed at 9 A.M. while your staff is stumbling around the statehouse corridors, bleary-eyed.

Certain famed workaholics–Hugh Hefner, for one–are said to hold actual staff meetings at 3 A.M.

Hefner is one of your great all-time workaholics, but even I would be willing to stay up working very late at night in the Playboy Mansion. Of course, it would be my luck that, the very night I came for an all-night session, Hef would nod off at ten.

Senator Dole is not only a workaholic but also a "perfectionist"; however, the two always go together. You never hear of a slipshod workaholic. They're always "demanding people who are as tough on themselves as on their subordinates."

If I were a workaholic, I wouldn't be at all rough on underlings, like I hear Ralph Nader can be. Nader, as you know, is another fiendish workaholic. Why, the man barely has time to change his clothes, and he is always depicted "gulping his meals between planes, scarcely aware of what he's eating."

I sort of envision Nader taking a shower in his suit and, at dinner, chewing on a lightly buttered government study.

The reason men like Nader get snappish at times is that–aside from leaping awake at 3 A.M. with big ideas–they "get by on only three or four hours' sleep and are always at their desks by 8 A.M. sharp." (You never, ever, read of a workaholic arriving at work as late as 8:30; nope–it must always be 8 A.M. *sharp,* if not 6:30.)

Your typical workaholic also is "able to grab a catnap anytime, anywhere," yet the articles never say what shape these supermen are in all day. Maybe all they *do* is catnap.

Indeed, for all we know their work is a perpetual mess and

must be done over again by subordinates. Most of the marvelous ideas I get at 3 A.M. look pretty dumb at 10 A.M., assuming I can decipher them at all.

Let's give all our top workaholics a decent night's rest and, in the meantime, scout around for a few "playaholics" who sleep all day and wake up at 3 P.M. with a wonderful idea to take off the whole afternoon.

A DAY AT THE HUMAN RIGHTS RACE

AN OLD FRIEND I hadn't seen for years, the Aging Liberal, told me over lunch last week that he's been hit by hard times.

"There's nothing unpopular to champion anymore," he lamented. "The moment I find a new cause, it's taken over by the media and within two months everyone in the country is behind it and movie stars are mouthing pious platitudes on talk shows."

The old graying radical sighed deeply and shook his head. "Back in the good old days, I was vilified by everybody and I had a mission. Now, it seems, I've become the leading defender of safe causes."

"Give me a for-instance," I said.

"Take old people," he said. "Suddenly, everyone wants to help the elderly. Until Mrs. Carter came along and popularized it, I had the lame, the halt and the blind all to myself."

"Why, that should make you feel wonderful!" I smiled.

"What's the point in championing a cause everybody believes in? I can't stand this new Bleeding Heart Chic. I think it all started when William F. Buckley went to bat for that convicted rapist. I may as well become an arch-conservative."

"Well," I said, "you could always come out *against* old people and perhaps take a firm stand opposing the rights of the handicapped. Those certainly would be two very unpopular causes."

"At least I'd be on my own again," he said. "If there's anything we flaming liberals hate, it's a popular cause."

After we ordered lunch, I said, "I guess there's no more zip left in the women's movement. Feminism seems to have joined God and motherhood as one of the safer causes to uphold."

He laughed. "In fact, it's replaced God and is edging up on motherhood. I briefly considered coming out for God, but Eldridge Cleaver and Charles Colson stole even that one."

"Speaking of motherhood," I said, "how about children's rights? That looks to be the hot issue of the 1980s, and you could still get in on the ground floor."

"Well, maybe," he said. "I seriously considered taking up the banner for short people after the Randy Newman brouhaha, but I'm too late. Nobody in America would dare speak out against short people."

"I suppose there's no point in becoming a gay activist at this late date," I commented. "That's about to be taken over by the middle class."

"Yeah, everyone wants to get into the libertarian act today," he said. "It's not worth my time. Every singer and comic around has inserted a pro-gay clause into his act and now does ten minutes attacking Jerry Falwell to show his heart's in the right place. I'm starting to feel sorry for Falwell, and a part of me is tempted to rush to his side."

"Hey, that would make a nice unpopular cause," I said, snapping my fingers, "although I fear the ACLU is already there."

"I doubt it," the old liberal said. "Right now, they're too busy defending Nazis."

"Now there's an unpopular position nobody else is into yet," I said. "Why not become the leading defender of Nazi rights?"

"I hate to upstage the ACLU," he said, "but maybe right-wing causes are the answer. So far, no liberals have come out for censorship, spoken about the injustices inflicted on management by labor or defended the rights of whalers."

"Nobody but Pierre Trudeau came out on behalf of slaughtering baby seals, so there's an opening for you," I told him, "although I suspect the ACLU may soon defend baby-seal killers."

"That appeals to me," he said, "I could become the first liberal to go after the environmentalists and that anti-smoking crowd. The country's chain-smokers are in need of a real battler."

"You're on the right track," I agreed, "and if you're too late for that, there's always the fight for death with indignity."

"You've made my week." He smiled at last. "I found a new way for liberals to go without losing their lost-cause identity."

"If all else fails," I said, "there's always the black movement."

"No," said the Aging Liberal. "I have to draw the line somewhere. Right now, that's a little too unfashionable."

BITING THE BULLETS

AFTER A seventeen-year study, my sub-subcommittee on gun control has come up with a compromise solution: bullet control.

By banning the large-scale sale of bullets, gun owners may keep their weapons, the average person (or squirrel) will be safe and criminals won't have to go around empty-handed.

It will, of course, still be possible to get conked over the head with a gun butt, but this is just a first step. The agreement should satisfy everyone except perhaps the hard-to-please National Bullet Association and its 728 members.

The ban on bullets will work this way: Starting in 1984, all cartridges fired by "Saturday-night specials" will be illegal—however, so as not to annoy the powerful pro-ammo lobby and collectors of antique bullets, all other ammunition will still be readily available.

By 1990, all bullets fired by "Sunday-through-Tuesday-night specials" will be outlawed (except in woodsy states).

Bullet control is designed to mollify the rifle groups whose favorite slogan is "Guns don't kill people—people kill people." When the committee looked into this, it found that, in actual (target) practice, bullets kill people.

The committee also discovered that, to inflict any real damage, the bullet should be inside a gun. To test this, several marksmen tried to pick off a moving target by *throwing* bullets at it. Results showed that the bullets merely ricocheted off the man and he escaped with only a few nicks.

When the same test was tried using bullets fired from a gun, however, the fellow died (presumably from the bullets). The committee concluded that guns and bullets can be hazardous to your health when "used in connection with each other," as our report phrases it. To be on the safe side, though, the committee temporarily recommends a twenty-minute "cooling off" period for people purchasing bullets.

As it now stands, any nut can walk into a gun shop and buy enough lead to wipe out a small town. Until the new law goes into effect, a ruling will require "all nuts to be registered and forced to cool their heels for half an hour."

Another popular riflemen's slogan—"When guns are outlawed, only outlaws will have guns"—is true enough, the committee agreed, but many outlaws who testified before the committee said they're willing to give bullet control a try.

"Look," said one gangster, "we hate to be unreasonable about this, but we'd look pretty dumb wandering around the streets without a gun. We can be every bit as terrifying with an empty .38 and then at least we won't be booked for carrying a loaded weapon."

Sub-subcommittee members foresee a day when Congress may pass a measure banning guns with handles and, eventually, triggers. Gradually, the entire gun will be phased out of existence, a part at a time. Remarks one congressman, "There's no reason to rush into this gun-control thing helter-skelter."

Sporting Chances

ANYONE FOR TENACITY?

SINCE EVERYBODY agrees that the basic problem with my tennis game is that I don't take it seriously enough, this summer I'm practicing up on my sincerity.

To prove to people how serious I am about tennis, I've signed up for fifteen lessons in "Advanced Tennis Behavior" with an instructor who works with me two hours a day on such fundamental problems of mine as poor resolve, losing wardrobe and duffer's jargon.

The class begins where "Zen tennis" leaves off. The idea is to get rid of all my silliness on the court so that I can play an entire set without either embarrassing my partners or boring my opponents. Last year, I was thrown out of several tennis clubs for my slovenly habits, juvenile manner and lack of grim determination.

The first day, the teacher told me my tennis attire was severely confused. "Your outer game is in even worse shape than your inner game," he said. "A sincere player does not wear Bermuda shorts, a Yankee cap and knee socks. Besides that, you have the tan of a rank amateur–your arms don't match your legs."

He assigned me to forty-five minutes a day of nonstop shopping at a tennis boutique, increasing my wardrobe a little at a time until I'd acquired enough chic paraphernalia to qualify for a private court.

After a few days, the instructor said: "That new headband is a vast improvement, but your shoes still lack the right number of stripes and you haven't even got a warm-up suit yet." He shook his head sadly. "I know you're capable of much better than that."

A day later, I showed up in a sixty-dollar mesh shirt, Arthur Ashe sunglasses and an elbow brace by Pancho Segura.

"Not bad," he said. "You're getting the idea, but that racquet needs a lot of work. A wooden model can ruin your total look. See that fellow over there with a big Prince metal racquet? Notice how deftly he zips the cover off in a single fluid stroke. Watch him strap on his sun visor—he has a beautiful follow-through."

After one week, I had the basic boutique moves down well enough to work out as a grade-C serious player. Although matched against a man with a B-level tennis ensemble, I won handily (largely on the strength of my Jimmy Connors wristband and Bjorn Borg ball bag).

My teacher was so impressed that he felt I was ready to move on to lessons in "Intermediate Silence."

"Your big problem is, you talk too much. A serious player never says more than 'Sorry,' 'Your add' and 'Out.' An extremely chatty game might include 'Good shot' or 'I should've had that.'"

With his help, I finally eliminated the feeblest jokes from my game and cut out the pratfalls, but I still razzed myself unmercifully and made mocking gestures. This is frowned upon in neighborhood tournament play.

By working long hours with me, the teacher managed to iron out nearly all of the fun in tennis, but he spotted a major new flaw. "You don't play nearly enough to be considered sincere," he explained. "A serious player is on the court at dawn and plays into the wee hours, even in the rain, when lesser mortals have given up."

The idea, he said, is not to win but to let everyone else know that you're twice as involved in tennis as they are, that this is no idle pastime with you. "When others go off for a swim, or to eat, you must learn to beg off, saying that you want to get in a few more games before dinner."

After a week of playing from sunup to sunset, I began complaining loudly how sore I was all over.

"Excellent!" My teacher smiled. "That's the spirit. If you don't let people know you ache from every joint, how are they to tell you're a serious player? Also, be sure to play in ninety-degree heat, and make everyone aware that you 'like to get in five sets before breakfast.' Display your blisters and even minor sprains. Sincere tennis players are constantly wracked with pain."

As we shook hands, he said: "One last word of advice: If all else fails, you can always become the most serious player on any court merely by remarking at once that 'the net looks a fraction low to me' or 'the surface plays slow today.' That'll show 'em you're not just out there for a good time."

WHO'S ON FIRST? (MACBETH)

AFTER LISTENING TO pre- and post-game baseball broadcasts, I've begun to realize that those of us in the entertainment game may be going about our interviews the wrong way, especially with so many athletes breaking into show business.

What follows is an interview held not long ago with a member of the Royal Vic Shakespeare Company, Ltd., a repertory troupe out of Bangor, Maine, after a particularly grueling exhibition performance of *Macbeth* (that noise in the background is the sound of some extras pouring wine over the director's head while three supporting players carry the wardrobe mistress to the showers):

Good evening, first-nighters. Tonight we're lucky enough to be talking with Hank (Mr. Ego) Downey. Well, Hank, how does it feel to get through an entire show without walking into a single piece of scenery or dropping a line? This hasn't been your year, has it?

No, Al, it sure hasn't. Of course, I was lucky tonight; I had a lot of help out there, don't forget. You don't do it all by yourself. I'd say I was pretty doggone fortunate to have a stage crew like ours. In a play like Macbeth, *it can be a matter of inches. One slip and there goes your tragedy.*

I'll say. Which reminds me, Hank, how's that elbow been feeling lately? We all remember the trouble you had with it toward the end of last season. Wasn't it Denver where you took that bad spill from the balcony in *Measure for Measure?* Gave a lot of us quite a little scare.

All I know, Jack, is that it seems to be healing up real fine. Just yesterday in rehearsal we had a fencing workout and it felt pretty good; only a tiny twinge in the shoulder when I follow through on a thrust, but that's just temporary. Sure did come at a bad time, though, right there before that guest shot on the Carson show.

Speaking of that, Hank, has the audience been much of a factor so far this season? I know that when you first joined the rep in mid-year after two years at Lincoln Center some of the folks were expecting too much.

Well, that's right, Lon, but that'll happen. They all got on me at first, as you know, for holding out for $1,000 a week at the Globe Theater, but like I told some of the fellas, I'm going on my twelfth Equity year, you know.

You certainly have a point there, Hank. Then, too, you've had the added experience of radio and TV spots, magazine promos and that off-season job as product advisor for Max Factor. I think most of the fans realize your position now.

Yes, Red, they seem to be pulling for me. I notice people seem to be laughing louder—not at me so much as with *me—and most of the real rude hecklers have laid off. That can make a difference in a fella's mental outlook.*

I'll bet. Another thing, Hank, what's it like to be up there against one of the all-time great ones—like a Shaw or a Shakespeare. Is it just another show, once you've been around a while?

Well, Bill, we just try to take 'em one at a time. You know what they say, Strindberg put his pants on one leg at a time, just like everybody else. Overall, I couldn't say there's a heck of a big difference, no.

Still, wouldn't you say, Hank, that the prospect of taking on someone like Shakespeare might give some of those younger fellas the willies? I imagine when you first came up from summer stock, it took you a while before you could think of someone like Gielgud or Burton as an equal . . .

That's about it, Tony. I've played all over—Stratford, Off-Broadway, daytime TV—and I'm here to tell you, there's no substi-

tute for your classics, your Ibsen and your Moliere. That's what this game is all about, if you ask me.

Any other advice, Hank?

Only this, Phil—that a young fella just breaking in shouldn't be afraid to take a walk-on, even in something like Barefoot in the Park. *Never underestimate a pro like Neil Simon.*

I guess you know that as well as anybody, Hank. I'm thinking now of that unfortunate TV comedy series you were in a few seasons back. It surprised a lot of people who thought you were incapable of that long a slump—thirteen weeks, wasn't it?

I'd just as soon forget that, Win. I've never been one to dwell on past errors.

I know you're anxious to get that damp costume off, Hank, but before we let you get back to the green room, how do you think you'll do next week in Chicago against Chekhov?

Well, Howard, as you know, we've come a long way in the past month since that triumph in Seattle, when we upset all the oddsmakers by taking both ends of that twi-night twin bill with the Russians, Uncle Vanya *and* Lower Depths. *I'd say that constituted a real turning point. I think we just might pull a repeat in Chicago.*

You'd say, then, that the company is "up" for this next tour?

No question about it, Vin. We still have a relatively young cast, but what we lack in depth we make up for in hustle. You won't find a more willing bunch of kids anywhere. They're always ready to hang in there against new, untried playwrights, and to put out that extra gesture that makes all the difference between success and failure. It's really been a lesson to some of us older players.

Well, Hank Downey, we want to thank you for taking the time out to chat with us today on *Backstage Warm-up*. Now, as we do every day, we'd like to present you and your lovely wife, Eulalie, with a carton of our sponsor's own spirit gum. So, until later, Hank, when we'll be talking to you and voice coach Dominic Giovanni in our intermission show in the prompter's box —break a leg, fella!

Will do, Joe.

ALL PSYCHED DOWN FOR THE GAME

"IT'S BEEN A real down week for me, Dr. Newberk, what with football reaching its annual fever pitch and me reaching my annual autumn ennui, not caring one way or the other who wins what."

"You're once again having difficulties facing up to your utter lack of interest in the Rose Bowl, is that it?"

"Exactly, Doc, and as usual I feel tremendous guilt about it."

"It must be hard on a man in our society who is apathetic toward football. Do you fear your masculinity being threatened?"

"Yeah. Darn it, I know I should worry whether USC or Stanford meets Michigan on January 1, but football holds no meaning for me. Office pools make me very bored and depressed."

"Does your indifference include pro football as well as intercollegiate?"

"Doc, I don't even read the stories on the sports page, like I used to, and all those weekend game scores on TV drive me nuts."

"Maybe your total rejection of football reflects a refusal to admit you might be a latent fan. Rather than accept that part of yourself, you're overcompensating. Do you ever long for season tickets?"

"Doc, I didn't even much like football in high school—that's where my guilt began. I just went to games because of the dances afterwards. Even there, you had to rehash the game with your date. I was forced to have an opinion of the team's chances for the title."

"Then you felt a need to show an avid interest in football merely to win the admiration of certain women early in your life, is that it?"

"Right, Doc. They all expected it of you."

"Did this sort of behavior later manifest itself in college?"

"It got much worse. At college, I could barely drag myself to the so-called 'big games,' and then only for the half-time events."

"What was it, specifically, about those half-time events that drew you to the stadium week after week?"

"It was the crisp fall air, the sound of crunching leaves underfoot, the aroma of hot coffee and roasted peanuts, the roar of the crowd–"

"Yes, yes, of course, but was there anything else?"

"Gosh, I don't think I want to probe any deeper, Doc . . ."

"Try. That's what we're here for–to reveal the darkest secrets in the innermost recesses of the mind . . ."

"Well, O.K.: I went to those games primarily to gawk at the song girls, cheerleaders and majorettes. It shames me to admit it, Doc."

"I'm sure it does. What you're saying, if I hear you, is that football was an explicitly sexual experience in college."

"I guess so, but everything was then. Even during crucial plays, my eye would wander from the backfield to the sidelines where the girls were warming up for the half-time show."

"Why does your hostility toward football disturb you?"

"I feel incapable of talking to barbers and cab drivers who keep asking me what I think about Jim Plunkett. I have a difficult time functioning in large male groups at this time of year."

"You feel stifled and unable to speak, is that it? Possibly you feel you've let these barbers and cabbies down in some basic way. You feel, in a word, inadequate."

"I think you've hit on it, Doc. When some guy mentions the Rams' passing game, I feel like a sissy. I try to hide my true feelings about the Rose Bowl by saying 'It looks like Ohio has it all locked up again.' Down deep I know I'm a fraud, and I sense that the taxi drivers and barbers know it too."

"Why do you feel so ambivalent about your alma mater?"

"They refused to win for four years, and it was a terribly ugly sight for a young man to experience, season after season."

"Obviously, you have an intense loathing for your Old Eleven. Thoughts of the team must stir unpleasant memories of your youth."

"They'd keep fumbling, Doc, all afternoon. It went on for years

—and the other team's interceptions were equally repellent to me."

"Perhaps you associate your own fumbles at that youthful age with your college team and, by extension, with all of football. I assume the Super Bowl brings out extreme feelings of apathy in you."

"I've tried to repress it, but I can't."

"It occurs to me that the two things you've focused on today—the song girls and the fumbles—are perhaps symbols to you of your own inept, bumbling ways with co-eds. Ignoring football is pushing aside your past. . . . Well, we're out of time, but next week I'd like to pursue this and get into your feelings about the Dallas-Miami game."

"I'm not quite sure what you mean."

"Don't tell me you missed it? Geez, it was a helluva battle! There was one incredible catch in the last quarter, when Miami was fourth and nine on the Cowboys' 38-yard line, and . . ."

SPORTS SOUPED UP WHILE-U-WAIT

UNDER THE HEADLINE "Baseball: Too Slow a Game in Jet Age," someone has once again suggested how the sport can be speeded up by such shortcuts as limiting games to seven innings, lessening the number of balls and strikes, forcing pitchers to hurry up, etc.

All worthy ideas indeed, but obviously this fellow hasn't heard of an ongoing study being made to make baseball even faster, by:

Permitting runners to go directly from first to third base, without having to stop at second and thus delay the game; eliminating right field entirely, as too dull (any balls hit here would be considered automatic outs); doing away with all pitchers (batters would toss the ball up and hit it themselves); increasing the number of shortstops to six (to prevent balls from going all the way out to left field).

Moreover, if the pennant winner is not decided by July 4, revised rules will declare the season null and void. The World Series, if any, would be decided by a "sudden death" verdict—the toss of a coin in the Commissioner of Baseball's office.

The man who wants to see baseball speeded up also suggests limiting arguments between players and umpires—a point worth considering. Such incidents, though lively and colorful, do hold up the game. By the same token, plays that tend to hasten the game along, such as pickoffs and double plays, ought to be made mandatory each inning.

Research into baseball reveals, alas, that much of what slows the game down is the dawdling of spectators, who insist on ambling to their seats when they should be hustling, who take seventh-inning stretches in other innings, make unnecessary trips back and forth to the hot-dog stands and take far too long parking their cars.

There's no use speeding up baseball if everybody is just going to squander all that precious time saved.

People who are anxious to speed up baseball are wasting their time when so much more work remains to be done in chess.

My own modest ideas to speed up chess include eliminating the first twelve moves, which are mainly ritual; doing away with some of the chess pieces that merely clutter up the board, such as pawns or knights; and shortening the length of time between major matches from five years to three and a half. The game would be decided by a round of arm wrestling.

There's no reason for games like baseball and chess to take so long in this day and age. In the era of the Cuisinart and the Concorde, they're slowing everyone up. If a jet plane can get you to Paris and back in six hours—the average length of a double-header—there's no need for a chess game to last several days. (It's no secret that Lindbergh was appalled by the famous Fischer-Spassky tournament. "I flew the Atlantic for this?" he muttered.)

Those involved in streamlining baseball propose using a stopwatch or egg timer. If a side is not out in ten minutes, say, the team in the field would be suspended from baseball for a week.

Any pitcher who walked a man on purpose would be sent to the penalty box.

Another sport in big trouble with the time-motion people is golf. Why all those endless holes? Surely six or seven should suffice. And why so many clubs? Is there a real need for all that distance between tees and greens? Why delay the game with water hazards and sand traps, where balls tend to lodge?

After a close look at golf, it was recommended to authorities in charge of speeding up sports that the game be reduced to one hour, if not outlawed completely. It was also suggested that all golf matches be taken off TV, where they make fans so lazy on weekends that valuable time is lost and no work is done around the house.

One other sport being scrutinized today is track—especially the 100-yard dash, which experts claim is perhaps *too* fast.

In the effort to standardize sports, officials hope to lengthen the 100-yard dash to 500 yards, even though this might make the 440-yard run seem redundant. (The mile run, they say, is just about long enough.)

Basketball is still the toughest sport to speed up, for it's about as fast as it can get, yet one idea is being studied. Since most major basketball games are decided in the final moments, it might help if only the last two minutes were played. This would cut down on the lengthy season, which careful scheduling might squeeze into a single evening.

The most stubbornly pokey sport is horse racing, but nothing can be done to speed up the horses. They refuse to go any faster, no matter how often riders are admonished. The jockeys blame it all on the horses, who in turn blame the trainers. It's a mess.

Impure Science

BUTTON UP FOR THE ICE AGE

I HATE TO sound like an alarmist, but I understand we may be in for another Ice Age. Don't ask me where I heard it—I think it was in one of the gossip columns.

Maybe you're too young to remember the first Ice Age but it was a dilly: water all over the basement, icicles hanging from everybody, cars that refused to start, and, of course, it was very cold —not as chilly as Chicago in December maybe, but plenty cold all the same.

The funny part about an Ice Age is, you sort of get used to the cold. It's so cold you almost forget there's an Ice Age on and just go about your normal everyday life, as people did in the Jazz Age.

Some species did curl up and die off, sure, but they lacked the proper mental attitude. No gumption. If you let an Ice Age depress you, you're a goner right away.

Species that bundled up warmly and took care to sip plenty of hot liquids usually survived the bad weather. Others—the brontosaurus, the mammoth—failed to take good care of themselves and became extinct before their time. It happens.

I have a surprisingly optimistic feeling about the next Ice Age. As I see it, we made it through the first one O.K., so let's not get carried away about this one. If it comes, it comes—that's my attitude. I don't know about you, but right now I have too many other worries—the sinking of the continental shelf, to name just one that springs to mind.

When we look back on that first big Ice Age, we're able to laugh. Many of us wonder how we ever got so upset at the time, but we were all much younger then and had never sat through an Ice Age before.

People got hysterical and assumed it meant the end of all life, but of course it didn't, though it certainly threw a good scare into everybody.

Now and then, mankind needs something like that. Mankind tends to get a bit smug, and just knowing we all may be snowed under soon allows us to value each and every century that much more.

How do we know an Ice Age is just around the corner? Easy. Many furry creatures have been seen heading south and, what's more, taking longer and longer vacations in Barbados and Puerta Vallarta.

Also, the global temperature is dropping. I haven't noticed it myself, but then I go around in short sleeves in winter, so an Ice Age could come and go and I'd never know it.

Finally, in the words of the National Academy of Sciences: "We are now entering the cold 10,000-year phase of the 20,000-year earth wobble cycle." I think in time we might learn to handle the cold, but I'm worried about that wobble. (This is *just* a hunch, but maybe if we could fix the wobble the earth would warm up again. It's worth a try.)

Anyway, if the Ice Age does arrive, here are some tips that may help you and your loved ones get through it alive:

1. Don't fall asleep. Many people, believing the first Ice Age was 10,000 years away, got careless and dozed off, only to wake up half frozen the next day. After that, they slept with one eye open for years and years.

2. Don't stand near a glacier. They move slowly, true, but when they move, brother, watch out!–they *really* move.

3. Keep gloves and ski mask on you at all times. It's easy to be caught off guard. The last Ice Age struck in mid-July.

4. Report any unusual polar bears in the region. This is usually a clear sign that an Ice Age is well on its way.

NOBODY HERE BUT US BALDIES

DOES ANYBODY KNOW whatever happened to the featherless chicken?

I am almost afraid to ask, certain it has gone the way of the square egg or the oblong tomato, both of which seem to have been announced for the sole purpose of making cheap headlines. (Scientists, you know, are not above having their little jokes too.)

Just about a year ago, there was a newspaper account that claimed science, in its inimitable fashion, had perfected a featherless chicken–if "perfected" is the right word. In 1910, a chicken without feathers would have been regarded as seriously defective.

The purpose of a defeathered fowl was to save money on plucking. A smooth chicken, I suppose, rolls down the chute easier. The drawbacks stated at the time were that a bald bird (1) gets cold, (2) bruises easily and (3) loses its balance. Well, who wouldn't?

My guess is that a featherless chicken was judged not commercial, or perhaps the Humane Society finally stepped in and put a stop to manufacturing silly chickens. A chicken without feathers, I should think, would soon become the laughingstock of any barnyard, or lab, although Dr. Max Rubin, a poultry researcher, is quoted as saying, "I don't think they're aware of the fact that they're naked."

This struck me as rather a heartless thing for a man to say who purports to be a friend of chickens. While I'm no poultry expert myself, common sense tells me that a chick born without feathers would realize within a week that something was awry. A chicken has eyes, for God's sake.

The delicate breeding problem, it was explained, is that smooth chickens can't get any traction in bed; they lose their footing. This in turn makes the naked chicken extremely embarrassed and uptight about "doing well."

It is rough enough to lay eggs, I imagine, without also worrying how you look and wondering all the time if you're being compared to a chicken *with* feathers.

What I can't figure out is exactly how they go about breeding a featherless chicken in the first place. Do you mate a slightly balding rooster with a middle-aged hen interested primarily in companionship and quiet evenings by the fire? Or is the chicken first shaved and then introduced to a kindly understanding rooster?

When science announces these major advances, they always leave out the sexy details. If I were a rooster, I'd probably be turned off by a chicken without feathers, but for all we know that's just what gets the boys excited.

We also presume that chickens would rather have feathers than not, but maybe they're a huge bother. Perhaps feathers are to chickens what toenails and whiskers are to people—annoying ornaments that simply get in the way and must be cleaned and clipped all the time.

According to this AP story, the nude chickens had less fat and 16 percent more meat on their bones, but were twice as jittery —and no wonder: They got nervous running around naked all day, with everybody giggling at them and making crude comments.

Possibly the idea didn't work out because poultrymen had difficulties with chickens catching nasty chills that couldn't be cured by slipping little sweaters on them. If you've ever tried to get even *one* hen to lie down and take two aspirin, you know what these chicken ranchers were up against.

I wish the reporters who write about these sensational scientific discoveries would do follow-ups. How is the featherless chicken faring? What has become of those square eggs we were promised —speaking of which, where is that oblong tomato?

It's easy enough to go around developing featherless chickens or tomatoes and eggs with corners, but not quite so simple to follow through on it. If you ask me, these are just cute stories that publicity men for the big science laboratories cook up to keep the public constantly amazed and titillated.

Probably there was never any serious intention to develop a featherless chicken, so I'm glad I didn't fall for it and get my hopes up a year ago. It doesn't matter if *I'm* left in the dark, but I think it might be nice if they told the chickens.

FOND MEMORIES OF THE GRIM REAPER

TWO ENCOURAGING BOOKS on death—*Life After Life* and *Journey to the Other Side*—prompt me to reminisce about my own experience when I was given up for a goner only to return to life fifteen days later and upset everybody's weekend plans.

It seemed like only a few moments, but I was told that I had, in fact, been "away" two weeks, a new record for round-trip travelers to the Great Beyond.

This doesn't count a lady in St. Paul who so enjoyed her preliminary death she taught herself to expire at will, using intense concentration and deep breaths, rather like TM.

"It's pretty scary sometimes," says her husband, "but Fran always makes it back in time to fix supper. She says it relaxes her and, afterwards, she has twice as much pep as before."

Generally, people were glad when I was back in the pink after my fortnight "over there," but some friends sounded miffed. They figured I'd done it on purpose, as a gag. I'm known for my wacky stunts.

The nurse wasn't so pleased. "I have enough to worry about without patients playing possum," she said, annoyed that I had cheated Old Mr. Death. "You have a very peculiar idea of fun."

My own doctor was equally unimpressed. When I got back to life, he chuckled, "Well, well—look who the cat dragged in!" He warned me not to try it again, for the shock of returning to life can put a strain on your heart, as well as your credulity.

When I got his bill, I was shocked and called him to complain that it seemed unfair to bill me for the time I was dead. "Take it up with the insurance people," he said, and hung up.

My coverage, though extensive, does not include a life-after-death clause, the agent explained, and I have to pay the difference myself. He told me: "We're thinking of offering a post-life insurance policy, since these incidents are popping up a lot lately. It would cover anything that happens to you while you're dead."

Most versions of what life is like in the so-called "hereafter" describe it as a pleasant experience not unlike going to East Hampton, so I decided to gather material for a book on people who had "died" but hated it. I found only six.

Reactions vary. Said one man: "I felt as if I was drifting into a new dimension; everything was white. It was like skiing, only bumpier." A woman remarked: "It reminded me more of Paris in the twenties." A third person told me: "I'd compare it to a poorly lit Italian restaurant with very slow service." Well, that gives you the idea.

When *I* got back to life, my wife asked, "Is there any kind of entertainment, or dancing? I mean, is it worth going back?" That's hard to answer. I wouldn't go out of my way to rush right back, but I've been to worse places.

"This is all very confusing to people who only die for a little while, because they don't know if they're coming or going," said one of the friendly, smiling hostesses who met me after I'd prematurely died and gave me a glass of wine. "Once you loosen your tie and relax, you'll enjoy your cosmic flight. Would you like a pillow or anything?"

Like many folks who have "died," I felt myself slipping out of my own body and was able to stare down at myself lying there. I looked quite content, though in need of a haircut.

"Hey, maybe I'm actually immortal," I thought. "Wouldn't *that* be a nice surprise!" (although the very idea made me blush).

The notion of immortality also scared me. Besides a trim, I didn't have nearly enough cash to last forever; there hadn't been time to get traveler's checks. I looked to see if I'd brought my house keys and was relieved that I had. If I did return to life, at least I wouldn't have to go to a hotel.

If you're really dead, of course, you needn't worry about any of these petty details, which are taken care of for you.

"Uh, how do I know if I've died–you know, for *good?*" I asked a fellow who told me he'd been gone since 1924.

"Well, if you arrive and there's a big basket of fruit in your room, you can be pretty sure that's it," he smiled. "Since these books came out, though, we have a new motto around here: 'Never say die.' We prefer to feel that we've only gone away for a while."

Real long-term death, he pointed out, is quite different from the temporary variety–for one thing, it's more boring than the shuttle version. "Even final death itself isn't half bad," he said. "I'll tell you one thing–it's much easier than moving."

OUR DECAYING CIVILIZATION

JUST AS I WAS about to sink my teeth into a dish of sweet potatoes larded with marshmallows, I came across this headline: "Fewer Cavities Are Hinted in Ancient Peru Indians Than Among Modern Man." I am not impressed.

I'm getting a little tired of always hearing how some ancient civilization was in such tip-top shape that it makes today's civilization look pretty anemic. Peruvian Indians, as it happens, had it rather soft compared to modern Americans, or even modern Peruvians.

Mostly, it seems, they sat around in their fancy Inca villages feeling quite smug about their terrific teeth.

Modern man is doing just as well as he can, under the circumstances, and one thing he doesn't need right now is to be reminded that his molars are in worse condition than some 1,200-year-old mummy's.

I wouldn't be at all surprised if, in another 1,200 years, residents of Peru look back and marvel at how healthy we in the United States were in 1983. "Gosh," they'll say, "those ancient

Americans had 97 percent fewer cavities than folks today. What sturdy people they must have been!"

We, of course, know exactly how *unsturdy* we are, but future races could easily be fooled by our bridgework. By the same token, there's no way for us to know how fit those ancient Peruvians truly were. O.K., so they had nice teeth, but maybe their toenails fell out at an early age or they had unsightly dandruff. For all we know, your *average* ancient Peruvian was a mess.

All of this fine talk about ancient civilizations is beginning to give modern man a severe inferiority complex. I don't see why we have to sit still for it anymore. If he had any grit at all, modern man would stand up and say:

"Hey, let's quit putting the knock on contemporary mankind, O.K.? If you haven't got something good to say about modern man, don't say anything!"

Anthropologists, I suspect, are duty-bound to say only glowing things about ancient cultures. I imagine they find a lot of stuff in Egypt that gets covered up again, very quickly, if it paints the old Egyptians in an unflattering light.

Just for once, I'd like to see a headline that said, "Ancient Race in Katmandu No Match for Today's Suburbanite," and read below that modern man, for all his failings, is twice as nice a fellow as his ancestors.

I'd even settle for a story that said: "Mummies recently examined by anthropologists were found to be stoop-shouldered, myopic and flat-footed, with evidence of high blood pressure and premature senility."

A dentist who studied the Incan mummies' incisors discovered that "cavities were not treated directly but relieved with herbs, such as coco leaves, which contains cocaine . . ." What these Peruvians did, it appears, was keep away from dentists and snort dope. Is this the sort of behavior we want today's generation to emulate?

I don't know why we always give ancient people credit for something they did naturally. I see no reason for us to go around feeling sorry for ourselves and envying the dentistry in old Peru. If these Incans knew so much, and were such a hardy culture, where are they nowadays? Believe me, there's a whole lot more to modern man than pretty teeth.

PUT ON A HAPPY FACE

A CULTURAL HISTORY of smiling—and the relationship between human and animal smiles—has just been completed by the New York Zoological Society. It is long overdue.

For too many years now, we (and by "we" I of course include our grinning little animal friends) have gone around smiling without knowing quite why. Maybe animals know why, but most of us up here on two feet are in the dark.

I'm not sure just what a "cultural history of smiling" should include, but presumably it will trace the first known smile—more of a smirk, actually—up through our modern-day belly laugh. At long last, we'll be able to pay a well-deserved salute to the first man, woman or saber-tooth tiger to smile.

Smiling did not begin, as you might think, with cavemen. While cavemen did plenty—more than their share, really—they did little smiling, per se. It was hard to find anything very amusing in a tar pit. He or she may have emitted an occasional sneer, but if a caveperson smiled you can rest assured it was an accident.

Smiling as we now know it did not begin in earnest until the Ice Age, and even then it was difficult to tell if people were "smiling" or simply grimacing from the cold.

Little work of any kind has been done on The Grimace, but there is every likelihood that what we blithely call a "smile" was in fact an indication of intense pain. Some 73 percent of infants' smiles, for instance, is due to gas, and as cultural historians are quick to report, "There's nothing funny about that."

Grimacing was popular at the time of Marco Polo, but it gradually evolved into snickering and, finally, smiling. Before that, people who felt like a smile had to slip out behind the barn. For 500,000 years, smiling was frowned upon.

How did this change from grimacing to full-blown grinning come about? It is thought by many to be largely the result of court jesters. Other scholars claim that smiling was more of an "overnight thing"–a sudden fad, like roller skating, that caught on with young people of loose morals who ran about with silly grins as the oldsters clucked, "What won't these kids think of next?"

In any case, we still take smiling too much for granted. Why do some people–New Yorkers, say, and certain tribes in Borneo–smile less than people in Austin, Texas, where the phrase "Smile when you say that, mister!" was first coined?

Other major questions come to mind: Where did the "smile button" originate and who posed for it? Were smile buttons worn by ancient Greeks? How did Mona Lisa get *her* cute smile?

None of which deals with the more complex relationship between human and animal smiles. Most of us have not given any thought to whether bears, horses, camels, canaries and wolfhounds do, indeed, smile–and why should we?

If a dog is smiling, how can we tell? I used to know a Labrador retriever who seemed happy enough yet never quite managed a smile, but then neither did I. If a dog ever smiled at me, I'd ask him to find another place to hang his hat. I couldn't cope with a dog I felt might be chuckling at me behind my back. I like pets to have regular noncommittal animal-like expressions.

I also had a nodding acquaintance with several cats and none of them ever gave me so much as the time of day. Cats have a neutral look that cannot, by any generous stretch of the imagination, be termed "smiling." At best, it's closer to glowering.

If many animals don't smile, possibly they've never been exposed to anything very funny. Maybe if a cow or even a cat were allowed to hear a few minutes of Henny Youngman, they would crack up like anybody else. Whether animals have a sense of humor, however, is a horse of another color.

UNLUCKY OL' SUN

EVERYONE IN THE scientific community out where I live is concerned over recent doubts by astronomers about the sun.

It seems that the sun may be a different sort of star than we thought and a less reliable energy source—not that I've made up my own mind one way or the other, understand. When it comes to theories about sunspots, I'll listen to almost anyone's ideas before deciding; I'm not at all dogmatic about the cosmos.

(I dislike a person who is narrow-minded about the sun, don't you? It shows a lack of growth.)

Most of the time, I avoid all discussion of the sun. It just gets people too upset. We had some folks in recently and I stupidly let drop a casual comment about the sun's interior and—well, it ended up with one astrophysicist in tears and two wives not talking. The party broke up early and did I catch hell about it later.

"I thought I told you *never* to bring up sunspots around the Dubins," my wife said, angrily lighting her cigarette. That was that for the sun around our house!

As you may have heard, we all depend on the sun for everything, and here is where I think we go wrong. Why must Americans, of all countries in the world, be so dependent on a single energy source? This isn't any way for a highly developed nation to behave. It's very humiliating.

Is the United States some sort of backward country, quaking at every little eclipse, or are we a civilized people? Why let the same "small star" keep us all on tenterhooks like this, year after year? If we're not careful, we could land in the same sorry fix we're in with the oil-producing Arab nations.

I say we should find ourselves a new star, one we can deal with easily and openly, an alternate fuel source we feel secure with, a star that won't just decide to burn out some fine winter morning. It makes no sense to let ourselves be pushed around the universe and bullied. Are we or are we not a major Western power?

In school, I was virtually guaranteed that if the sun ever burns out "it won't be for a million years." Or maybe it was a billion years; in any case, it was a pretty reassuring-sounding figure and gave a boy of fourteen a good solid feeling.

I remember how we all smiled rather smugly at each other when we heard the sunny long-range forecast, and chuckled: "Well, I guess *we* won't be around to worry about it—ha, ha!" How little we really knew; how naïve and trusting we all were!

At fourteen, we believed when scientists promised you that the sun is good for a million or more years, the warranty will at least hold up through 1990.

Science teachers all led us to believe that the sun was "our friend" and that, while the oceans and mountains might do us in someday behind our backs, we could always rely on good old smiling Mr. Sun.

When I grew up, I simply assumed that the sun was one of those basic areas that scientists understood, if they understood nothing else. Now, suddenly, they "don't know" why the temperature fluctuates, what causes tremors on the surface and why certain "neutrinos" seem to be dogging it.

Next, I suppose, astronomers will report that the big yellow thing we've been labeling the "sun" is, in fact, a sort of planet lit from within by a large volcano.

I'm older now, and less sure of a lot of things and the sun is one of many uncertainties in life we must learn to adjust to. I don't want to sound bitter after all the sun has done for us over the years, but I must admit I'm just a little disappointed in it.

SCARE TACTICS

A REPORT BY the Stanford Research Institute claims that many people besides Uri Geller are capable of ESP; they just don't know it. I am one of the few people to whom this does not apply. I am 100 percent ESP-proof.

It's a deep mystery. Famed doctors, psychics and magicians who have studied me carefully pronounce me otherwise normal. "Why, there's nothing wrong with this boy that a haunted house won't cure," said one parapsychologist, ordering me to a clinic to be spooked.

In Transylvania, I underwent a week of therapy—sitting alone in a dank castle, listening intently for rattling chains, banging shutters, moving nightstands, an owl, anything. I gobbled tania root morning, noon and night; I ran around in wolfbane. Nothing happened, except the wolfbane made me sneeze.

It got so dull I came home and watched *Psycho* on TV, but a psychic experience can't be hurried. No self-respecting ghost likes to be pushed into these things; it only turns him off.

In desperation I visited Uri Geller, who gave up on me after a week when I still couldn't bend a spoon—not even using a vise. "You're just not trying," he pouted. Kreskin was paralyzed in my presence. He got no signals of any kind; I suggested charades. "Hey, get this guy out of here," Kreskin said, finally. "He gives me the creeps."

When I tell believers I'm beyond help, they won't accept it. "You must train your psychic powers, like a muscle," they insist. "Anyone can do it, but it takes practice. You have to work at it."

I began very simply, hoping to bend a pipe cleaner telepathically (possibly into a little giraffe). When that failed, I tried unbending paper clips. After some knee bends, I stared at a needle; the eye stared back. The trick, I'm afraid, is to concentrate hard, and my attention span is just under ten seconds.

Experts claim we're all continually having psychic "experiences." Some people manage two or three before lunch. What we call a "coincidence" may, in fact, be genuine ESP. Well, if that's the case, I say forget it. I want a real ghost or nothing. I want to bend silverware with brain waves. When it comes to ESP, give me the works!

Once, I went to a séance, but it was called off on account of sunshine or something. Instead, the clairvoyant held a reading. Unable to read much more than a newspaper, she blamed me, labeling me a warlock. Maybe I'm not getting any psychic action because I'm a demon myself. That would be a fine joke on me, all right.

Most so-called psychic experiences you hear about are borderline incidents that would barely qualify as everyday occurrences without a few nice dramatic flourishes. "Y'know," somebody will say (popping their eyes for effect), "last year I dreamed I was on a boat headed for South America and–not six months later–I was on a paddle-wheeler headed down the Mississippi! I think there's something to this ESP."

As for Loch Ness monsters, Venusians and other phenomena, I remain unconvinced, snapshots or not. Anyway, suppose there *is* a Loch Ness monster, or even two? What then? I wouldn't be surprised if there are scads of monsters and Martians out there in the lagoons. I would be more surprised if there aren't. What are lagoons for?

When a monster is at last hauled from the deep and we get a good look at him in the light, I predict worldwide disappointment; the old horror films have spoiled us. And nothing from another galaxy can hope to live up to even a third-rate punk group.

THE SOLAR UNIT ALSO RISES

PEOPLE SEARCHING FOR new energy sources obviously aren't looking ahead far enough to what is sure to occur once the nation turns to sun, wind and garbage for fuel:

Husband: Edna, did you see this March bill for wind? I can't believe it. I'm sure we didn't burn up that many breezes. We were away for a week, or did you forget to call and have all the windmills turned off?

Wife (*sighing*): How much is it this month?

Husband: If I read this right, we've been billed for 6,000 zephyr units of power. That's ridiculous for a house this warm.

Wife: Didn't you see where Con Energy just upped the rate for paddle-turns-per-hour?

Husband: It's those damn wind hogs next door who are using up all the best air in the neighborhood. What a bunch of gust guzzlers! Now I see they're a two-windmill family.

Wife: Well, the President warns there's a limit to how much wind is left in the world, but nobody listens. Everyone just assumes there's an infinite supply of natural air.

Husband: I read an article that says if people keep on squandering wind like they do now, by 2100 there won't be enough velocity left to power the country's major windmills. It suggests cutting down on the use of weekend sailboats.

Wife: What will happen when we finally run out of wind?

Husband: We'll just have to turn to alternate energy sources, such as mule teams or chain gangs.

Wife: Americans are so wasteful when it comes to blowing air wisely. The kids still think nothing of leaving the mill running when they're not home.

Husband: Well, at least our solar-heating bill hasn't gone up. It's still 78 cents a year, although I see they're trying to get a rate increase to $3.50 a year. The Sol Company insists that the cost of running the sun has gone up.

Wife: How can that be?

Husband: Beats me. They're blaming it on "overhead."

Wife: Speaking of which, we'd better stock up on some fresh solar panels for next winter. Those original tar paper slats we got in 1978 are on the blink–I think they're buckling again. If you weren't so chintzy, we could get a classy nuclear system.

Husband: Do you have *any* idea what nuclear repairmen are charging these days to install an atomic cell? It's highway robbery –assuming we can even get one to come out within six months. Those nuclear repairmen make a fortune. I think they're all crooks.

Wife: Why don't we just give away our old solar unit to the maid and buy a nice new reflector, like the Crimmins have on top of their house? It makes the roof look so much prettier.

Husband: I guess we are wasting good sunbeams with these old burned-out panels. When the solar man comes around again to check the meter, tell him we're using too much energy.

Wife: He was here this week and said we might be fined for inefficient energy consumption. He thinks we have an energy leak somewhere.

Husband: Maybe that's what's causing me to sweat all night–a solar leak in the house. Has he any idea where it's coming from?

Wife: He checked all the cotton batting around the doors and it's not that. He suspects there may be some sun escaping through the windows in the downstairs guest room. I wish we could get our whole house re-solarized next year.

Husband: We'll see . . . right now, I'd better get down to the energy shop before it closes and pick up some extra bags of garbage to keep the fireplace going this weekend.

Wife: Good idea–but this time don't buy any of those cheap presto-manure logs. Get the good rubbish cubes. They're more expensive but they burn longer and don't smell quite as funny.

MEASURE FOR MEASURE

A CITIZENS' LOBBY opposed to the metric system in America has hired me to devise a better way of measuring, so I've invented a method that not only wipes out metric but does away with all numbers—the new Poetic System of Weights & Measures:

IOTA: One iota is equal to 2 inches under the old system, but in Poetic measure an iota is equal to 3 whits.

WHIT: A whit is half an inch long, except in Europe, where they use a long or a short whit, which is one third of a smidgen.

SMIDGEN: A smidgen equals 14 inches (or golden rule). Metric users can make the conversion easily in their heads simply by figuring, "It doesn't make a centimeter of difference to me."

YEA HIGH: "About yea high" is now officially anywhere from 3 to 5 feet tall, depending on the country in which you're standing. In the U.S., yea high is just a tad over 4 feet.

TAD: One tad measures 26 iotas on a standard tadstick, or 48½ old inches. In discussing weight, however, a tad is 9 ounces, or approximately 2 tidbits.

TIDBIT: Half a bit or the same as 4 wee bits.

BIT: In time, 15 minutes (as in "I'll be over there in a bit"). In cooking, it's equal to a teaspoonful (as in "Could I have just a bit of that shortcake?"). Should not be confused with a "bite," equal to 9 bits, or with "2 bits," which is 25 cents.

NIT: Now equal to one fourth of a tad. Nits come 110 to the pick. Thus, a pick of nits equals 22 tidbits. (A good memory device is the old riddle: "How many nits could Peter Piper pick if a nitpicker could pick nits?").

HAIR: There are 200 hairs to an ordinary gram (or 15 per gramps).

HAIRSBREADTH: One ten-thousandth of a snippet.

SNIPPET: One third of a snip, also equal to 7 scintillas.

SHADE: A shade equals a mile and a third, which is computed by taking the square root of a standard oak tree.

JOT and TITTLE: A jot is half as large as a tittle (10 tittles thus equals a jot), but is twice as big as a dot. Six cubic jots are the same as a square smidgen.

GOB: Two bunches (or in military terminology, equal to one standard U.S. sailor).

BUNCH: There are 21 batches to a bunch.

HUNK: Equal to 3½ gobs.

ITSY (or EENTSY): One hundredth of a bit, or what was formerly known as a "millibit."

STONE'S THROW: Exactly 102 feet, equal to 85 piano throws.

PIANO THROW (as in "I'd trust him about as far as I can throw a piano"): Equal to one regular-size liar (or, musically, 27 lyres).

ARM'S LENGTH: Two feet formerly, or one sixth of an earshot.

EARSHOT: Twelve feet, or the same as one spitting distance.

SPELL (as in "Let's sit a spell"): 27 minutes.

MANY A MOON: Three months, or 144 spells; also one eighth of "a coon's age."

TWO WHOOPS AND A HOLLER: Exactly 650 feet (it takes 25 hollers to make one whoop).

BIG AS A MINUTE: Two feet high. Thus, one may refer to someone as 3 minutes tall.

FOREVER AND A DAY: One week, or the same as 5 blue moons.

SLIP (as in "a mere slip of a girl"): 97 pounds; in Europe, 6 "slips" = 4½ girls.

KNEE HIGH TO A GRASSHOPPER: Equals 3½ years and/or 2 feet 2 inches, whichever comes first. It takes 27,000 grasshoppers to make one knee-length.

SMALL FORTUNE: Two small fortunes equal one "king's ransom," now worth $348,096.13, which rounds off to $350,000.

POOR AS A CHURCH MOUSE: An official U.S. church mouse now earns $2,320, well below the poverty line.

FAT AS A PIG: According to the new Poetic System, a pig officially weighs 318 pounds; it takes 85 pigs to equal one standard whale.

COUPLE OF BUCKS (as in "Can you lend me a couple of bucks

till Monday?"): The equivalent of $20; "Monday" is two weeks, or one standard "mañana."

POETIC LICENSE: In most states, renewable every 6 years unless you have had three or more moving violations and seriously injured public sensibilities, in which case the license holder may be suspended up to 90 days, or "a baker's month."

EAT, DRINK AND BE WARY

FOLLOWING THE CAFFEINE scare and the news that babies are endangered by their pajamas, I asked the Food and Drug Administration and the Federal Trade Commission for a list of items that are in no way harmful to people. After some prodding, they produced the following:

PAPER NAPKINS: People who have had to give up eating may be encouraged to hear that little or no harm has resulted from using paper napkins regularly; however, ingesting them over a long period may be dangerous (though no more so than eating tomatoes).

CHARD: Unfortunately, Swiss chard is *very* good for you, despite the fact that 98.7 percent of those who ate it in FDA tests expressed an intense dislike, or at best extreme indifference. Even rats who were regularly fed the weird dark-green substance failed to die later, though they weren't exactly crazy about it either. Said one: "I'd rather be dead than eat much more of this stuff."

RADIO: TV rays may render you impotent, but there is no evidence so far that links radio waves to sterility, no matter how close you get to the dial. People in laboratory tests were allowed to sit next to radios for six months and afterwards appeared to be as healthy as before, if twice as bored.

PEACHES: After extensive scientific tests, lab animals fed a steady diet of sliced peaches produced no ill side effects of any kind–until sugar and cream were added, often resulting in death.

(Raw Elberta peaches eaten alone, with the skin peeled, were given a tentative "green light" by the FDA; however, the agency has decided to attach a precautionary label to each peach, warning potential eaters to "Beware of Huge Pit Within.")

WICKER CHAIRS: While generally considered safe, even for long-time users, the government now cautions people against the over-use of such chairs and the possibility of tumbling off them onto the floor, severely injuring themselves, perhaps for life.

"The weave in the seat can give way at any time," notes one FTC scientist. "We still believe the safest place to sit for any duration is on the floor itself." Recent tests proved that fewer people fell and hurt themselves while sitting on a floor than any other place. Only half as many Americans in 1982 died on floors as in bed.

BUBBLE BATHS: Rats who were soaked several hours a day for 2½ years in lavender-scented bath water came out somewhat more wrinkled than they went in but otherwise were none the worse (albeit rather more peevish).

The FDA, therefore, has decided to permit the sale of bubble bath, with a warning not to soak rodents in the tub for longer than two years. Such rats, they caution, may emerge from their bath in a testy mood, overheated and wringing wet, and are likely to take a mean nip out of anybody nearby.

POSTCARDS: It was found that 89 percent of all people who handled postcards came down with serious sunburns, leading the FTC to wonder if there was any direct cause-and-effect relationship.

"We discovered that the postcards are not at fault," says the agency, "and that the unusual skin condition may be due to a continued wearing of sunglasses." (A new series of tests is planned.)

PAPER BAGS: These potentially dangerous sacks were once on the FTC's list of "potentially harmful objects" following incidents of children sticking their heads inside the bags and crashing into tables, inflicting nasty gashes. This resulted in an immediate ban on paper sacks as "hazardous to children's shinbones," since lifted.

Recent tests found that paper bags often leak or, if overloaded, have faulty bottoms that "break open," injuring people untrained in the proper way to carry home heavy bags of groceries. This defect has now been corrected by the addition of double-strength sacks.

BREATHING: Scientists now question if *not* smoking may be just as hazardous to one's health as cigarettes, given the uncertain condition of the air, but new tests indicate that by and large it is better to breathe than not.

ARMAGEDDON RACE

THIS MAY BE a bad time for some people but the doomsayers have never had it so good.

At a recent doomsday convention in Atlantic City, the keynote speaker was Dr. Thadeus Moribund, Visiting Professor of Gloom at Stonehenge University, who said this is the worst period in history for mankind. It's also the world's worst year, but Moribund looks forward to an even bleaker 1984.

"They tell me the Dark Ages was no picnic," he says, "but at least man survived, so how bad can it be? The universe, as we know and love it, will not be here by 2001." Moribund claims the world will either freeze, starve, choke, crowd, poison or tickle itself to death. "My pet theory," he confides, "is that we'll all be eaten alive by hamsters."

I asked him about the oft-mentioned fear that the continental shelf is slipping half an inch a year and that Canada may slide into the sea any day now, taking the U.S. with it.

He shook his head gravely. "There's a real chance of that, but it's even more likely we'll drown first when the glaciers melt." I asked, "Say, how *are* those polar ice caps doing, anyway?" "Due to nuclear tests," he frowned, "they're melting faster than ever and may well wash away northern California by 1985—providing a massive quake doesn't wipe it out earlier."

I asked whatever happened to good old strontium 90. "It's still poisoning generations yet unborn," he assured me, "but twice as fearsome as that are these aerosol sprays, easily the most ghastly development for man since July."

"They're scary, all right," I said, "but what about this talk that someday we won't have any more drinking water?" Professor Moribund said it was an old scare. "The hot trend today in doomsday circles is that we're running out of land."

I asked him, "You mean people may suddenly start shoving each other off curbs and out of windows? Will it finally come to that? I've never been able to picture exactly what goes on."

"Beats me," he sighed. "Look—we doomsday experts only predict cosmic catastrophe; we leave the details to others. We can't do everything. We're too busy forecasting to worry about the whys and hows." He wondered if I wanted to hear some current perish favorites. I said I surely did.

"Cloning shakes people up pretty good," he said, "but there's just no end to end-of-the-world notions. You must have read how the planet is growing colder and that eventually we may sniffle ourselves into extinction." His eyes lit up. "Or have you heard the one about the earth slowing down?" He rubbed his hands together gleefully.

I told him I had indeed but wasn't sure what it meant. He said, "If the planet slows down, we'll all lose our balance one day and go crashing into one another. It's a very messy way to go . . . Of course, there are worse things that can happen."

Such as? "There's a new study that warns of a certain breed of insect now proliferating faster than man can smack it with newspapers. Scientists fear it could someday gobble up all of mankind and much of New York City."

Dr. Moribund said his only worry as a prophet of doom is that people have begun to take the end of civilization with a grain of salt, forcing cataclysm leaders to dream up even more horrid specters of tomorrow. Through clenched teeth, I said, "Give it to me straight, Doc. I can take it."

"Well, I hate to sound like an alarmist," he said, "but the human race is now in danger of slowly sinking to death as the earth turns to quicksand. It's a very real possibility if we don't learn to control our environment. Several people have already had narrow escapes in their own backyards. The mud, which has always been our friend, could turn against us just like *that.*"

A TOAST TO THE COCKTAIL HOUR!

JUST RECENTLY, I read somewhere that Evelyn Waugh "invented" the cocktail party. (I could have sworn it was T. S. Eliot.)

Oh, sure, it would be nice to get credit for the electric light or the automobile, but to have actually devised the world's first cocktail party–well, that's something mankind will be applauding long after light bulbs and automobiles are forgotten.

I suspect this is how the cocktail party first dawned on Waugh:

MRS. WAUGH (*enters Waugh's workshop carrying tray*): What could you possibly want with all of my best glasses and four big bags of potato chips? Not another crackpot idea, I trust.

WAUGH: *Shh-h-h-h!* I'm working on the final details of a little brainstorm of mine. I call it the "cocktail party." I don't like to boast, my dear, but it could alter the course of social history–assuming, that is, it's not used for destructive purposes.

MRS. WAUGH: Cocktails at a party? I don't get it. Why roosters?

WAUGH: You're just like all the rest–no vision! No foresight! I call this little shindig I'm tinkering with a "cocktail party" because it sounds catchy and–well, commercial. I've *nearly* got it. If I can just figure out where these blasted swizzle sticks go, I'll be home free . . .

MRS. WAUGH: What are "sizzle sticks"?

WAUGH: Swizzle! Swizzle! These thin long-stem gizmos with knobs on one end. I tried sticking them in avocado dip but nothing happened.

MRS. WAUGH: Why couldn't they be used to stir drinks with?

WAUGH: Of course! That's it! Dear, you're a genius. It's so obvious. Why didn't I think of that? Now, if I can just think how to skewer these tiny meatballs without them rolling onto the floor.

MRS. WAUGH: Dear, I hope your "cocktail party" idea is going to be—well, practical. If only you'd invent something people can use—like brunch. Now, that was something everyone took to naturally.

WAUGH: You know brunch was *my* idea originally! Someone stole it.

MRS. WAUGH: Yes, yes, of course, and now you've worked so hard to perfect the cocktail party too. I hope you're not neglecting your health. Is all this liquor and cigarettes really necessary?

WAUGH: I've got to try every possible combination of alcohol until I find the true cocktail itself, a rare elixir that continues to elude me. I'm having some new people in today around five o'clock to help me sample a new drink I just concocted in the lab.

MRS. WAUGH: I wish you'd told me some people were dropping in today. This garage is a mess; it's no place for any kind of meeting. We'd better hold it in the living room instead.

WAUGH: I'm sorry, but there wasn't time to call you. Last night at 4 A.M. I got this inspiration for gin and vermouth and had to scribble down my notes in the dark. These may be the crucial ingredients I'm after to make the "cocktail party" a reality at last.

MRS. WAUGH: Well, who did you invite?

WAUGH: Oh, everybody, but I know they'll hit it off. I told them to drop by anytime around fiveish. It's nothing fancy.

MRS. WAUGH: Fine, but what happens once they get here?

WAUGH: Everybody will just sort of mingle . . .

MRS. WAUGH: "Mingle"? I wish you wouldn't use so many technical terms.

WAUGH: It means to mix and make chitchat. Don't worry, it'll work out fine. When people come, you simply go to the door and say: "How nice of you to come! Just toss your things in the bedroom. The bar is over there and help yourself to food!"

MRS. WAUGH: Hmmm. It sounds risky to me. How do you know all these strangers will have anything to say to each other?

WAUGH: They won't immediately. That's the point of giving

everyone "cocktails" first, see? After six or so, everything should start to hum and, if we're lucky, we'll witness the birth of the very first "cocktail party." In a few years, I'll be on easy street.

PROBING THE KNOWN

WHILE MANY SCIENTISTS still hope to discover life on Mars, Professor K. E. O'Ryan is excited by the even more likely possibility of death on Mars.

"I've felt for years now that there must be some form of primitive death on Mars," he told me recently while preparing to launch a private probe of the earth's neighboring planet.

"What makes you so cocksure?" I asked Dr. O'Ryan.

"Well, we already know that ideal conditions for death exist on Mars–lack of food, poor air, little or no water, inadequate housing. It stands to reason that death of some kind will await us when we arrive. I expect my mission should be a great success."

"Why hasn't anyone else considered the prospect of death on Mars?"

"Oh, they've thought of it, all right," smiled O'Ryan, "but nobody has dared bring it up except yours truly. The idea of life on Mars is so much more *appealing* and–well, upbeat. It's hard to get NASA funding for Mars exploration if you go around talking about death. The government won't go along, because the public doesn't want its tax dollars spent on such a depressing space probe."

When I told Dr. O'Ryan he sounded very confident of finding death on Mars, he said: "Well, I've been watching Mars since 1936 and I see no sign of life whatever, nor any reason to believe it could possibly survive. Why do you think Mars has been so damn quiet for centuries?"

"I wonder if you're not just a pessimist," I said.

"I don't let emotions rule my work," O'Ryan said. "It's obvious there's nothing on Mars but death and more death. Why not face facts? The less movement I see in my telescope, the surer I am of it. After years of being laughed at, I'm about to be proved right."

"I guess you've been pretty much alone in your theory that Mars contains all of the necessary conditions for death," I commented.

"That's the lonely road of the original researcher," he sighed. "Most scientists only want to look on the bright side of interplanetary study, but I'm not influenced by my cohorts' Pollyanna approach to Mars."

Dr. O'Ryan said that when his private spacecraft lands on Mars, he expects it will send back photos of total nothingness. "I can hardly wait!" he grinned. "It's gratifying to realize that my life's work is soon to become accepted fact. I'll be known in all the science textbooks as 'the man who discovered death on Mars.'"

"I hate to be a wet blanket," I said, "but if there's death on Mars, there must have been life."

"There you go!" he snapped. "Don't leap to conclusions. You sound like my colleagues. Nothing is going on out there in space, my friend, and the sooner we get it through our heads, the better. My studies show conclusively that Mars is dead as a doornail—*deader*."

"Just what species of death do you hope to find on Mars?" I asked him.

"Even the smallest evidence of non-life would make my mission worthwhile," he explained. "I expect to find absolute devastation of all living things—the fewer the better—but for the time being I'll be satisfied to bring back a few Martian rocks."

"Yes, that *would* be exciting, all right," I said. "That would be almost as deadly a find as moon rocks."

"Later on, in more sophisticated Mars landings, I expect to find all sorts of dead organisms," he went on excitedly.

"What do you suppose they will have died from?"

"Many of loneliness, I suspect," said Dr. O'Ryan, "a few of weightlessness. Some may have committed suicide upon learning where they were. Mars is a pretty bleak place to call home."

"I guess the notion of spending your whole life in a crater is enough to discourage even the most ambitious organism," I observed.

Dr. O'Ryan added that many Martian organisms expire of sheer ennui. Those that try to leave Mars early in life are soon frustrated and turn to drink—only to find that all there is to drink is water, which makes any would-be life on Mars even more morose.

"It's a damn shame," I said. "They can't even drown their sorrows."

Dr. O'Ryan nodded: "If scientists had discovered earlier that life on Mars existed, it might have given life there something to live *for.*"

"I admit it's hard to get very excited about a little moisture on Mars," I said. "That's sure not my idea of life. So, as you say, Professor, death on Mars looks like a real possibility. May I be the first to shake your hand . . ."

SOMETHING OUT THERE DISLIKES ME

DESPITE ALL THE talk about ESP, UFOs, demons and other unseen forces, nobody has mentioned a major phenomenon that I call "Extra Spooky Perception," which is sort of a reverse ESP that works on—rather than in—you.

A common example would be the "disappearing newspaper item," in which a little story you saw in the paper—and want to find again—is on the *only* page of the newspaper that's missing. You can have 100 old papers in the house, but never that particular page.

When I was younger, I regarded this as sheer coincidence, or just lousy luck, but as I grow older I realize it is nothing of the kind. It is something more than that—a very real force, directed at me and perhaps a few others.

As I burrow madly through stacks of newspapers and magazines, muttering, "Dammit, I *know* it's here somewhere—I remember the exact spot on the page it ran!" I can hear, chortling softly behind me out of sight, those little ESP spooks.

Another instance of reverse ESP is how the telephone will always ring precisely twelve minutes after I lie down for an afternoon nap. You may scoff and say, as I used to, that somebody is bound to call at 4:30 or 5:00, which I could accept if the phone didn't ring no matter *what* time I put my head down.

I can attempt a catnap at 11 A.M., 2 P.M. or 8 P.M. and the phone will always ring, even if I should be in a strange country where I don't know anybody. It's bound to be a wrong number or a man selling magazine subscriptions.

In fact, if I want to talk to someone, I'll *purposely* lie down, shut my eyes and pretend to be asleep. Within twelve minutes, the phone is jangling merrily away. This doesn't always work, of course, because the folks at ESP headquarters can often tell when somebody is trying to put one over on them.

You want *more* proof? I'll go into a restaurant with my heart set on some favorite dessert, and needless to say they aren't making it that day or they just sold the last one two minutes before I came in. You call that normal?

I've grown so aware of Extra Spooky Perception that I can almost feel when it's about to strike, so rather than waste time going to a favorite restaurant for a special dish, or catching forty winks, I avoid both.

Don't worry—I've got plenty of other examples. Say I'm in line at the bank (where I tend to be most of the time): As soon as the ol' ESP force spots me coming it'll make sure that right in front of me is a chatty butcher with four bags of money to deposit.

Nobody can tell me that man was there before I arrived; it's another of several supposedly "innocent" events that I can no longer wish away, or ignore.

If I have to go to a post office, ESP springs into action and it turns out to be either (1) the day after a holiday or (2) the day all the crazy people in town are sending money orders to Alaska. Why, I wonder, did they *all* descend on my branch at that very hour? Pretty darn strange, if you ask me.

ESP will occur anywhere I am, such as on a plane, bus, or in a waiting room when a blonde and a bum both enter and search for a seat. If there is one next to me, and a spot next to someone else, I think by now you can guess who goes where.

Or take any grocery store I choose to walk into at random: ESP is invariably in the air, planting people in front of me who are trying to cash a check without proper identification, or having the clerk run out of change as soon as it's my turn.

It has to be ESP that's also responsible for checkers and tellers and postal clerks who close down their counter as soon as they see me approaching, or who make sure that the person who waits on me is a trainee.

ESP obviously accounts for the scads of stores I arrive at just as they're locking the doors; I'd have made it on time, but the spooks already thought of that and arranged for me to try the side door first, the one reading: USE SIXTH AVE. ENTRANCE. It must be ESP, too, that determines the very phone booth I need will be occupied by a teenage girl breaking up with her boyfriend.

Plenty of people would allow incidents like these to make them paranoid, but I know what's out there and I realize there's nothing I can do to keep Extra Spooky Perception from working its will on me whenever it pleases. It is simply another very real presence that we do not completely understand.

I don't know about you, but *I* am not alone.

WHEN A BODY GREETS A BODY . . .

A LOT HAS BEEN written about body language, its uses and abuses, but nobody has dared discuss how it works in actual practice, or even if it *does* work.

It's all well and good to say that if a pretty girl lifts one arm over her head, and extends a knee slightly, it means she has a crush on you, but what happens next? Can you just sidle up to someone at a party and whisper, "Say, I couldn't help noticing the way your toes are turned inward . . . Your place or mine?"

May you assume the person sending out signals *realizes* he or she is making advances, is telling you to get lost, etc.? Also, do you reply in basic body language or is plain English O.K.?

To cite a personal experience: The other night, a lovely woman at a coffee shop was holding her cup with the thumb at such an angle as to be almost lewd. Her left shoulder was also cocked and —well, I think you get the idea, all right.

As you can imagine, I was in quite a tizzy. In desperation, I strolled over and winked, which in body talk translates roughly into: "I am interested." She moved away quickly, called the manager, an ugly scene followed and I was finally taken downtown and booked on two counts of "impersonating a masher."

I've tried speaking body language, but I get nowhere—not even as far as using my voice. Crossing one ankle over the other (said by body language swingers to be a surefire opener), I tried catching the eye of any of seventeen women at a little bar that advertises: "Body Lingo Spoken Here."

When that failed, I became more explicit, cracking my knuckles and pulling up a sock. This told the girls I was (1) single and self-employed, (2) interested in tennis, Truffaut, caramel sundaes and a good time but was (3) a lovable lug at heart.

One of the gals scratched her ear, thus informing me she was a recent college graduate (either UCLA or USC) with an art history major, dug Michel LeGrand and was partial to films by Francis Ford Coppola—or she may have said Frank Capra; her neck has a tendency to mumble.

When I replied, "Huh?" (by cupping my ear), she walked off in disgust. I'd offended her somehow and we had missed making contact by *this* much, but then body language is not a pure science, like, say, phrenology.

Or maybe I'm just not adept enough, though I have a pretty fair kinetic sense and my forehand is improving. I've read the classics in the field—"30 Days to a More Powerful Posture," "Why Johnny Can't Read Jane"—and taken a course in speed-reading bodies. (People ran back and forth in front of the class and we took down what they were saying. I got so I could read up to 250 women a minute, with 77 percent rate of comprehension.)

In a recent interview with the author of a body language book, he explained the basic grammar: Open hands means "openness," a sideways glance indicates "suspicion," chewing a pencil or biting nails shows "insecurity," wringing hands means "frustration" and —most startling of all—whistling, perspiring and a "whew sound" all are clues to "nervousness."

This was all news to me. No wonder I have such rotten luck with women, am a total business failure and can't change a tire.

Nonetheless, here are a few inside tips I've learned over the years and want to share with other body language novices:

—If the individual is smiling and laughing (upturned mouth, teeth bared, rapid intakes of air, hair neatly parted) while seated in a "casual attitude"—i.e., with a drink in one hand, slouched in his chair, on the floor, etc.—he may be regarded as "HAPPY."

—A wrinkling around the eyes (or "peepers" as they're termed at the Body Institute of Applied Speech), scowling or "frowning" about the lips and loud noises emanating from the throat indicate the person is what we call "ANGRY." If fists are clenched and both arms raised, he is said to be "PRETTY DARNED BURNED UP."

FUTURE SHUCK

I HAVE SEEN the future and I'm tired of it. In fact, about all I see nowadays is the future. Today has vanished, swallowed up in forecasts of what tomorrow holds. Nobody likes yesterday anymore and the present bores people, a fact that professional futurists have neatly turned into a giant industry.

Every magazine includes at least one piece promising that by 2001 (why is it never 2004? or 1997?) man will be living in caves, be working at home an hour a week and flying to and from the grocery. This conflicts with futurecasts that claim we'll all be shopping by computers, or the one about running out of food by 1990.

Futurism has grown by leaps and bounds since the Computer Epoch began. Before that, future-gazers had to hedge their bets a little, but now anything goes. Dodging distasteful specifics, they issue some awesome catchall pronouncement: "Soon, computers will be commonplace in the courtroom." Or maybe it's the bedroom. Nobody quite knows what they mean, but it sounds so irrefutable. Anything doable can be stored in a silicon chip the Size of Your Thumbnail. I predict that by no later than March of 2001, our fingernails will be made of silicon chips, or vice versa.

The newsstands are full of futurezines, with spooky names like *Omni* and *Discover,* that print tea readings done by University of Chicago professors. In November's *Omni* I read that "handwriting analysis is increasingly being accepted as a science." Right. (In *Omni* anyway.)

Today's futurist was yesterday's swami. I date the dawn of the Future Age from Alvin Toffler's *Future Shock,* which showed that if you said something scary enough about what Life Will Be Like, many people would buy it. In Toffler's new book he doesn't quite take it all back, but he tells us that we can do something about the future. It seems that the future can be stopped after all: We Have the Know-How. And the best sellers.

The typical future scare is entitled (in eerie printout letters) "City of Tomorrow," depicting funnel-like buildings with little pancake-shaped cars scooting through the streets and nobody on the sidewalks. In the city of the future, if I recall, everyone lives underground and everything runs by a computer in Danville, Ill.

When you can't quite prove anything, you simply say it (whatever *it* is) will be done by computer, satellite, cable, data banks or freezing. You won't hear a peep out of anyone.

All this talk of future wonders makes me nostalgic, taking me back to my school days when there were regular banner headlines in the *Weekly Reader* that, by 1970, man would be eating meals made up of pills on a plate; that by 1975, man would be flying around with a jet strapped to his back, and that by 1980, easy, man would be dialing people on picturephones. The picturephone flopped before we got a look at it. Man is no dummy.

Those were the hot predictions of the fifties. The things we actually have now, I notice, nobody predicted–Atari games, call-forwarding, lapel mikes, designer chocolates, indoor football, no-fault divorce, snooze alarms. Where were today's futurists then?

Underlying futurespeak is the premise that the guy writing the book or the article knows something we don't, that he's been conferring with major specialists, technicians and think tankers, and that, according to their careful prognostications and whatnot, the Future can be plotted on a graph.

In flipping through an old *Omni,* I see an item about "lunar billboards," which is your basic future shocker. Here's a dilly about "plastic brains" and yet another on "do-it-yourself dental fillings." Read all about it!

Actually, if you read enough about it, you can write this stuff yourself. How about Underwater Condos! Body Telephones! Martian Graveyards! Fish in Space?

What you do, see, is you formulate a preposterous juxtaposition and then write that "given the current rate of modern technological breakthroughs, it will be possible within the decade to . . ." That's Futurese. "Within the decade" gives you a little leeway, though not quite as much as good old 2001.

The nice thing about future shucking is that, by 2001, or even by the end of the week, nobody is going to remember (or possibly be around) to contradict the most outrageous futurizing. The sky's not the limit, for The Future Is Limitless. There is no such place as the future. It's just sci-fi with a Ph.D.

Futurism wouldn't fool anyone for a minute in the world we all know a little about. Imagine someone writing that, by the year 2001, people would be 3.5 times funnier than they are today; or that within the decade, sex, as we know it, will vanish from the face of the earth, or that 50 years from now every child will clean up his room as a matter of course and sonnets will be big business.

One thing I've learned in hanging around Tomorrowland is that, if you wait long enough, the future never gets here. It's something to look forward to.

IT ONLY HURTS WHEN I BLUSH

IT IS ENCOURAGING to see that shyness is finally gaining acceptance in the scientific community.

For hundreds of years now, people have been tiptoeing about, all tongue-tied and red-faced, trying to pass themselves off as healthy, normal individuals. The shrinking violet and the timid soul were not taken seriously until Dr. Philip Zimbardo opened a "shyness clinic" at Stanford University and wrote a book about this social disease that nobody dared to discuss in public before.

Like sex and death, shyness was one of those taboo topics people avoided mentioning in polite company. Today, however, in our new open, freewheeling, anything-goes society, we're able to confront shyness with the same blunt honesty we bring to aging and transsexuality.

We are, after all, grownups, are we not? And this is 1982, not 1882, is it not? There is no need to whisper behind closed doors that "Stanley sure is a shy one, all right" or "Louise never says boo."

You wouldn't guess it, to see what a big strapping bruiser I turned into, but for years I was considered a helpless 97-pound mouse. It was all I could do to bring in the morning paper without flushing bright scarlet. Today, of course, I am a mesmerizing raconteur and man-about-town, up on all the latest dance steps—all thanks to a few sessions at Dr. Zimbardo's shyness clinic.

My problem was, I could not admit my own shyness to anyone, not even myself. I thought I was a natural-born dummy. Finally, I saw a physician and confessed the trouble to him. "Doc," I said, "I must talk to you about something that's been bothering me for the last thirty-seven years. I think I may be . . . socially impotent." (I could not even utter the word "shy.")

"Now, now," he said, trying to calm my worst fears that I had contracted something more severe than chronic shyness. I was worried I might be—well, aloof, perhaps even a closet hermit. I had heard that people like me were often regarded as social lepers. In some cases, incipient shyness is mistakenly diagnosed as trichinosis.

I recall reading that Hitler was actually a shy, retiring fellow, riddled with insecurities and self-doubts, and that Napoleon and William the Conqueror were uncomfortable on dates.

Many people appear to be friendly and outgoing, even warlike, when in fact they are simply covering up a tremendous lack of social confidence. This makes it hard to tell who is truly shy and who is only pretending to be a brash boor but is shy *underneath*—what Zimbardo terms a "shy extrovert." We will leave the "bold introvert" for another day.

Such people, it seems, are shy without knowing it, and here is where the danger lurks. Dr. Zimbardo claims that "shy people may, in fact, form the backbone of the silent majority which supports the political status quo—especially a dictatorship."

Too many shy folks in one place, in short, can lead to a fascist regime, led by a meek *führer*. The reddening cheeks, the downcast eyes, the toe in the rug, the coy fluttery eyelashes—these are all the familiar signs of your latent tyrant.

Attila the Hun, it is said, was known to blush furiously when about to invade a new country. After sacking a city, he would often mumble, "Oh, gawrsh, now look what I've gone and done."

Other "shy extroverts" include: Joe Namath (secretly afraid of both girls and sports); Teddy Roosevelt (built the Panama Canal to avoid asking directions to California); Yasir Arafat (afraid of his own shadow—the arrogant manner shields a demure soul); and Mick Jagger (became a rock singer to hide his fear of people in groups).

Dr. Zimbardo reveals that "shyness is universal"—not, as many had assumed, confined to the United States and Canada. Zimbardo has found shy people everywhere—Paris, Tibet, even New York City—and claims that "60% of the people in Japan and Taiwan" are shy. Some nations, like Russia, are simply ashamed to report soaring shyness statistics for fear that other countries will decide to walk all over them.

Contrary to myth, people are not born shy. "There is no evidence that shyness is an inherited trait," Dr. Zimbardo concludes. "It is learned." Well, that's reassuring, but I have proof of my own that shyness often skips a generation. If your grandmother was a pushy so-and-so, there's a good chance you may become a despot any day.

Going in Literary Circles

THE ORIGINAL UNABRIDGED BLURB

AFTER YEARS OF admiring his way with words, I've finally found the man who writes all of the lively blurbs that appear on book jackets and in the ads for would-be best sellers.

I met J. R. McPuph at a literary cocktail party last week where he was in the midst of discussing his latest discovery.

"It's the work that everybody should read if they never read anything else," he said, "the best book to date on the subject, a serious effort that takes a calm, rational look at a controversial subject many have found too hot and unwieldy to handle . . ."

"It sounds good, all right," I said.

"It's not merely good," he went on. "It shows unusual insight. The author is obviously a man of rare intelligence who has finally written a long overdue book . . ."

"How many days overdue?" I kidded McPuph, but he was too excited to hear me, and babbled on:

"It's by a brilliant young regional writer from the South who is a voice of the newly liberated, an author with a keen feel for the small but telling effect, the memorable phrase and subtle nuance that reveals character. It sent shudders up my spine and gave me that rare shock of recognition. This is the real thing, a fully realized work."

"I can't wait to read it," I said. "It seems to have everything."

"How did you know?" said McPuph. "It's the book everybody said couldn't be written–the one that everyone is talking about this season, a shocker being whispered about from Southampton to North Korea, a *roman à clef* that has the entire nation trying to guess the identities of its thinly veiled yet memorable and full-blooded characters."

"It sounds sensational," I smiled.

"*Sex*sational!" corrected McPuph. "This is a book that many in the halls of power will cringe at, not to mention the book that the labor unions, the CIA and Hollywood tried to suppress."

"Tell me more," I said.

"Actually, it's just a marvelously funny book by an incredibly gifted new face on the scene, a former milliner from Nebraska who worked nights for eleven years to finish this teeming saga of life on the Nile."

"I thought you said it was amusing."

"Oh, it's a giggle, all right. It'll make you laugh but perhaps also shed a tear or two at its fond—but haunting—recollections of what it was like to be at war in the 1860s and a mother of six in a little Nova Scotia fishing village in the early days of the Russian Revolution."

"It's all of these things?" I asked.

"Yes and somehow much more," added McPuph. "To read this book is to experience the world of a small boy growing up for the first time in the Southwest, when time stood still. It will take you back."

"It sounds like a pure delight," I said. "That is to say, a charmer."

"You took the clichés right out of my mouth," said McPuph. "This is a powerfully but skillfully written, finely wrought novel that far surpasses the author's earlier work and shows promise; it foreshadows something even greater to come. The writer is not merely a shrewd observer of the human condition but a born storyteller too. He spins a dandy yarn."

"Does he remind you of anybody?"

"Indeed he does. He's sure to make you think of Mark Twain, Dostoyevsky and Dickens, who had best look to their laurels."

"But will it make me forget *Gone With the Wind?*"

"Perhaps not *GWTW,* but it may make you forget *An American Tragedy, The Green Hat, Stella Dallas, Young Fu of the Upper Yangtze, Arms and the Man,* Chesterton's letters to his son and Fitzgerald's letters to his daughter."

"Would you go so far as to say this book is as crisp and zesty as the first day of autumn or as sweet as the first sip of May wine?"

"Both," he said. "I'd even go so far as to say it's a stunning evocation. I might add that if Hemingway were alive today he wouldn't be able to put this book down."

"What you seem to be getting at," I said, "is that this is a darn good read."

"Not only is it a darn good read, it's a real page-turner, as well as an alternate Literary Guild selection, and is soon to be a major motion picture."

"I can't wait to get it. Where can I snap one up right away?"

"It's available at fine booksellers everywhere."

"I'll see you later," I said, walking out the door.

"If I were you, I'd run, not walk, to my nearest bookstore."

"What was the title again?" I asked.

"I don't remember, but it's going to be the Big One for '83. . . . Mark my blurbs."

DON'T "QUOTE" ME ON THIS

AS LONG AS everyone else is becoming a language scold, I may as well jump into the fray with a pet grammatical peeve of my own, an affliction approaching herpes-epidemic scale called "quotationitis," or Bartlett's Disease.

This is the reckless, helter-skelter use of quote marks around words, phrases or entire sentences that don't need them, the sort of thing you see in hand-lettered signs in store windows that read "OUT TO LUNCH" (quotations all theirs).

What happened to plain old humble OUT TO LUNCH? Another example of quotationitis is APARTMENT "FOR RENT": INQUIRE WITHIN. When I see that, it sounds as if the landlord doesn't really mean the apartment is for rent at all; he's just kidding.

One day, I saw a sign on a door that read "BACK" AT 2:30, so I looked to see if it was an osteopath's office, in which case the "BACK" AT 2:30 would make sense as a lame pun, but the "BACK" had no clever point at all. It was simply BACK with a little scrollwork around it.

I suspect the purpose of people who go in for rampant quoting is to sound breezy or folksy or something. I've even seen OUT TO LUNCH written OUT TO "LUNCH" as if "lunch" was too slangy a word to use without quotation marks. You wonder if "LUNCH" is a code word for, say, dope.

These quirky quotation marks (or "quarks," as I think of them) are obviously a desperate cover-up by people who somehow feel that if a phrase occurs in common speech it should wear some sort of punctuational finery when it's meant to be seen in public.

How else do you account for "WET PAINT"? Is the paint wet or isn't it? "WET PAINT" hints that it's probably dry.

Formerly simple understandable commands, such as DO NOT DISTURB, suddenly sprout little quote wings, in a vague attempt to seem cute, if not forceful. Half the time, extra quotation marks appear to be replacements for the bold old no-nonsense underline.

That would help explain why menus everywhere now prefer to say "WE DELIVER" rather than the more humdrum–and somewhat less personable–WE DELIVER. "WE DELIVER" also seems to promise a little more speed, just like classified ads that claim to GET RESULTS "FAST." It's almost as if the quotation marks are trying to pass themselves off as four little exclamation marks.

Menus are full of such anonymous quotations, memorable lines like "NO SUBSTITUTIONS PLEASE" (or sometimes NO "SUBSTITUTIONS" or even NO SUBSTITUTIONS "PLEASE") and that old hot-weather favorite, "T-SHIRTS" AND "HALTERS" NOT PERMITTED. This last one implies that T-shirts and halters (or "SANDALS") are so sleazy or risqué that the restaurant would not even mention them by name if some less grubby word were available. At the same time, it seems to be mocking T-shirt and halter wearers.

Bartlett's Disease can occur anywhere the written word is publicly displayed. The excess quotes often seem to be a modest apology by amateur scribes for daring to scrawl something that all the world can read, for fear "WET PAINT" might be taken as some kind of graffiti.

On the other hand, maybe it's simply a harmless little "Hi, there!" from the author, a way of saying: "Sorry I can't be there in person, friends, but if I were, I'd say: 'Wet paint!' "

Nonetheless, I think maybe it's time to form an organization to oversee, if not actually stamp out, the wild, unthinking use of quotation marks so as to prevent such baffling phrases as FOR INFORMATION, "CALL" PL 8-0455. (One imagines somebody standing out in the street shouting the telephone number.)

After all, there are plenty of famous lines that require quotation marks, but we're cheapening all the truly great quotes by sticking meaningless little ditto signs around everything in print, elevating "NO SHIRTS GIVEN WITHOUT RECEIPT!" to the same status as "GIVE ME LIBERTY OR GIVE ME DEATH!"

Indeed, whenever you come across a ringing phrase such as "NO SHIRTS GIVEN WITHOUT RECEIPT," you feel like asking, "Say, who said that?" To prevent this, let's insist that anything quoted from now on must carry a source, for example:

"NO REFUNDS. PLEASE EXAMINE DATE ON TICKET AT TIME OF PURCHASE"—Sam Shubert.

"ALL SWIMMERS MUST TAKE SHOWER BEFORE ENTERING POOL" —Johnny Weismuller.

"IF YOU BREAK IT, YOU'VE BOUGHT IT!"—Auguste Rodin.

"WE RESERVE THE RIGHT TO REFUSE SERVICE TO ANYONE"—Jilly Rizzo.

ALL THE PEOPLE FIT TO PRINT

OFFICIALS AT THE International Academy for Human Beings are encouraged by recent strides taken by *people,* who suddenly have been rediscovered by the press and given their own little newspaper columns, magazines and TV shows.

Last year alone, 1,826 "people" sections began in U.S. newspapers, plus several periodicals devoted to this unique, fun-filled phenomenon as well as magazines about virtual nobodies (*You, Us*); a TV series, "Who's Who," also zeroed in on the species.

According to an academy spokesman, People have surpassed Places and Things in national priorities. Since 1974, a banner year for folks, interest in *Homo sapiens* jumped an astonishing 78.1 percent, overtaking such hardy perennials as Cars, Pro Football, Gourmet Cooking and House Plants; only Cats showed a comparable increase.

In 1939, a lousy year for the human race generally, people were almost unheard of. By 1959, the situation had grown so desperate that People had all but vanished as a viable editorial commodity (replaced by Warehouse Fires).

"People in the news—or 'newsmakers' and 'names and faces,' as they're often termed—are going over big nowadays with the general public, and they're the people who count," says R. V. Dote, head of the Academy for Human Beings at Cornell.

"In years past," Dote notes, "most 'people' stories were strewn willy-nilly throughout the paper, as filler items. Now they've been neatly organized into their own cozy corner of the paper and are enjoying a healthy revival, I'm pleased to say. It is quite an advance in news gathering."

It's now much easier, Dote reports, to locate genuine "people" stories in a hurry. Before, readers were confused as to when they'd come across an authentic peoplesque item. "Readers today realize," says Dote, "that if a story is clearly labeled 'People,' they're about to be titillated and maybe even moved."

There's still a lot of uncertainty when a "people" item deals, say, with a pregnant whale or mating pandas. "Technically," says Dote, "whales and bears are not people. We at the Academy feel 'people' must not become a catchall term to be misused or distorted by publicity-seeking animals. Let 'em get their own column."

In 1976, there was a flap when *People* magazine named King Kong to its list of the "25 most influential people."

"We called the *People* people to demand a retraction," Dote says, "but they stuck by their choices. They claim Kong has 'near-human emotions' and stands on two legs, but we weren't at all satisfied with that explanation."

A Missouri paper received several angry phone calls when its "people" department ran items about the Loch Ness monster and pet rocks. "The paper later apologized and promised to use all such non-people items as traditional filler stories."

I asked Dote to explain the difference between a hard-core "people" item and plain old-fashioned gossip, and he says: "It's a very fine line, like the one between art and pornography. I can't really define it; it's just something you feel."

Dote credits the New York *Times* with playing a vital role in the nationwide resurgence of people by starting seventeen new "people"-type columns, thinly disguised as "Notes." "Thanks to them, people are finally respectable as well as hot news. Editors who once considered the subject too offbeat or controversial are printing all sorts of people stuff, no matter how trifling. It's a major breakthrough for people large and small."

CATCHER IN THE RYE CAUGHT OFF GUARD

AFTER FIFTEEN YEARS of sending futile letters to Corning, New Hampshire, I finally placed a phone call to J. D. Salinger:

"Just wanted to wish you a happy sixty-fifth birthday," I told the aging reclusive author of *Catcher in the Rye,* who has granted only one interview in two decades (to a high school reporter) and been glimpsed publicly on but two or three occasions.

"I hate birthdays," said Salinger. "I say you're only as old as you feel—and I still feel like a preppie. Well, go ahead—it's your dime."

"I guess the first thing is, when will your next book be out? It's been twenty years now. Maybe you're fussing with it too much."

"Oh, golly, I'm not writing books anymore," said Salinger. "I'm trying to sell a TV pilot and—well, it takes time. But I've come awfully close. I got a couple of screenplay assignments, but they later farmed 'em out and I didn't even get a goddamn credit."

"Which pictures did you work on?" I asked.

"I had a hand in *Benji* and I did the seventeenth rewrite of *Star Trek.*"

"This helps explain your lengthy literary silence. You're not being coy after all. You can't sell an original to Hollywood?"

"It's very embarrassing for a man of my stature," said Salinger, "but you know what they did to Fitzgerald . . ."

"Treated you shabbily, eh?"

"They put me up at the Beverly Hills Hotel and at first everything was great. Then they forgot I was even out there. I did get to meet Clint Eastwood, though, so it wasn't a total loss. He's a very down-to-earth fellow actually, a sweet guy."

"So I've heard." I shook my head: "I can't believe that J. D. Salinger is into TV."

"Well, I wasn't getting anywhere with all that Zen business, and my agent finally said, 'Hey, Jerry, cut the mystical crap.' So I started working in films. I did a low-budget horror picture to start and a couple of Bruce Lee movies."

"You must have been sorely tempted to finally sell the screen rights to *Catcher in the Rye,*" I remarked.

"Oh, right away. I got ABC to take an option on a sitcom about Holden Caulfield, but they ruined it—naturally."

"You mean they actually shot it? What happened?"

"You ever see 'Happy Days'?"

"*You* wrote 'Happy Days'?"

"Well, the pilot, and I was consultant on the first few episodes, but the producer started messing around with the concept and it didn't turn out as I'd hoped. Ron Howard isn't quite what I'd imagined as Holden. And as you may recall, in the original story there was no 'Fonzie' character. But I did make a nice piece of change on the deal."

"This also explains why you refuse to emerge from hiding."

"Oh, I'd be laughed out of New Hampshire if they ever learned what I'm really doing in my little rustic retreat. When I go into town every week to get my mail, the groceries, and go to the barber, they all assume I'm still writing sensitive stories about brilliant young doomed neurotics."

"When, in fact, you're just trying to land a TV series, like every other writer today."

"I'd give anything for a prime-time show like 'Hill Street Blues,' or Newhart. I can't even get in to see Grant Tinker."

"I had no idea you had gone so commercial. I figured you'd become more private, interior and—well, eccentric."

"You don't think I *like* sitting up here cranking out schlock."

"But nobody suspected you were doing sitcoms and Kung-Fu movies."

"It puts bread on the table, pal. And don't forget the greeting cards I'm writing on a free-lance basis."

"Incredible," I said. "So I guess we can all stop holding our breath waiting for your next spiritual novella on the Glass family, or the further adventures of Holden Caulfield."

"Well, I did try a sequel, called *Catcher Out of the Rye,* but my agent never even sent it around. He said it was too short. The thing only ran fourteen pages."

"You must have got a lot of reading done in the last twenty years."

"Mysteries, mostly. I hate anything too heavy, although I did enjoy *The Betsy*. Boy, that Robbins sure knows how to churn out the words. I wish I knew his secret. I've got scads of good ideas for stories but I can't get myself to sit down at the typewriter."

"I know the feeling all too well."

"I've got this one short story I've been putting off since 1966," sighed Salinger.

"You really should try to be more disciplined. Do you ever read *Writer's Digest?* They often have some good tips in there on how to get started. You just have to set aside a certain time each day for your novel and stick to it. It's a matter of good work habits."

"Yeah, you're right," said Salinger. "I've vowed to do that this year. No more of this procrastinating. . . . Well, I have to run now. I've got a Mother's Day verse due tomorrow and I haven't the slightest idea what I want to say. Thanks for calling."

"My pleasure," I said. "And good luck with your TV stuff. Don't worry–something will click for you sooner or later."

MEN OF LETTERS CROSS PATHS

A CONVERSATION OVERHEARD on the street between two old crossword puzzle addicts at the corner of Down & Across:

"A five-letter salutation, Sam!"

"Greetings (colloq.), Joe! Also Halifax Island (abbr.)."

"Indian phrase for a lengthy passage of time between meetings."

"So what's transpired since we last met (slang, reverse of 'What's down?')?"

"Oh, less than one. How's by the second-person singular?"

"Gershwin musical 'Oh, Kay!' (abbr.)."

"And how's the diminutive female spouse?"

"Superlative meaning large or expansive."

"You still merchandising footwear?"

"I haven't done that in a twelvemonth. We just got back from a globe-girdling journey via aeronautical conveyance to a southern European country of Latin origin; also home of Sophia Loren."

"Gosh, I haven't been to the seat of the Renaissance in a demi-score. Did you see the famed two-letter river beginning with P?"

"No. The opposite of 'Mr.' and I spent most of our twenty-four-hour spans in the ancient metropolis that burned while King Nero operated a traditional string instrument."

"Did you have an audience with the Vicar of Christ?"

"Oh, yes, and we spent the entire day beneath a chapel ceiling made famous by the sixteenth-century Italian muralist."

"Did you enjoy the four-letter isle where Napoleon died?"

"Military for confirm; also first name of Yankee slugger Maris."

"Tell me, are you engaged in your usual sustaining occupation?"

"No, I quit my job and am now an agrarian supplier of foodstuffs; also one who deals in husbandry."

"Besides domestic fowl, do you raise any animals indigenous to a British Commonwealth country below the equator (same as swimming stroke, or crawl)?"

"If you mean a ewe or kiwi, the reply is a brief declarative negative; also Northwest Orient (initials)."

"Ah, then you surely must breed a strain of African antelope."

"Opposite of false! I do indeed raise gnus."

"Are you content, i.e., in a state of sublime satisfaction?"

"I'm happy, yes. I assume you're still busy as a familiar dam-building river denizen; also TV character played by Jerry Mathers."

"My pursuits involve printing measures and electrical units. Would you like me to show by example?"

"Obviously, you mean ems, ens, ohms and ergs."

"Yowsah, in the six-letter catchphrase of conductor Ben Bernie."

"Hey, have you been back to the land of Lincoln lately?"

"If you mean the area in an old folk song where there's no place like, the answer is a positive hyphenated expression of sixties radicals."

"How was it to be back in a medium-size Illinois town that was the birthplace of Amos 'n' Andy's creators?"

"Peoria never changes, but you'd hardly recognize the city of the big shoulders and hog butcher to the world anymore. The home of Mrs. O'Leary's cow and Ernie Banks is getting more and more like the 'Fun City' purchased for $24 from the Indians."

"Speaking of our native American tribesman (plural), can you lend me some wampum? I'm low on pocket money; same as last name of popular Western singer."

"I can let you have the equivalent of $100 in underworld lingo."

"A 'C' would be plenty, ample or sufficient. I'll give it back to you tomorrow (Spanish)."

"You're a real close acquaintance, or chum, in GI parlance; also first name of rotund Brooklyn comic."

"I'd better be returning to my residence or domicile. It must be five o'clock, post meridiem (initials). We're having a pair of people—or any two items—in for a mixed beverage of vermouth and a clear alcohol distilled from mash and juniper berries; also a two-handed card game."

"Well, so long until we meet again (German)."

"See you, first name of Dashiell Hammett detective hero played by H. Bogart!"

THE GREATEST STORY EVER CONDENSED

THE *Reader's Digest* has recently condensed the Bible to the size of an ordinary novel, a 40 percent reduction of the 750,000 words in the standard version, but the *Digest*'s editors claim it wasn't any harder than their condensing of *The Odyssey* and *War and Peace.*

I don't quite know how they handled it, but I can imagine the scene up at the *Digest* offices:

Executive Bible Editor: "O.K., gentlemen, let's see if we can't get through at least a few of the five books of Moses by lunchtime. We have a big week ahead, what with the Brooke Shields biography we have to cut, and then there's that damn *Iliad* to condense."

Copy Editor (*growls*): "Yeah, and don't forget, we also have to have the new annotated Shakespeare collection ready for the printers by next Friday."

Old Testament Editor: "Why don't you give me Genesis and Leviticus and—uh, Al, you want to take Exodus and Deuteronomy?"

Copy Editor: "Sure, no problem, but it looks to me like most of the fat is in Revelations."

New Testament Editor: "No, no, that has to stay. It's the whole point of the story. I'd say the first thing that could be squeezed is Exodus, which is old-hat by now."

Junior Executive Bible Editor: "Well, I'd hate to lose too much of the Passover sequence. There's some pretty good stuff in there about the Jews' flight out of Egypt and all."

Copy Editor: "Aw, come on, you guys. Let's not be so damn precious about this thing. We'll never get it cut by spring at this rate, and they want it for an April selection. There's an Easter tie-in."

New Testament Editor: "I know, Al, but it *is* the Bible, after all."

Copy Editor: "Bible, schmible–it's still too long, let's face it. The Old Testament has thirty-nine books, which we've gotta trim to twenty-one, somehow; I skimmed it last night and it's just too repetitive. First thing I want to do is go through and X out all the 'ands.' There must be 20,000 'ands.' I don't know who put 'em in, but it's worse than Hemingway."

Executive Bible Editor: "Well, we should try to retain a few of these biblical phrases–for rhythm and poetic flavor and so on. No?"

Copy Editor: "This ain't a poem, for cryin' out loud! It's gotta tell a story and get to the point quicker. The reader just won't stay with a plot that rambles like this. It's worse than Michener."

Executive Bible Editor: "Maybe we'd better go at this chronologically. I think we all agree on keeping most of Genesis."

Copy Editor: "Lemme have it, will ya? I'll show you guys how to boil these first 200 pages down to a few lines. You gotta be ruthless!"

Old Testament Editor: "Gee, it's fairly succinct, isn't it? I was always taught that the Bible was a model of tight writing. It only takes seven words to relate the creation of the universe–'And God said, "Let there be light."'"

Copy Editor: "We can cut the 'and God said . . .' There's another of those damn 'ands.' It's just not necessary to tell the reader all that. We all know who said it."

New Testament Editor: "We can still tighten up 'Let there be light' a little. It seems ambiguous to me, and the average reader is going to wonder what the exact meaning is."

Copy Editor: "O.K., let's just make it 'The Universe started.'"

Old Testament Editor: "I don't know."

Copy Editor: "Look, we can't quibble over every little phrase. We still have sixty-five more books to go after this (*glances at watch*). It's already 11 A.M."

New Testament Editor: "Who do you fellows see as our typical reader?"

Copy Editor: "We got to think of the suburban housewife—that's who this book is aimed at. No fancy writing but plenty of narrative and snappy quotes. Keep the plot moving, with enough spice every few pages to hold her interest."

New Testament Editor: "I say we get rid of all the funny names and throw out those 'begats' and the 'harken-untos.' If there's one thing that puts a reader off, it's a lot of extraneous 'harken-untos.'"

Executive Editor: "Well, let's have a whack at Genesis and see if we can crunch it by 50,000 words by the end of the day. Tomorrow morning, we'll take a hard look at the Psalms . . ."

I'VE GOT A LITTLE LIST . . .

THE FOLLOWING EXCERPTS are from the forthcoming *Nachman's Almanac of Lists and 101 Other Surefire Best-Selling Ideas:*

NINE STATESMEN WHO NEVER FOUGHT A DUEL: 1. Dean Rusk; 2. Talleyrand; 3. Golda Meir; 4. Harold Macmillan; 5. Bernard Baruch; 6. André Malraux; 7. U Thant; 8. Elihu Root; 9. Clare Boothe Luce.

FIVE FAMOUS ACTORS WHOSE FIRST NAMES ARE WILLIAM: 1. William Holden; 2. William Powell; 3. William Conrad; 4. William Windom; 5. William (Bill) Macy.

ONLY FAMOUS ACTOR WHOSE FIRST NAME IS STAATS: Staats Cottsworth.

TWO PRESIDENTS BORN IN AUGUST: 1. Benjamin Harrison (August 20, 1883); 2. Lyndon Baines Johnson (August 27, 1908).

SIX PHILOSOPHERS WHO WERE LIGHT ON THEIR FEET: 1. Martin Buber; 2. Immanuel Kant; 3. Alfred North Whitehead; 4. Ludwig Wittgenstein; 5. Spinoza; 6. Friedrich Nietzsche.

EIGHT PITCHERS WHO FAILED TO HURL WORLD SERIES NO-HITTERS: 1. Vic Raschi; 2. Grover Cleveland Alexander; 3. Bobby Shantz; 4. Chief Bender; 5. Preacher Roe; 6. Lefty Gomez; 7. Mike Garcia; 8. Mordecai ("Three-Finger") Brown (see also: "Pitchers Named Mordecai with Fewer Than 10 Fingers").

NINE GREAT WRITERS WHO COULD BARELY SPELL: 1. Count Leo Tolstoy; 2. Edgar Guest; 3. Victor Hugo; 4. "George Sand" (born Charles Dickens); 5. Honoré de Balzac; 6. Anthony Trollope ("Ring Lardner"); 7. Colette; 8. Bret Harte; 9. Lewis Carroll ("Boz").

FOUR MINOR DAMS: 1. Pardee Dam (Calif.); 2. Upper Baker Dam (Wash.); 3. Smith Dam (Ore.); 4. Reservoir No. 22 Dam (Colo.).

FIVE MUSICIANS WITH BAD BACKS: 1. Dame Nellie Melba; 2. Johannes Brahms; 3. Paderewski; 4. Kid Ory; 5. Georges Bizet.

SIX FAMED INDUSTRIALISTS WHO REGULARLY SKIPPED BREAKFAST: 1. Alfried Krupp; 2. Charles Eastman; 3. P. K. Wrigley; 4. Andrew Carnegie; 5. Howard Hughes; 6. A. P. Giannini (see also: "Twenty-six Tycoons Who Liked to Use Initials").

FOUR PAINTERS WHO WERE ALLERGIC TO PAINT: 1. El Greco; 2. Van Eyck the Elder; 3. Edward Hopper; 4. Leonardo da Vinci.

SIX FISH THAT ARE REALLY VEGETABLES: 1. Sand dabs; 2. Abalone (or "Marlin"); 3. Bananafish; 4. Pike; 5. Broccoli; 6. Gefilte fish.

NINE COUNTRIES THAT HAVE NEVER WON A WAR: 1. Lapland; 2. Tibet; 3. Ecuador (formerly "Persia"); 4. Chad; 5. Sumatra; 6.

Costa Rica (now "Persia"); 7. Paraguay; 8. Canada; 9. Fiji (formerly Oklahoma Territory).

SIX MOST COMMONLY USED LETTERS IN THE GERMAN ALPHABET: 1. U; 2. E; 3. T; 4. G; 5. O; 6. N and H (tie).

FIVE ANCIENT GREEKS WHO WERE UNDER FIVE FOOT TWO: 1. Sappho; 2. Plutarch; 3. Aesop; 4. Aristotle; 5. Xenophon.

SIX EXPLORERS WHO WERE ALSO LEFT-HANDED: 1. Ferdinand Magellan; 2. Commodore Peary; 3. Meriwether Lewis; 4. Marco Polo; 5. Leif Erikson; 6. Ponce de León (was ambidextrous but batted left).

THREE COMPOSERS WHO WERE HEAVILY ADDICTED TO TAPIOCA: 1. Edvard Grieg; 2. Stravinsky; 3. Otto Harbach.

FOUR DWARFS (OR MIDGETS) WHO COME TO MIND: 1. Tom Thumb; 2. Billy Barty; 3. Toulouse-Lautrec; 4. Sneezy.

SEVEN RULERS WHO DRANK, SMOKED AND RAN AROUND: 1. Ivan the Terrible; 2. Nero; 3. Henry IV (Part II); 4. Montezuma; 5. Claudius II (The Goth); 6. Kublai Khan; 7. Wilbur Mills.

SIX ENTERTAINERS BORN IN 1929: 1. Betsy Palmer; 2. Jackie Vernon; 3. Jeanne Moreau; 4. Buck Owens; 5. Beverly Sills; 6. Bob Newhart (also Dick Clark, Rita Gam).

FOUR WOMEN SAID TO BE PIGEON-TOED: 1. Mary Queen of Scots; 2. Emily Dickinson; 3. Isadora Duncan; 4. Sacajawea ("The Bird Woman").

THREE GENERALS UNABLE TO CARRY A TUNE: 1. General Pershing; 2. General Custer; 3. General LeMay.

ALL BOOKED UP FOR CHRISTMAS

OF ALL THE grandiose coffee-table books I've seen for Christmas, here are a few I'd like to find under somebody else's tree:

The Letters of Harry James (edited by Jules Peterkin, with a preface by Zoot Sims; E. W. Dirndl Sons; unpaged; $45):

Flipping through this marvelous glimpse into the world of "big brass," one is amazed to come time and again upon an intimate passage, such as this note, written by James to a BMI agent during his early "cornet period": "I won't be able to make that Steel Pier gig on the 17th, since that night I expect to be at the Coconut Grove . . ." Here is a James we haven't seen before, a musician caught in the riptides of doubt, pulled between his art and the tempting fleshpots of Hollywood.

Heave!: An Almanac of World Shot-Put Champions (introduction and page numbers by Parry O'Brien; Big Boy Publishers; 1,017 pp.; $75 till Jan. 1, best offer thereafter):

Is there a heavyset lad on your list with an eye on the 1984 Olympics? If so, this is surely the book for him—assuming, of course, he can pick it up. With actual finger diagrams and toe position in the ring, *Heave!* reveals all the fine points of throwing lead things—not just the 16-lb. shot, discus and hammer but bowling balls, bookends and doorstops.

The Films of Stu Erwin (Wesley Thrum, Jr.; Idolatry Press; 918 pp.; $19 until June 1):

Even if you're not sure exactly who Stuart Erwin was—and I happily consider myself among those who do—you must own this book, if only to prominently display your love of cinema. The many complex, indeed paradoxical sides of Erwin are shown here in more than 650 still photos, many from Thrum's private collection, and, though badly focused, invaluable for all Erwin students.

The Bedside Book of Mugs (by Mortimer C. Scroggin; Hobby Horse House; 1,208 pp.; $50 till April 26, 1985):

"Muggery"—the ancient art of sipping coffee or tea from earthenware cups—is at last given proper treatment in this handsome compendium tracing the history of mugs, urns and jugs from Grecian times. Author Scroggin, who himself owns the largest mug collection in England (and also the largest mug itself), describes the 3,000 basic shapes and designs, including many rare varieties, such as the famed cracked "King Yuban Mug" of Brazil, said to be worth $1.7 million.

Encyclopedia of Goats (Meyer Thornblad; M. Thornblad Press; 769 pp.; $60 till Jan. 1, remaindered thereafter):

Another finely researched work by the author of *The Boy's Book of Gophers* and the *Fireside Guide to Giraffes.*

In *Goats,* Dr. Thornblad discusses the sudden resurgence in goatherding and shows us the world of the goat as it seems to a typical ewe. Mountain goats, nanny goats, the Three Billy Goats Gruff and the Los Angeles Rams–all play a part in this joyous celebration of goatdom.

The Complete Hat Book (by Morley Druid; Scribbler's Sons; 871 pp.; $45):

All about hats, their history, purpose and sizes, with data on how the first hat was made (and why) and when hats were first introduced in America (and to whom).

This lavishly illustrated volume, containing a foldout porkpie hat you can actually wear, puts an end to all of those barroom arguments over the difference between a derby, a homburg and a bowler. The book, a must for every serious hat wearer, is by the author of *Gloves of All Nations* and includes a brief introduction by Senator Mark Hatfield.

Ancient Pittsburgh in Photos (by Walter O. Bleaty; Klumpf; 186 pp.; $32.50 till Dec. 25, $4.50 thereafter):

Here–for collectors of antique Pennsylvaniana–is a remarkable compendium of amateur snapshots of Pittsburgh from its early settling through 1911, end of the Iron Age.

Rare close-ups of smelters at work and play, plus a color section of grids, girders and amusing smokestacks, make this easily the finest book ever done on Steel City. For that special Pittsburgh buff on your list.

Batboys, Ballboys, Waterboys & Caddies (by Amos Roy Frew; Doubleplay; 388 pp.; $27.80, plus wine and tip):

At last, an affectionate look at the art of toadying. Frew interviewed some 750 aging batboys, etc., who reminisce from their unique vantage points and reveal what went on down there on the sidelines, foul lines and base lines. They tell it like it was–and if nothing went on down there, these old-timers say so.

We learn, however, what ounce bat Babe Ruth used to clout No. 60 (and which size he used to clout Miller Huggins), what number iron Arnie Palmer asked for on the 18th hole at Augusta in '68, and whether Don Budge and Budge Patty were ever related, as often rumored, or just good friends.

The Curtain Rod in Fact and Fancy (by Lenore Krindle; Pantheneum; 718 pp.; $48 till Jan. 2; checkout time 1 P.M.):

If you think you know all there is to know about curtain rods, take another peek. As editor of *Rod & Cornice,* Ms. Krindle has collected many lively anecdotes in her travels, plus 116 miles of curtain rods, all of which she shares with us in her definitive work on this underappreciated *objet d'window*.

Great Pickpockets of North America (by Elias Pumphrey, Jr.; Jovanovich, Geohegan & the Pips; unpaged; $25; introduction by Karl Malden):

From Artie ("Two Fingers") Newmeyer to the amazing Omaha, Nebraska, supermarket team of Hal and Lois Haggis, this book does justice to many of the misunderstood criminals of the century.

Pumphrey, renowned for his earlier volume on subway mashers (*Gotcha!*), recalls some historic moments in purse snatching and "dipping," with a list of famous pockets picked. Did you know that Ed McMahon once "lost" his watch at the Macy's Thanksgiving Day parade? That House Speaker Tip O'Neill has had his wallet stolen 28 times in the Senate? Or that Frank Sinatra has no pockets at all?

The Golden Age of Nostalgia (edited by Jed Groff; Stein & Ale; 1,109 pp.; $50 till Dec. 25; $12 in 1950):

From 1928 onward, America has been awash in nostalgia, much of which Groff recounts in examples of the nation's fondest memories.

"Remember the old days?" he asks, and goes on to reveal some of his own favorite remembrances: When Fiorello ("The Little Colonel") read the Dow Jones averages over the radio . . . Stanley's famous remark to Livingstone, "Dr. Christian, I presume?" . . . Bob Burns and Fred Allen's "Who's on first?" routine . . . Lindbergh's triumphant return to the Philippines . . . and the day Jessie Owens went 4 for 4 at Hialeah.

The Fireside Book of Oatmeal (edited by H. J. Loontz; Simon & Schuster & Simon; 724 pp.; $41.35):

A compendium of the best that has been thought and written through the ages on the subject of hot cereal; Cream of Wheat is discussed as well as rolled oats. This bulky work includes eighteen handsome color-plate reproductions from the brush of the world's most celebrated 18th-century illustrator of porridge, Jacob Gottschalk, whose paintings were once sought after by German royalty and regarded as "good enough to eat right off the wall."

The Unmaking of "Abbott & Costello Join the WACs" (by Lyle Fanzine; Little Brown House; 817 pp.; $23.50):

Veteran filmland correspondent Fanzine takes us back to the year 1947, when Hollywood was in all its postwar glory and Abbott & Costello were in their decline. Using close-ups, Fanzine reveals what went wrong—frame by frame—in this ill-fated production that film scholars now realize was a forerunner of many doomed Abbott & Costello movies.

"The basic problem," writes Fanzine, "was that director Hershey Whiffle couldn't remember which was Abbott and which was Costello—and what's more, he didn't care." This misunderstanding got the comedy off to a poor start from which it never quite recovered.

Nonetheless, A & C admirers will revel in the rollicking—at times sad—glimpses behind the scenes of a disastrous near-epic: How Abbott held his fork (and why) . . . what Costello whispered to a prop girl on the first day of shooting . . . why the camera ran out of film . . . how much the food cost in the famed "mess-hall scene" . . . and much much more.

Leonardo da Vinci—The Prairie Years (edited and stapled by Norris H. Xerxes, Jr.; Oversize Press; 17,201 pp.; $2,415 before Jan. 1, 1978—$2,400 thereafter):

Before Da Vinci was plucked off the streets of Venice and made it as a "Renaissance Man," he had a brief but unsuccessful career as a farmhand in Poland. While others labored in the fields, young Leo was hiding behind haystacks tinkering with levers and pulleys, painting free-lance murals and attempting the earliest crude sketches of what later developed into the first successful tortellini.

It was during his lonely days as a prairie hand that Da Vinci laid the groundwork for many of his inventions. The author has generously provided original foldout Da Vinci doodles of the modern-day horse, the spray shower and what appears to be primitive versions of the Cuisinart, the felt-tip pen and rhythm-and-blues.

There is ample evidence here that Da Vinci devised the first "expansion baseball team." By means of a series of cranks and ratchets, he showed how a simple nine-man team could be stretched to ten and moved without effort to any city.

The Menus of Lazlo Scudder (translated into the Portuguese by Juan Luis Borges; Chas. Scribner's Daughters; 814 pp.; $35):

Scudder, who was a marginal but pushy figure in several literary movements, traveled freely from the Algonquin Round Table Set to the Bloomsbury Group to the Chicago School of Poetry to the St. Louis English Teachers Prayer Breakfast. Always overshadowed by more dazzling minds than his, Scudder nonetheless made his mark wherever he sat while freeloading his way through some 1,850 meals at posh restaurants on two continents.

Scudder jotted down his impressions on the backs of menus, some of which are reproduced here. A typical Algonquin entry, for Oct. 8, 1923, notes: "Veal very stringy . . . ditto Geo. S. Kaufman . . . Woollcott ate six desserts . . . FPA again ordered brisket . . . Dotty Parker didn't touch her soup . . . Bob Benchley still on a diet . . . Edna Ferber says her crab Newburg 'quite tasty.' "

A Lot of Old Doorways (introduction by Otto von Van; Museum of Moody Art; 489 pp.; $27.75):

This companion volume to Von Van's *A Lot of Old Walls* and *7,000 Peeling Billboards* is another view of the Depression as seen through the dingy lens of America's master photographer of "old stuff." Von Van evokes an era in a doorknob. He's equally noted for his alleys and frumpy old folks.

In the preface, Von Van tells why he refused to take a picture of even a middle-class person or a door not falling off its hinges: "The economics of social realism dictates: the seedier the subject, the more honest the photo and, thus, the more dough I could get for it. There's nothing classier than a shabby old guy on a stoop . . ."

MANY UNHAPPY RETURNS

EACH YEAR AT this time, our resident tax expert sets up his little card table in my office to answer your questions:

Q. I am a single man—and not half bad looking, either—with an unmarried son who owns his own business and employs me to take care of my mother at their home. Can I claim either of them as dependents and, if so, what is the status of the house? Does it qualify under the "home used as dude ranch or spa" section?

A. According to a recent change in the tax laws, you may claim your mother as your "son," provided she has moved within the last year and has not forfeited any interest on a bank loan. Your house is just a house.

Q. I am a hotel clerk who has married four times, twice to the same woman, one of whom now supports me as well as my children from another marriage. May I claim her as my "employer" or is she still my wife?

A. Neither, unless you received 50 percent of your income from gross ("adjusted") capital gains during the years prior to 1978, and had fewer than four exemptions last year but more than three. If so, attach Form 357-A (Schedule E), which covers "multi-married hotel clerks."

Q. My wife is on social security but is also employed by a foreign government and does not live with me. May I claim a foreign tax credit or do I simply qualify as an Italian citizen and thus am exempt from the new "separate-nation domicile" status?

A. Yes, and you should have a refund coming.

Q. I sleep in my office and use my home as a work area. Am I allowed to deduct my food bills and kitchen upkeep as a legitimate business expense?

A. Only if two or more dependents live at home at night and you have a non-alien status, are not the sole support of your *brother or sister and have not previously deducted more than $1,000 in state gasoline taxes ($500 for a four-cylinder car).*

Q. May I claim depreciation on a deceased spouse?

A. Yes, if he or she does not qualify under the "net long-term loss" provision (attach 1982 National League Schedule.)

Q. I run a small disco on my farm, which I recently incorporated. The farm earned no taxable income in 1977, but the disco did. Should this be entered under "nonfarming activities"?

A. You have answered your own question.

Q. I am a financial institution with no "capital loss carry-over from years beginning 1970" but I'm supporting a fiduciary from a former marriage. May I claim a dependent?

A. Only if your fiduciary lives at home.

Q. As part owner in a religious order, do I include the rental value of my parsonage, as referred to in Schedule SE, Part Two, Line C, as earned income?

A. It depends if your parsonage earned a profit last year.

Q. My entire 1982 fishing income was from a small business I own with my grandmother, who is legally blind. Is there any way to deduct the amount of fish we threw back or should she file separately?

A. As a limited partner in a small business with a blind fisherman (or fisherwoman), the government allows you to claim up to 25 percent of her income unless she regains her sight before April 15.

Q. I am a qualifying widow who also receives alimony from my next-to-last husband, who was out of work last year and lived with me. Do I claim him as a dependent, head of household or moving expense?

A. If he earned less than $400, you may claim him as a "bum" or not at all.

Q. My wife is 65 or older and I am a U.S. citizen living on government-owned property. Which of us should file a return since neither has ever had a dual-status tax year.

A. Your wife is not eligible to be married to you this year.

Q. I made repairs on my son amounting to $11,993 but he failed to return a profit, unlike his sister. Do I deduct him under "bad debts," "losing joint ventures" or "casualty and theft loss"?

A. On Line 19, enter your son or daughter, whichever is smaller.

Q. Our dog is practically a member of the family, so may I deduct Taffy as a dependent since she is 13 years old and infirm?

A. Only if Taffy did not have an income last year of more than $750, and is not covered under the Railroad Retirement Plan.

Q. If I should die before completing my return, am I entitled to death benefits if it is determined my Form 1040 is the sole cause of death?

A. No, but you may be entitled to a Work Incentive Credit if you received no payments for special fuels, etc.

YOGI ACE WINS IN CREATIVE BURST

Sri Chinmoy, the Indian yogi, surpassed his own unofficial record for poetry writing in a 24-hour period by writing 843 spiritual poems between midnight Saturday and midnight Sunday. —New York *Post*

INCREDIBLE AS CHINMOY'S hoped-for record mark is, it must remain unofficial in the light of a more recent attempt by a Yuma, Ariz., housewife who claims to have penned 1,608 poems in 23:7.8 hours.

Authorities at the National Amateur Poetasters Union must now decide if Mrs. Norma Swilph's 1,608 poems is a new indoor mark.

The record for outdoor poetry writing (wind-aided) is 946.7 rhymes, held by Isadora Stanpool, a 31-year-old English teacher from Athens, Ga., who set the mark in May 1974 at a Vermont writers' conference. At the time, it was hailed as not only the fastest poetry ever written by an American but quite possibly the worst.

Yogi Chinmoy's fans insist that, while many poets can knock out 800-plus poems a day, it is doubly difficult to compose a poem —and a spiritual one at that—under world-mark pressure.

A true "spiritual" poem, say NAPU rules, is worth 18 points more than a regular (or "sandlot") poem, since it cannot deal with such amateur topics as unrequited love, death, spring, autumn or the look on a child's face at Christmas. (Mrs. Swilph's 1,608 poems have already been attested to by two poetry editors and a notary yogi.)

Mrs. Swilph—who has made something of a name for herself among Southwest balladeers as the "Arizona Flash of Genius"—wrote her poems nonstop. During her attempt to bust the U.S. indoor versifying mark, she refused all food and drink save for a swig of Gatorade when her meter began to flag in the closing stanzas.

As she told a reporter from *Poets Illustrated:* "When you're going for speed, baby, you got to sacrifice something, even if it's beauty. Any hack poet can write pretty-sounding lyrics."

There is no indication whether the Indian speed merchant was creating his verse under strict NAPU-sanctioned conditions that require at least two grammarians, a punctuation judge and three former world poetry champions be in attendance.

As it happens, many of Mrs. Swilph's best efforts were disqualified for various minor infractions—mixed metaphors, limping meter, hanging dactyls, fuzzy imagery and faulty interior rhymes.

If accepted by the NAPU, Chinmoy's claim of 843 poems will entitle him to a place in the Minnesinger's Hall of Fame at Clarkston, Wash. (birthplace of modern poetry), which now houses bronze plaques of such fabled greats as Vern ("Mr. Cadence") Pfeiffer, winner of the 1921 iambic pentameter and 440 quatrain.

Others enshrined include: Walt ("Highpockets") Derkin, legendary middle-distance ode man; Chuck ("The Iron Quill") Biggers, beloved 1936 blank-verse champ; Sam ("Flyin' Fingers") Robin, first black poet to be inducted in the Old-Timers Wing (poets who composed prior to the Chicago School Era); and Hank C. ("Doc Dithyramb") Larrabee, holder of an all-time mark in epic verse.

This summer at Lake Tahoe, Mrs. Swilph was at her typewriter by 5 A.M. for a light-verse workout, tapping out 150 poems per hour on a small Hermes portable.

Mrs. Swilph now hopes to challenge Yogi Chinmoy to a muse-to-muse encounter at Madison Square Garden, scene of the annual Homeric Relays.

This fall's poetic games will draw competition from around the world to take part in such classic events as the 22-syllable haiku hurdles, the canto, the couplet sprints, the roundelay, the cross-country pastorals, the W. B. Yeats free-style medley, the 400-line sonnets and, always a thriller, the Alexandrine half mile.

"Meeting Chinmoy in person on my own home turf is a chance I've been waiting for all my life," says Norma, who at 26 packs a wry 98 pounds on a compact five-foot frame. She concludes:

"At last the world can witness the two fastest rhymesters under one roof. I've long admired Sri's work from afar, but I've been preparing for this moment ever since I took third place in limericks at the 1974 Edward Lear Memorial Open."

THE GUILTY READER'S GUIDE TO LITERATURE

SENATOR KENNEDY claims to have read every book on a list of 20 classic works of literature, or 18½ more than me.

Somehow, I slipped through the clutches of education without ever cracking *Paradise Lost, Great Expectations, The Communist Manifesto, The Sound and the Fury, Robert Frost's Collected Poems, The Republic, Walden,* the Bible, *The Divine Comedy, The Stranger, Ulysses, Madame Bovary,* and the *Iliad* or the *Odyssey.* Not bad for a man with a college degree.

It seems more of a feat, almost, than having read them all, which anyone who tries can do. The head of a Boston department store, this survey reports, has read 18 of the books. Bill

Lee, a ball player, finished 13—but then they both have much more spare time than I do.

I've read parts of many of these fine books, but I don't suppose that counts. Can you count half of *Herzog* and a third of *Moby Dick* as one book? For all I know, Senator Kennedy only read part of *Ulysses*. I'll bet if you hauled him up before a committee, he'd confess he never got through it. Nobody has.

I could do better with this list if they gave partial credit for having begun a book, or for having seriously considered reading it, or for having thumbed through it several times. Few people have flipped through as many great books as I have.

Indeed, I even own some of these classics, and it seems only fair that this be taken into account, since obviously I'm going to read them sometime. Maybe next year I'll give *Walden* another chance.

These lists are always compiled by English professors who have already read the books and feel pretty good about it. I know when I've knocked off even a semi-classic work, it's as if I've just come through successful brain surgery and want to recommend it to everyone. How else will people realize I've finished an actual book?

It's annoying that this list doesn't include *Les Misérables,* a classic novel and—more importantly—one I happen to have read in junior high school. Isn't one big fat Victor Hugo novel equal to a Dickens, or even a thin Camus and a third of Yeats's poetry?

While I never finished *Hamlet,* I did read *Macbeth* and *Julius Caesar* (also in junior high, where I did the bulk of my scholarly work); and although I ducked *The Sun Also Rises,* I did polish off much of *A Farewell to Arms* and would like to be compensated for this.

Many of us have been working away at these books all our lives and deserve credit for it. There should be a way to salvage your literary reputation by gaining points for (1) thumbing through a book enough to get the drift, (2) seeing the movie and (3) soaking up the plot by hearsay, thus allowing you to venture bold opinions at parties.

Unfortunately, however, it's possible to go through life and never once be asked if you've read *Les Misérables.*

To help those of us who scored rather poorly on the great-books query, here's a list of 10 classic works for people who don't like to feel totally illiterate—books I've read, can vouch for and suggest everybody else read too:

1. *Make Way for Ducklings;* 2. *How to Be a Jewish Mother;* 3. *Movies on TV;* 4. *Beginning Spanish;* 5. *The New Yorker Cartoons—1925–1950;* 6. *Here's Johnny!* (biography of Johnny Carson); 7. *The Underground Gourmet* (both New York *and* San Francisco editions); 8. *Penthouse Annual;* 9. *Great Front Pages from The New York Times;* 10. *One Hundred Famous Plots.*

I'm sure I'd read more classics if only they had little drawings and were more concerned with baseball, like most of the 538 books I read between the ages of nine and fifteen. Surely, 538 boys' baseball novels are worth one *Paradise Lost* or *The Communist Manifesto.*

There are plenty of ways to learn about life, I always say, without reading books about it. In fact, you don't want to spend a lot of time immersed in stuff like the *Iliad* and *The Divine Comedy* if it means passing up Life's Great Experiences. That'd be terrible.

I'd also hate to be asked how many of life's twenty great experiences I've had. Once again, I doubt if I'd do nearly as well as Senator Kennedy or even that department store president—at best, two out of twenty. I guess it's also possible to miss out on both the books *and* the experiences.

ALICE IN ADULTLAND

AFTER READING A recent roundup of the latest winners in children's books, I've come away with a few ideas for literature aimed at the modern, totally liberated kid:

I'M GAY! WHAT ARE YOU?: In this droll, charmingly illustrated book, nine-year-old Benny Brown moves into a new neighborhood and encounters problems in the schoolyard when the other kids meet their first gay classmate.

At first Benny is ignored and even ridiculed by the other children, but eventually he wins them over with his outgoing personality and natural instincts for color and fabric.

Benny himself must learn to cope with the hangups of suburban youngsters in Shaker Heights, much less enlightened than those in his native Mill Valley. Dick and Jane, his straight parents, teach Benny how to face the issue squarely and, despite a few bloody noses, he wins over the school with innate wit and good taste.

The book, by noted gay children's author Noël Durbish, is every bit as delightful as Durbish's last book, *Dori and Didi Visit Lesbos,* in which two young girls take an imaginary journey to a secret island where they learn tolerance for alternative sexual preferences.

ARTIE FLIPS OUT: Again author-illustrator Moe Fertig takes young readers into the grim nightmare world where children harbor perverse desires, like normal kids anywhere.

In *Artie,* a young man has a nervous breakdown on his thirteenth birthday when he fails to get the Shetland pony his grandpa promised him. Artie begins acting strangely at the party, tries to stab granddad with a cake knife and is finally taken away to a clinic for autistic children.

Here Artie meets kindly Dr. Kindley, who explains to Artie that his subconscious feelings of hatred for his parents are "perfectly normal–swell, in fact," and that all children frequently feel like bumping off their folks. Many do. Artie learns not to be frightened of psychiatrists and comes to enjoy his weekly shock treatments, which he calls "the Big Buzz."

In this frank and honest book, author Fertig shows young readers that flipping-out can happen to any boy or girl, and that "it doesn't always mean you're crazy." The book offers an amusing look at the dark underside of the confused child and teaches young readers that going bananas is often curable.

SLOPPINESS CAN BE FUN: This book, fast on its way to becoming a classic in the best-selling series of Permissive House books (*Banging Your Dish Can Be Fun, Whining Can Be Fun, Ignoring Mommy Can Be Fun,* etc.), shows how other kids all around the world also don't pick up after themselves.

The purpose of the book is to make young children feel less put upon by their parents, relieving them of any nagging guilts they may have about being slobs.

IF MRS. O'MALLEY HAS A BABY, WHY CAN'T I?: Betsy Budd, prize-winning author of oversexed girls' books, has a new book, and it's a beaut!

Ms. Budd, who helps boys and girls learn all about life before the age of ten, delves into the libido of a young girl, Nancy, who wonders why her Catholic next-door neighbor has so many babies and yet she can't have *any*—a problem worrying many a nine-year-old.

Budd, *so* wise about how children feel about their bodies, confronts not only the issue of kiddie-porn (in the chapter where Nancy meets a beguiling gym teacher), but the abortion question. When Nancy asks her mom, "Why can't Mrs. O'Malley stop having kids?" she's sent to her room and told not to come out until she's twenty-one.

In Chapter 2, Nancy goes to church with Mrs. O'Malley and meets the priest, who comes away from the rectory with a keener knowledge of the complexities involved, and is a finer person for it, too.

CHARLIE MEETS MR. GOD: This book, which whimsically answers kids' worries about what becomes of them when they die, is a sequel to author Loren Bletchner's earlier masterpiece which introduced youngsters to the realities of the graduated income tax.

As always, Bletchner makes clear that it's never too early to spoil a boy's fantasies.

Media Blitzes

EXTRA! MUCH OF EUROPE FEELS BLAH

EASILY THE MOST envied job in journalism is that of mood reporter—the foreign correspondent who determines how vast multitudes of people feel at any given moment.

Recently, for instance, there was a lengthy analysis of "Germany's mood" ("a pervasive sense of deadlock and immobility, touching almost every aspect of national life"), which ran just in time for Ronald Reagan's meeting with the German Chancellor.

It permitted our President to greet the head of state, as he stepped off the plane, with a consoling embrace. "There, there, old man," Reagan told the Chancellor. "I'm sure that pervasive sense of deadlock and immobility will vanish in no time! You just wait—almost every aspect of your national life is sure to look rosier by morning."

A mood specialist continually roams about Europe and Asia, stopping in world capitals long enough to take the nation's pulse and analyze its psyche, after which he writes a dispatch that begins: "The mood today in Belgrade is one of great calm, but there are undercurrents of unrest."

In Spain, he cables home: "The mood in Madrid now is one of unrest, but there are undercurrents of great calm." Or in Tokyo: "The mood here is one of calm unrest, with undercurrents of Spain."

Reporting on the mood abroad is nice work if you can get it, for it's hard to imagine an editor back home questioning your acute description of the state of mind of, say, Paraguay—although perhaps there are occasional conflicting views:

"Hello, McGuinness? This is Garbel on the foreign desk in New York. Look—you say here in this piece that the mood in Paraguay today is 'extreme anguish and fear, tempered by a faint glimmer of hope.' This doesn't jibe at all with a Reuters story that just came in and claims that the Paraguayans are 'happy as clams.' Now which is it?"

The problem in doing mood stories is that you must keep coming up with a hot new mood to satisfy the editors. You can't very well cable New York that there's been no noticeable shift in Israel's mood since Lebanon.

"Get off the dime, Perkins!" editors would yelp. "We can't go with this article on 'Israel Today' without a paragraph or two on the national mood. Get your butt out there and find me a mood—and we need it by eight o'clock tonight, no later!"

Today, there's a major industry devoted to plumbing the mood in America from hour to hour, and everywhere you turn you bump into it. In reviews of *Annie,* theater critics in 1977 remarked as how the musical "somehow caught the mood of the new Carter Administration, with its hope, optimism and openness."

Even veteran journalists were impressed by this refreshing twist in mood-divining. Nobody had ever thought to compare a Broadway show—let alone Little Orphan Annie—with government policy. Mood experts, though, are always on the lookout for anything to hitch their angles to, such as:

"The tall ships floating confidently down the East River on July 4 seemed to reflect the feeling in America of a new hand at the helm in Washington."

People who do nationwide mood stories at news magazines must first check with their bureaus to nail down the mood in Chicago, Atlanta, Seattle, etc., before reporting a major coast-to-coast mood. Luckily, the moods always dovetail nicely, otherwise chaos might result at *Time* and *Newsweek.*

"Say, Fred, how's the mood down there in Dallas these days? I'm writing a cover story on 'America: A New Buoyancy.' Would you say it's pretty buoyant in the Dallas–Fort Worth area? Joe tells me that Miami is buoyant as hell, and I understand Boston was never perkier."

"Sorry, Pete. Texans here are grouchy as all get-out nowadays."

"Uh-oh. You wouldn't even want to say they're less grouchy than usual?"

"I really can't, Pete. It's not just here—the grouchiness is spreading as far west as Phoenix and even into parts of California."

"Hmm . . . Well, maybe I'll see if we can switch the angle slightly and do a cover on 'America: The New Grouchiness' . . ."

THE AMERICANIZATION OF ALEX

ALTHOUGH Alexander Solzhenitsyn is still unhappy with how things are in the United States, he's sure to come around eventually once the various forces of modern America go to work on him. I foresee the following chronology:

August 1983: A Welcome Wagon calls on Solzhenitsyn at his remote Vermont farm but he remains adamant, accuses Welcome Wagon lady of being "the very symbol of decline of Western society and typical of America's spiritual weakness." He says she "lacks courage to face moral dilemmas," but Welcome Wagon woman leaves basket of goodies on the kitchen table and replies: "Glad to have you in town, Mr. S! This neighborhood needs men of your intellectual vigor." He is charmed by her total innocence, decadence and cute smile.

October 1983: After staring suspiciously at basket of goodies for two months, Solzhenitsyn samples Cheese 'n' Potato Chippers, peanut butter-coconut-chocolate cookies and Pop Rocks. He writes major address, delivered at University of Vermont, criticizing Americans for their love of evil foods.

November 1983: Solzhenitsyn goes on long thoughtful walk in woods to ponder America's demise and meets joggers, who tell him life here isn't so bleak if you run every day. They explain how jogging builds up one's spiritual strengths as well as calf muscles.

December 1983: Solzhenitsyn takes up running, buys custom-made jogging suit (all black) and decides he can think better while running. He delivers harsh speech at Boston Marathon denouncing out-of-shape Western civilization. Holds press conference where he links new social order to jogging. Claims old commissars in Russia were able to do ten miles a day, easy, while today's Communists merely bicycle. He lashes out at bicycling, surfing and skateboarding.

February 1984: Solzhenitsyn invited on "The Phil Donahue Show" for in-depth two-parter on moral sickness of America. He declines in favor of "The Tonight Show" so as to be seen by more decadent American masses. Carson books Solzhenitsyn with Dom DeLuise, Dr. Joyce Brothers and Robert Blake, who tells him, "Go back where ya came from, ya grungy ol' right-wing Russki creep–and dat's da name uh dat tune." Solzhenitsyn walks off show in protest, which makes news. He blasts Western press for playing story so small, says it was worth two-column head on front page with an inside jump and boxed sidebar.

April 1984: *People* magazine devotes "Couples" section to Mr. and Mrs. Solzhenitsyn at home in Vermont, with cozy photos of the pair playing Ping-Pong, going down to the post office for their morning mail, chatting with farmhands, studying private stock ticker in farmhouse and feeding their agent, Sue Mengers.

June 1984: Liz Smith prints item revealing that "Solzy" was seen at Studio 54 snuggling on arm of "well-known tennis cutie and recent Chinese defector, tennis star Hu Na." Rona Barrett gives her opinion of latest Solzhenitsyn address at Brandeis denouncing détente and signs off with "Keep thinkin' those big thoughts, Alexander."

July 1984: *McCall's* reprints Mrs. Solzhenitsyn's favorite warm-weather borscht recipes and she reveals in article how he courted her with letters from Siberian *gulag* praising her cabbage borscht and blinis.

September 1984: Solzhenitsyn does first TV commercial for American Express, in which he says: "My name is well known wherever I go but not my face, so when I travel to the West to cite America's failure to understand the world struggle, I make sure they know me as well as how to spell my name."

October 1984: Solzhenitsyn sells small Vermont farm and moves to Manhattan to "be nearer the bourgeoisie." Takes part in Alan King's Celebrity Tennis Tournament and is partnered with Bill Cosby in doubles against Clint Eastwood and Art Buchwald. Frequents Elaine's with Nureyev and Balanchine. . . . *New York* magazine does cover story on how Solzhenitsyn has redone his new East Side flat to resemble old pre-Revolution peasant hut.

May 1985: Dean Martin "roasts" Solzhenitsyn on TV special, gently razzing him about his pessimistic view of Western lack of will, love of Czarist Russia and dreary speeches. Rich Little does a devastating impression of him, Don Rickles cracks him up with insults about his impenetrable prose style and lousy singing voice. . . . Solzhenitsyn does guest stint on "Saturday Night Live."

August 1985: His transformation now total, Alexander Solzhenitsyn changes his name to "Al Morgan" and writes best seller telling how he's come to love America despite its moral stagnation and failure of courage. He lists his favorite things as Cocoa Puffs, Pac-Man, Garfield and the *Reader's Digest*.

THAT LITTLE OL' WINE EXPERT, ME

THIS CERTAINLY has been a vintage year for wine experts—not quite as good as '78, but then the sun hasn't been as hot either.

I haven't counted the number of working wine experts—and official estimates vary so much as to be virtually useless—but I would put the current figure at somewhere around 28,000, as of this morning; the total could jump by 500 overnight.

Exactly what constitutes a "wine expert," as opposed to someone with merely home-grown credentials, is equally difficult to define. If you know how to remove a cork from a bottle without splashing anybody, and can distinguish a red wine from a pink one, you are ready to go into the connoisseur business.

How do we know when a person crosses the fuzzy line from wine drinker to wine expert (and then, from wine expert to wino)? How does he persuade people that he knows his grapes? Is there an *académie vin* in Paris where one can learn the fine points of a Chablis? I'd hate to be told by just any newsman what kind of zinfandel to order.

I have no idea myself what a zinfandel really is, but it has such a nice ring. If you're going to discuss wines you must be able to sling words around like "zinfandel" and know the world of difference between a "tart" wine and a merely "sour" one.

Mainly, I'm ashamed by how much there is to know about wine today. Frankly, I suspect there's a lot of faking going on, but that is not for me to say. As perhaps the world's leading wine ignoramus, I shouldn't even be taking on such a vast, complex subject, but this has never stopped me before—and if I don't, who will?

Perhaps it's time that a complete outsider took a good hard look at the wine-expert industry and told the lay drinker what's going on.

Almost every newspaper over 4,000 circulation now has its own house wine expert (a modest little chap with professional pretensions). I listen to wine authorities on radio with intense fascination, astonished at their dazzling display of knowledge about recent crops in Bordeaux. I draw the line, however, at outright wine *tasting*.

The wine beat, it seems, is every bit as intricate as covering city hall, maybe more so.

Years ago, I'd have thought you could easily sum up everything about wine in six columns, but as so often happens when I don't know my subject, I'm wrong again. There's so much to say about late-breaking developments in wine that it barely can be handled in a weekly column.

I suspect that wine reporters have legmen these days who phone in hot stories from major wineries and that the larger newspapers hire stringers in France, California and the Rhine Valley. Soon, I imagine every paper will have a man who covers wine news from around the globe:

"Hi, Ed? Jean-Claude here. Look, I think I'm onto something

big at Christian Bros. They won't verify it, but I got a reliable source there–a Brother Aloysius–who tells me they're about to announce a new Pinot Noir. It sounds wild, I know, but I checked it out . . . We can't sit on this any longer, Ed. How would it look if *Gourmet* scooped us? I say we try for the early edition tomorrow. . . . O.K., here are the details–I'll dictate:

"A big beautiful wine–one might even go so far as to say piquant–was released yesterday in Napa, shocking vineyard observers across the nation . . ."

I wonder, moreover, if wine writers hang out at the same cellars and tell each other things like: "Hey, Harry, that was a helluva piece you did last week on that delicate ruby port. You must've busted your butt on it. I didn't know you knew so much about dessert wines . . ."

If wine has its own experts, there really ought to be someone equally knowledgeable on the subject of, say, bread. It is time that some bright young hotshot reporter began covering the pastry beat the way it deserves:

"Levy's Bakeries this week announced it would soon bring out a pungent new pumpernickel to satisfy the demanding palates of those who feel the traditional Russian rye is too light and dry a bread to be served with duck or quail. The new loaf is a darker, more robust version of Levy's classic corn rye . . ."

MEDIUM-HIGH SOCIETY NOTES

A SOCIETY COLUMN for the newly affluent and upwardly mobile:

Paula and **Bert Timkin** (she's the former Kelly Girl) joined with close friends last week to celebrate their recent admission into the Literary Guild, the swank event of the fall season . . . **Mrs. Waldo** ("I'm-just-a-housewife") **Cobb,** very active in Diner's Club circles, had a no-host cocktail party at the airport for **Les**

and **June Hummert,** new members of TWA's One-Million-Mile Club.

Fred Merwin—one of the Botany Club 500—gave the **Roger Gibbles** a dinner when Rog and wife **Della** returned from their annual cruise to Mexico City with the Club Med crowd. . . . **Artie Fenwick** (Famous Photographers School '63) and **Sammy Muldoon** (prominent in the Humane Society) gave an *intime* midnight supper in the Playboy Club's VIP Room for their wives, **Flo** and **Ruth,** both of whom are recent initiates into the League of Women Voters; **Flo Fenwick,** of course, is affiliated with the Fruit-of-the-Month Club.

Cora Purvis went to Victoria Station after being accepted in the Erno Laszlo Institute. Quipped Cora: "Herb always said my face was my fortune!" **Herb Purvis** is, as you know, a charter member of the Columbia Record Club . . . The **Chuck Kirbys** (longtime supporters of the Horchow Collection) are switching from the National Auto Club to the American Automobile Association, causing several raised eyebrows at last weekend's Policeman's Ball.

Lou Ambrose (Berlitz '72) gave a tea for daughter **Josie,** who has just joined the *très élégant* Jacques Cousteau Society. Josie, quite the gadabout, was glimpsed earlier that night at the Sierra Club . . . **Gloria Kneef,** with new beau **Joel Pennyman** (of the ultra-smart Mensa Society), toasted her tenth year in the Christmas Club at a lunch in her honor in the members-only dining room of the Downtown Merchants Club.

It was tennis and swimming at the Yountville Young Republicans Club for the **Hal Bigelows** (she's the former **Fran Moody,** a Carte Blanche regular for years). Bigelow, one of Our Town's major culture vultures, told pals he's joining the National Geographic Society and letting his membership in the Smithsonian Association lapse. Busy! Busy! Busy!

Ed Binks had a lavish coming-out party for **Toby Dobbins,** who announced he's joining the Mattachine Society. The chic soirée was attended by **Ethel Dinsley, Selma Venable, Marta Tuttle** and **Velma Zimm** (all matrons in the Daughters of Bilitis). . . . **Harv Anther**—registered with the Society for the Preservation of Barbershop Quartet Singing—is leaving No. 1 wife **Shirley** for the winsome and oh so clever **Judi Zinger,** a docent at the Reptile Museum.

News to Me Dept.: That the **Morty Neubarts** are just back from a two-day visit to the European Health Spa. . . . That **Lois Garth** is off on a whirlwind Tauck Tour of upstate New York. . . . That **Maggie Hunniker** has her eyelashes dyed at Elizabeth Arden's. . . . That the **Brad Ruggleses** are no longer in the Theatre Guild.

Betsy Biggs, whose daughters both attend the Katharine Gibbs School, is switching affiliations after fifteen years from MasterCard to American Express, amid whispers about the sudden chichi changes in Betsy's lifestyle (last month she was accepted into Common Cause) . . . **Greg Mickles, Jr.** (Academy of TV Arts & Sciences '57), is seeing a lot of that gorgeous **Vera Loffler** (Columbia School of Broadcasting trustee). They met on a charter flight to London last summer with the teddibly exclusive British-American Club.

THE WISHBONE IS FATHER TO THE THOUGHT

THE CHRISTMAS SEASON is a joyous time of year for just about everyone except the poor old dog-eared columnist, who each holiday period must pull yet another chestnut out of his typewriter and roast it to a golden-brown turn.

Once we get Thanksgiving under our belts, there's still Christmas to worry about, and after that it's New Year's. A columnist's work is never done, children. All in all, it's a thankless time of year for us, but we try our best. A little love and respect is all we demand in return.

There are several surefire recipes for cooking up the annual Thanksgiving Day column. The best idea is to go out in the country and shoot yourself a nice plump hunk of nostalgia, which you generously baste with lip-smacking descriptions of acorn squash, apple pandowdy, corn relish and plum pudding.

Many of your finest Thanksgiving columnists have never actually tasted most of this stuff, but they're only too happy to reminisce at great length. Look—we're pros. We city fellers can paint as lush a Thanksgiving Day mural as Grandma Moses. One glimpse at a Currier & Ives print is all it takes to rekindle those crispy adjectives and start the smoke curling out of the ol' potbelly Underwood:

"Stamping fresh rain off our rubbers, we all stood in the doorway of Uncle Gramps's farmhouse and sniffed the aroma of stuffed celery turning on the spit. 'Y'all come in!' Aunt Ned would shout, tossing another fresh nephew on the crackling fire as she gulped a steaming brew of warm whiskey sour.

"Wiping her hands on li'l Tad, Granny would wave from the kitchen, where the bracing scent of candied grits mixed with the odor of newly minced clichés and damp overcoats. Cried li'l Tad: 'That thesaurus looks mighty tasty to me!'"

This sort of column usually runs a tidy 750 words and is reprinted every Thanksgiving. Columnists who have been in the holiday game awhile soon learn the harmless dodge of reprinting "by demand" last year's column, preceded by this line:

"As usual on this day—as we've done for the past forty-two years—the *Evening Foglight* proudly reprints Lyle Mulvaney's beloved Thanksgiving at the Mulvaneys' column." (The thinking here is that, if it's an annual column reprinted since 1932, it ought to be pretty damn good by now.)

I don't see why columnists shouldn't be allowed to rerun their best stuff all year—like TV networks, movie revival houses, comedians and pop singers. It's unfair to make columnists crank out terrific material day after day while a singer can get away with doing the same seven hits for twenty-five years.

Literature-wise, Thanksgiving is a tough number, ranking just below Veterans Day and Washington's Birthday. Not enough really happens to dwell on and yet the pressure to do just one more Thanksgiving piece is enormous.

Not even sage political columnists in Washington can resist the temptation to bat out a fast Thanksgiving-in-the-Heartland ditty, just to show they've still got their thumb on America's pulse:

"As the President sits down to Thanksgiving dinner today, he may wonder what the folks down here in Turkey Trot, Ark., are thinking as they ask for more cranberry mold.

"From every home and hamlet in this traditional conservative stronghold, the people are voicing concern—not just about more cranberry mold but about more oil, sugar and foodstuffs. As Mr. Reagan says 'Pass the pumpkin pie, please,' voters here are asking themselves: 'Will there be any pumpkin pie at all next year?' "

As for your so-called "humorous" columnists, they're uneasy with Thanksgiving. It is, after all, a sober holiday with patriotic-religious overtones, so about the best way to circle it is by interviewing a turkey. The gobbler interview (usually entitled "Talking Turkey") is a proven crowd pleaser.

I'm afraid I interviewed a turkey myself this year, but I tried to get it out of the way early—so now I'm stuck. God knows what I'm going to write about today.

CHARMED, I'M SURE

THE PUBLISHER OF *Working Woman* magazine claims that "Prince Charming has died," which seems to have gone unreported elsewhere.

I always read the obits first, but I may have missed this item, so I checked it out and found that the prince hasn't passed away at all—he's simply been in hiding since the advent of women's liberation.

Charming's castle was picketed by NOW in the early 1970s, after which he fled to a quiet cottage in England, only to be discovered by Marabelle Morgan and her "Total Woman" followers, who tried to tear his place down. The prince now has an unlisted number; when you phone the old castle, his answering service insists he's "out of town."

Sources in the fairy-tale industry reveal that Prince Charming has escaped to a family estate near Sussex, where he putters in the rose garden, looks after a stable of white horses and each morning works on his memoirs, which he promises could "blow the lid off Never-Never Land."

Charming is writing his memoirs in longhand and has already sold the rights for $1.7 million, according to his agent, Lord Sterling. The book is expected to "tell all" about Snow White, Cinderella, Rapunzel and other ex-amours. A TV movie, to star Robert DeNiro, is in the works.

Through one of the prince's old chums—a frog who knew Charming during his days in a lily pond before he made it big in bedtime stories—I got in to see him. We met at the Dorchester Hotel in London, where he always stays when in town on business; he has a charming royal suite there.

Prince Charming looked incredibly fit for his age (173), and with his silvery hair and mustache resembled Doug Fairbanks, Jr. (For all I know, it *was* Doug Fairbanks, Jr.) Out of habit, the prince asked for my hand in marriage; his eyesight is failing. From then on, our interview went very well:

GN: I'd like to jump right in and ask your opinion of Prince Charles, or is that too controversial? I mean, is he truly charming enough?

PC: Well, he sure knew his way around the gals. Boy, to be thirty again!

GN: Very clever, Your Highness. I never thought you had any sense of humor. I used to wonder what the secret of your great "charm" was, because you always struck me as an awful prig.

PC: It's all Disney's doing. He turned me into a simpering ninny every chance he got.

GN: That *is* your image. So, O.K.—what is Prince Charming really like? How *do* you feel about the ERA? Should wives work? Is the nuclear family in danger because of the swinging-single ethic that you embody? Here is a chance to defend yourself.

PC: Look—I always encouraged Snow White and Cinderella to

keep working and become their own person in case things didn't work out.

GN: It always says you lived happily ever after, but now that I look back you were a no-good philanderer, forever cruising around the kingdom picking up helpless maidens.

PC: Well, sure, but see, that was my job.

GN: Nice work. How often were you married anyway?

PC: Who mentioned "marriage"? It only says "lived happily ever after." Most of the princesses just moved in until I had to rescue some new beautiful damsel from a dragon, witch or wicked stepmother. I couldn't be tied down like that to one fair maiden.

GN: Yet you claim all that didn't turn you into a chauvinist pig?

PC: I respected my women. Often, it was the maidens who rescued me, but I got the credit because the Grimm boys always gave the public what it wanted. They'd write anything if it sold fairy tales.

GN: Then you believe in women having careers?

PC: Sure, but I'm still old-fashioned. I like to see a girl in a velvet gown and glass slippers. Jeans and tank-tops are a real turn-off at a ball.

GN: Can you give me a tiny scoop now—just one juicy tidbit about Snow White before Barbara Walters grabs you? Was she really all that pure of heart?

PC: I don't kiss and tell. All I'll say now is that Snowy and I had a lot of laughs together, despite our breakup over whether her seven dwarfs should live with us. We're still close. I get a Christmas card from Snowy every year. . . . Cinderella was a sweet kid too, a very basic feet-on-the-hearth girl, but Cindy had family hangups—guilt about deserting her stepsisters and all . . .

GN: Say, how did you and the Jewish American Princess hit it off—coming from such mixed backgrounds and all?

PC: The Jewish Princess has been as maligned as I have, but I hope to set the record straight on all this when my memoirs are published.

GN: I can't wait. Until then, thanks for the time. You've been a real prince.

FOUL-WEATHER FRIENDS

WINTER WOULDN'T SEEM quite as miserable if it wasn't so overreported.

In the old days, weather was simple. A person was content to shiver, "Boy, is it chilly out there!" but now–through the miracle of TV weathermen–you can say "Boy, that wind-chill factor must be 20 degrees!"

The wind-chill factor is to winter news what the humidity index is to summer–one of TV forecasting's most enterprising advances, along with pollen counts, degree-days, air-acceptability levels, rainfall averages and satellite photos. (Ski reporting is now a separate division of weather journalism.)

The point, it appears, is to create bigger and better seasons. Plain old-time weather won't do. If a TV forecaster just came on camera and said, "It's going to snow tomorrow," he'd be back teaching dancing next week.

Without weathercasts, we wouldn't know what all those wet drops were in the air, why men's hats are suddenly rolling down the street or how cold it was yesterday in Minot, N.D.

TV weathermen never fail to reveal the coldest spot in the country, where the temperature habitually falls to 12 below zero ("Brr-r-r-r! *That's* cold, Van!"), as if it'll make you feel any warmer.

In spring, they ought to report: "If you thought today was pretty, Van, they sure had a lovely one out there in Clovis, N.M., which registered its most beautiful spring day since April 17, 1903. A record!"

Since weathermen are so dazzled by these weather marks, they could hold a winter and summer Olympics, pitting the coldest December 21 in Yakima, Wash., against a similar icy day in Muncie, Ind., or perhaps give a medal to the mayor of the hottest town for July 10 in history.

Local TV got involved in weather reportage thanks to newspapers' hard-hitting stories in the field.

Each winter, all papers send out photographers to take close-ups of the rain (the Jumping Over a Puddle picture), the wind (your Inside-Out Umbrella and Skirts Flying classics) and the cold itself (the Cute Kid in Fur Parka Blowing Steam shot).

One year, the New York *Daily News* dispatched four men to snap photos of four *different* people's umbrellas being whipped about. Well, you can't trust a single umbrella on a big story like that. You don't dare run one chintzy shot of a broken umbrella, and surely you can't get by using *last* year's umbrella pictures.

TV stations go even further, sending out entire film crews to get live action shots of snow falling and people clapping their mittens together—plus eyewitness accounts and personal weather experiences: "I just got my snow tires in time." . . . "It's a good day for ducks." We call this the story *behind* the winter.

Nobody grasps the meaning of rainfall levels, but they do sound impressive, even dire—the Dow Jones average of weather broadcasting: "So far, we've had 2.79 inches of rain already this month, which is .37 inches more than this time last year." To which the viewer can only shake his head in wonderment.

If rainfall figures astound you, satellite photos of cloud covers can make your day. These depict how the earth's atmosphere looks if you live on Jupiter—and a darn good likeness it is too. It never hurts to know the latest position of a Canadian cold air mass if you're planning a picnic.

I don't mean to sound indifferent to weather. I suffer as much as anyone, but I do it in silence. My personal method of coping with winter is to ignore it, if not defy it. I only wear boots, scarves, and carry umbrellas to stop it from storming; the best offense, I've learned, is a smart defense.

I won't give Old Man Winter the satisfaction of talking about him all the time (that's exactly what he wants). My attitude is, the less said about winter, the better. Let's keep all the weather outdoors, year-round, where it belongs. When I was a lad, winter was never allowed inside the house, but that was before they invented the wind-chill factor.

WE INTERRUPT THE NEWS FOR AN URGENT MEMO

AT A LITTLE-NOTICED local television station, WHIM-TV, producers of the evening news have been pondering ways to bolster their ratings and make a dent in ABC's "Eyewitness News." If they've had no luck so far, it's not for any lack of ideas. Here's a chronology of their recent efforts:

January 2: In bold move, news director replaces 6 P.M. anchorman with two-man anchor team of identical twins. As he explains in memo, "Two talking heads are better than one."

January 11: Ratings slide, so news director switches left-hand anchorman to right, right-hand anchorman to left, pulls sportscaster over more toward center. After no visible surge in ratings, anchormen resume old positions—with a third, taller anchorman in the middle. WHIM tells press: "We'll use as many anchormen as necessary to improve the news," cites No. 1 station in Idaho that employs eleven rotating anchormen and no reporters.

January 17: Ratings plummet. WHIM decides to make first anchorman funny, second anchorman tragic. Says news director: "We feel a serio-comic approach to news will appeal to our diverse audience." Promotion ads emphasize WHIM's "sincere zaniness."

January 24: Nielsens tumble to new lows. To improve coverage, WHIM hires black anchorman, Puerto Rican woman consumer expert, Polish weatherman, French-Italian sportscaster, Jewish science editor, Irish critic, Eurasian man-in-the-street interviewer, Swiss bell ringer.

February 2: No change in ratings. In station shake-up, Italian moved to weather, Jew to sports, Pole to science, black to Irish.

February 8: Nielsens now unmeasurable, so station hires Charles Eames to redesign chairs, Andrew Wyeth to redo backdrop, I. M. Pei to revise set. Newscast features reporters on stools revolving around a modernistic globe and fountain. "We're going to more of an oval look in news," confirms WHIM spokesman. "These stories need to be busier. The old horizontal approach was causing our sources to dry up."

February 16: Ratings slip to −18. Station manager fires news staff, hires gagman from rival "Comedy News" but vetoes use of laugh track, vowing, "We'll do our reports before a live audience." Adds news director: "There's nothing intrinsically wrong with local news that can't be helped by a little better timing."

February 23: WHIM brings in up-and-coming anchorman team from the Second City. Nielsens leap to −12 and entire news show gets weekend booking at Grossinger's. *Variety* reports WHIM to do all-singing, all-dancing public-affairs special on inflation, says "Three's Company" rumored going to all-news format.

February 28: Socially aware reporter upbraided for refusing to "have fun with" story on migrant workers. "He's a sharp enough newsman," states WHIM, "but the guy doesn't know how to have a good time." Newscast changes name to "The Six O'Clock Movie."

March 5: Ratings sink below "Zoorama" reruns. New hard-nosed news policy adopted. Announces WHIM: "News is nothing to joke about anymore." Station goes to all-frown format: recruits haggard newsmen dressed in black, puts hat with press card on anchorman's head, replaces folksy weatherman with Nobel geophysicist.

March 13: Anchorman winks on opening show and is suspended for overacting. Grim news approach fails to stir viewers. WHIM tries publicizing reporters' personalities. Promos depict newsmen double-dating, going to church together, pulling taffy. Anchormen share camera with wives, kids, mothers, puppy dogs.

March 19: Weekly ratings hit all-time TV low. News team replaced by "men who have been on the other side of the news and can be trusted to tell it like it is." WHIM team includes ex-mayor of Elko, Nev., ex-Fort Myers, Fla., fire chief, deposed Haitian dictator, ex-Mets bullpen catcher, former rainmakers.

March 27: Nielsen cancels WHIM contract. Station calls in Halston to advise on jackets, Vidal Sassoon to reshape reporters' hair. News director orders tinted aviator glasses for everyone.

April 2: In final effort to boost audience, WHIM forgoes Playboy Look for all-out naturalism. Newsmen instructed to affect Tweedy Look–pipes, elbow patches, mustaches, rumpled hair, open collars. Told to slouch, cross legs, appear bored.

April 10: Anchormen now delivering news in simulated saloons surrounded by correspondents carousing at bar.

RATINGS CLOBBER CLASSICS

AFTER SEEING HOW ruthlessly the networks now deal with new shows–canceling some after a few weeks due to lack of an instant following–I realize how handy the A. C. Nielsen Co. would have been years ago had ratings then been available:

BERLIN – Future symphonies by young local composer L. v. Beethoven have been yanked by the Municipal Philharmonic after overnight ratings revealed that his first four symphonies failed to pull the expected share of the total German music-going audience.

The musician's projected special, a Fifth Symphony, is thus being "shelved for the time being," according to a Philharmonic vice-president in charge of concertos and etudes, Rudolph Ding. "We hope to reschedule the Beethoven Fifth at some future date," said Ding, "possibly Sunday morning at 8:30."

PARIS – New fall canvases by much-touted Impressionist Vince van Gogh have been termed "disappointing" by museum curator Henri Canard, and the eccentric Dutch painter's series of oils is being replaced by an exhibit of sad clowns and kittens.

"The public just isn't responding to these sunflowers and wheatfields like we'd hoped," said Canard.

Van Gogh complained that his show–which includes a self-portrait, his room at Arles and some drawbridges–wasn't given enough of a chance to catch on with viewers. "I know there's an audience out there for drawbridges," he said. "What do they expect, anyway? I'm doomed to fail. They got me right up there next to Cézanne."

Canard said that in the first few days of the exhibit, Van Gogh's show failed to "pull sufficient numbers." He adds, "We had no other choice but to take his paintings down."

Cézanne's canvases, proven winners in recent years, are back for a seventh season in local galleries.

ATHENS – A newly sculpted statue, "Venus de Milo," has been canceled at the elbows because a local museum vice-president for statuary maintains the figure is not drawing enough viewers each week to justify continuing to display the controversial work.

Sculptors here are crying "censorship" since the partially draped female form has become the object of parents' concern over the fact that the figure depicts a nude woman in the prime time of life. Explains Greek marble executive Leo Zeus, "Early responses to Venus indicate that, while people are looking at her once, out of curiosity, they are not returning for subsequent viewings."

LONDON – Charles Dickens' new novel, *Oliver Twist,* has not survived the early Nielsens and will be dropped next week after the third chapter.

"We felt the plot had plenty going for it, atmosphere-wise, but the readers aren't buying it," said editor T. E. Dulwich, "and our advertisers were upset by the downbeat tone of the early episodes set in an orphanage and a workhouse . . . This just isn't the year for mawkish kids' stories."

STRATFORD-ON-AVON – Due to increased demands for more plays to run in the "family viewing" period, a new series by Bill Shakespeare about the lives of English royalty–under the umbrella title of "Masterpiece Theater"–has been bumped as "too violent."

For the Globe Theater's "second season," the company will substitute a comedy about a widowed court jester who moves to Ireland.

Thus the just-began "Hamlet" show will close after its fifth performance. Martin Burbage, Globe vice-president for programming, terms "Hamlet" "too melancholy"; he says the play was sixty-seventh in the October 5–18 ratings, just behind "Saturday Knight Live."

"We're proud of our commitment to live drama," vows Burbage, "but I'm afraid the groundlings are tuning us out."

POP TIME POPS CORK

YESTERDAY, AS "Father Time" (Bertram H. Griswold) was celebrating another birthday, I got in touch with him at his condominium in Shady Manor, N.J., to ask if he'd like to be interviewed for a story on how it feels to turn 1,983.

"Nothing doing," he snapped. "I've read enough of these 'centenarian reveals longevity secrets' articles to last me an eternity. You never read about old folks until they turn 100 and suddenly become all cute and newsworthy. The instant someone hits 100, the press sends a guy out for a fast interview, but by then it's too late–the poor guy can hardly stay awake, let alone come up with a lot of snappy answers."

He said he contacted a local paper about doing a first-person piece on his last 1,982 years, but an editor told him: "If you're not exactly 2,000, forget it. Our readers are only interested in round numbers."

I asked Griswold if I could just come out and hear his gripes about old-folks interviews. He agreed, but only if I promised to tell it like it is and not refer to him anywhere in the article as either "spry" or "chipper."

"If there's one thing a person over 100 is not, it's spry," he snarled. "I've felt crummy since I was 65." I asked the "Old Year" to list any other phrases he'd just as soon not see in print again.

"Just don't write that I'm 'surprisingly alert and articulate for a man of 1,983,' have 'an amazing memory,' once met Lincoln and have 'a twinkle' in my eye. None of it's true, and you know it. Turning 100, let alone 1,983, is no picnic."

I agreed to the old man's ground rules and drove out to Shady Manor, N.J., a pleasant retirement community where all of the best years from 1900 on reside in the pink of condition.

After a long siege of ill health, 1929 was looking alive again; 1920 through '27 appeared incredibly fit; the 1930s were sitting up and taking solid food; the '40s were jitterbugging out on the terrace; downstairs, the '50s sat silently; the 1960s were flaked out all over the place, exhausted; and the '70s were gazing in a mirror at themselves, still primping.

When I arrived, old Griswold was there to welcome me in a dapper three-piece checked suit and straw hat. He had a walrus mustache, big bushy eyebrows and looked a lot like the late Melvyn Douglas. He wasn't the emaciated wraith I expected.

"What's going on?" I said. "Where's your long-handled scythe, white beard, hourglass and big floppy sheet?"

"What a corny image," he sighed. "For 100 years, cartoonists have been drawing me like that. I've tried to get them out here to look at me and update the sketch, but they tell me the public won't accept any other version of 'Father Time.' I think the media is out to get us."

Griswold was full of annoying examples of how the press has been portraying old-timers like himself.

"First off, they pester the heck out of you to learn how to live to 100—as if anybody knows. To humor reporters, we make up all sorts of gibberish about eating ten bananas a day for fifty years, taking a nip with each meal or going dancing every night. They lap it up. I guess it sells papers."

I asked "Father Time" what else bugs him about the stories.

"Well, they always want to know the most astonishing event of our lifetime," he said. "If we try to name something original—like sugarless gum, night football or see-through blouses, the newsman always switches it back to the same old boring discoveries: jet planes, color TV, going to the moon."

Any other problems you old-timers have had with the press?

"Worst of all is surrounding us with 35 grandchildren, none of whom we see until we turn 100 and some photographer hauls 'em all out here. What a racket! Then they buy a cheap cake, put 100 candles on it and call that a birthday. We don't even get any cake, we're so busy answering dumb questions like 'Do you have any regrets after 100 years?'"

"Well?" I said, unable to resist the ageless query. "If you had your 1,983 years to live over, would you change anything?"

"Just today," he barked, and hobbled off toward 1984.

KEYHOLE KAPERS

ACCORDING TO HIGHLY placed rumors, the gossip column is making a big comeback, so now I may have a chance to write one.

It isn't as tricky as it looks. You don't need any real gossip, actually, so long as you have the right names and can string them together in such a way as to make each item *sound* juicy and exclusive. Here's my modest effort:

Barbra Streisand isn't speaking to any of her future co-stars—and don't ask why! . . . Truman Capote, seen at Le Côte Cheque, was dining *au gratin* again, poor boy (something wrong, Truman?) . . . Don't invite to the same party: Red Skelton and Susan Sontag. . . . Nothing to whispers that Earl Wilson and the "B.W." are pfffft . . . Warren Beatty . . . Johnny Carson to change phone numbers again? "Could be," winks John.

Spiro Agnew, the former vice-president, looks mighty fit for a man who once was regarded in Washington social circles as "nolo contendere." . . . Jack Nicholson . . . More rumors that gossip columnist Walter Scott will wed Robin Adams Sloan.

When Howard Hughes died, he left behind a string of unaccounted-for girlfriends . . . Seen huddling together at Le La, the chic new Greek restaurant: Orson Welles . . . Audrey Hepburn, now 46, dropped by our table at the Blue Angel when she was in town and confided she would soon be 47 . . . Julie and David Eisenhower . . . London gossipist Nigel Dempster has been reading N.Y. *Daily News* gossip Liz Smith on the sly (Ta-ta, Nigel!).

QUIRKY QUOTE OF THE DAY: "One if by land, two if by sea, and I on the opposite shore shall be."

Jackie O and daughter Caroline (no relation to Princess Caroline) make a nifty twosome wherever they go these days. . . . Overheard backstage at *Dreamgirls,* the Broadway musical: "Act II is running a little long!" . . . Cute sign on the door at P. J. Clarke's: "Enter Other Door." . . . L.A. *Herald Examiner* gossipist Jim Bacon to ex-L.A. *Times* gossip Joyce Haber: "Whatever happened to you?" . . . David Frost broke up with himself again.

TUESDAY'S CHUCKLE: "Heh-heh-heh."

Joel Grey, now four feet eleven inches, is taking on his biggest role to date in order, says Joel, "to stretch myself." . . . Barbara Marx. . . . Speaking of which, Barbara Howar, the famed Washington, D.C., famous person, will not marry Norman Mailer.

A bouquet of plaudits, orchids and huzzahs to syndicated gossip columnists Marilyn Beck and "Suzy" (nice scribbling!). . . . Liza Minnelli . . . Barbara Walters and Harry Reasoner shared an elevator at Sardi's last week, but Harry got off first. . . . Frank Sinatra packing 'em in.

PARDON OUR SLIP DEPT.: Oops, that wasn't Bob Dylan, David Bowie and Mick Jagger who checked into the S.F. Travel-Lodge last weekend, as we reported here—just three very hip hardware dealers in town for an annual confab. Sorry, fellas!

Second City gossip Irv Kupcinet and Chicago may be talking splitsville; seems Kup has big eyes for Miami . . . Muhammad Ali . . . Still no word on that Beatles tour, but Ringo and Yoko may team for a one-nighter in Cincy. . . . See ya tomorrow, Keyholers!

Culture Shocks

AW SHUCKS

IF PEOPLE SIMPLY had a fuller understanding of "corn," they would be a lot less frightened by it. In time, they might even come to love it, as I do, and be able to stand up before a large crowd like this and gobble it down openly.

Nobody treats corn seriously enough—or else they treat it too seriously and label it "camp," which is what happens to fine wholesome corn when it grows up and moves to New York. Camp is your fancy canned corn off the cob and I can't get it down anymore without choking. Honest-to-gosh corn is a personal thing that pops up out of the ground organically—Steve and Eydie, say, to pick a prime example at the peak of perfection.

Steve and Eydie are twice as corny as Kansas in August, but what of it? The important thing is, do you really like them? At first, you may not like yourself for it, but once you get over that you'll have the proper healthy attitude toward corn and corn by-products.

Beware of cheap imitations like Carmen Miranda, who is campy and as safe to enjoy as Lena Horne. What I'd like to know is, do people truly like Carmen Miranda or are most of them faking it? Do they, deep down, really dig Steve and Eydie and secretly loathe Carmen Miranda?

At one time, during that fuzzy period when it wasn't yet chic to savor her, Carmen Miranda was mere corn. People probably liked her all along but didn't dare come out of the closet until the coast was clear. Someday, Steve and Eydie may be designated official camp, but right now they're still just good juicy lip-smackin' corn. This is the time to sink your teeth in.

A while back, Rona Barrett slid from high corn to low camp. Now, of course, everybody rolls his eyes and quite adores her, but try to wring a confession out of a single avid *National Enquirer* reader.

It's getting tougher to tell the difference between private home-grown corn and the socially accepted plastic variety—soap operas, horror movies, beauty pageants, Nelson Eddy–Jeanette MacDonald musicals, etc. Lately, I notice a lot of bending over backward to embrace alien corn, dreadful stuff you don't enjoy at all but feel obliged to wink at—game shows, Spiderman, rock 'n' roll groups from the 1950s.

The only corn test is: Would you indulge in it all by yourself? I know I love barbershop quartets, because I once went out of my way to hear a regional competition, but I'm not sure about parades. You have to like corn for its own sake, not because you're supposed to or it's cute. You must be scrupulously on the level about it.

For instance, I sincerely like Roy Rogers (and Dale—but *only* if she's with Roy), and part of it is that he's not ashamed of himself or defensive about Trigger or "kidding himself" like Dean Martin and Liberace. Roy never swerves a foot from pure cowboy; it's all he knows and that's plenty for me.

As a kid, I liked Roy (well, I was a pretty corny kid, too—I read *Archie* and *Little Lulu* rather than *Plastic Man* or *Wonder Woman*), which explains a basic appeal of corn. It's just a small part of you that won't go away or grow up. Roy's charm is, he has never gotten any older himself; he thinks he's Roy Rogers. I was worried when *The Village Voice* discovered Roy, but I doubt if it'll go to his head; he's just not the type to go campy on you all of a sudden.

I used to dig Peanuts dolls, I swear it. On my lunch hour, I'd kind of *casually* drop into a stationery store to see what was new at the "Peanuts Gallery," making believe I was hunting for a get-well card, when in fact I'd be wondering whether to buy a Lucy figurine. (The thing was, see, I already *had* a Snoopy bank and a perfectly good Charlie Brown, so I really didn't need a Lucy doll.

It took years for me to acknowledge that I am hip to Muzak. People go around maligning it carelessly, but there's good Muzak and lousy Muzak. Maybe there's a little too much of it around, but in the right lobby, at the proper moment, Muzak can set me humming; no wonder all those dairy cows tap their feet when they hear it.

I'm unable to leave an elevator if an especially nice medley is playing, and once I went six floors past my office to hear a terrific banjo solo all the way through; it would have been rude just to walk out. In any case, as elevator listening goes, Muzak's an improvement over strangers asking me if it's started raining out yet.

I guess this is the place to divulge my long-term infatuation with Lawrence Welk's show, which I think is just grand and so did my grandmother and there was nothing wrong with her. She'd be the first to complain if Welk had a "bum show," as she did once when there were too many Hawaiian songs she'd never heard of. I could understand that. I hate hearing songs I don't know, and Lawrence Welk plays fewer of them per square minute than any conductor this side of Meyer Davis.

Welk once said that if you wake up a jazzman at 3 A.M. he'll reveal he likes Welk. We've reached a darn sorry state in America when you have to go around knocking on doors in the middle of the night to rouse a few champagne-music lovers out of bed.

Were it not for Welk, what's more, there would be no Lennon Sisters, and what sort of a world would that be? Even people reluctant to say they watch Welk can be nudged into conceding that, yes, they, well, always *kind* of liked the Lennons.

Why be shy about it? Can't we all be big enough to admit those were four adorable girls who sang yummy close harmony? It was like discovering a quartet that did Gregorian chants and was perky to boot. If the Lennon Sisters were the Andrews Sisters, everyone would be falling over each other in ecstasy. Just remember: Someday they *will* be the Andrews Sisters and then we'll see who eats crow.

Speaking of food, when I'm out on the town alone, with nobody around to see where I go, I'm almost sure to tiptoe past a massage parlor and instead slip quietly into a Steak & Brew or International House of Pancakes. Next to these, McDonald's and Colonel Sanders are trivial dining experiences.

McDonald's is where you go on your way home from something

else—it is not the thing itself, unlike Steak & Brew or IHOP, which require you to lay your plans early. You must find the courage to say, in a clearly audible voice: "Hey, why don't we all go to the House of Pancakes for dinner Saturday night?" The reason, should anyone ask, is simply that dollar-size buttermilk hotcakes don't grow on trees and neither do German pancakes lolling in butter and lemon or Swedish crepes with lingonberry jam.

The basic pull of Steak & Brew, needless to say, is the salad bar; I'm partial to *any* place with a salad bar and chilled plates. The top sirloin and all the beer I can drink are secondary. What I'm in there for, let's face it, is all the croutons I can sprinkle.

In the annals of cornography, there may be nothing more damaging than a frank admission that you are a blatant Jerry Vale fan. If you will just bother to listen to him, however, it's quite apparent that Vale is one hell of a crooner, about the last of our throbbing Italian singers who is not afraid to pull out the throttle on his tremolo all the way. Believe me, this man does not mess around with a love song.

I like Vale, but most of all I *love* Eddie Fisher. People laugh when I sit down to play my Fisher records, but it's only because they forget how just plain wonderful he sounds. If they'd stop snickering at me for a second and listen to a few bars of "I Need You Now" or "Tell Me Why," I guarantee they would be a lot less smug, smiling indulgently and saying, "Oh-h-h, I *used* to like Eddie Fisher." Your hard-core Fisherphile can't dismiss him so easily and may still be found sneaking an old album off the shelf, pulling the shades and hearing him let loose on "Downhearted."

Most of the time, you like somebody who's considered "corny" and don't know why. It's impossible to defend a heartfelt yearning for Steve and Eydie or Steak & Brew because it's pure passion and you can't discuss it without being reduced to babbling.

God knows what I like about Billy Graham, but you can't deny the Rev. Billy is tops at it. I easily can understand why Richard Nixon wanted to have Graham around: If I were President, I'd ask Billy over all the time myself just to hear him talk in that gorgeous North Carolina drawl. I've long been a Graham disciple but not until now have I been willing to stand up and come forward.

Mind you, none of this is meant as an excuse for soft-core corn, which is something else and mustn't be tolerated. There's sweet corn and mushy corn. Overripe corn includes the Johnny Mann Singers, sad clowns and pussycats on black velvet, Ferrante and Teicher, redwood burl coffee tables, Three Stooges comedies, candles shaped like banana splits, Doc Severinson's wardrobe, abalone ashtrays, anything labeled "World's Greatest Mom," "Sue the Bastards" or "I Love You THIS Much" and Amtrak food. I mean, that's just plain horrible stuff and an insult to golden sunkissed corn.

If you want the real thing, help yourself to any of these rich kernels of goodness spilling out of America's cornucopia:

Ozzie and Harriet. The Nelsons lived in a corn-bread house, spoke corn-fed lines and did cornball things, yet what I wouldn't give for a crack at some reruns now. While everyone else loved Lucy, I found solace with Ozzie and Harriet.

No show could duplicate their nifty dimension of life as art, but most of all, the Nelsons were just so damn *nice,* the soul of corn. It took a real effort not to like that family. Things came apart when Ricky got hold of a guitar and combed his hair forward, but that happens in even the best homes. Say what you will, the Nelsons were classic hot-buttered corn.

Woolworth's. This is another lunchtime diversion of mine: aimlessly wandering the aisles of an ancient corn palace, checking out the latest line of vegetable graters, bathtub toys and porcelain birds–plus, of course, a candy showcase featuring such hard-to-find items as orange marshmallow peanuts, cinnamon bears and Mexican hats. While Halloween and Valentine's Day are throwaway holidays, they're taken to heart at Woolworth's, and around mid-October and early February you can't get me out of there. The candy corn is in season.

Ice Shows. Critics who set out to mock the frilly pants off ice shows always return to their typewriters chastened; as a former ice-show reviewer, I can vouch for this. The stupid things are absolutely superb; you just have to admire all that "wizardry over ice," as we call it. (Footnote: I also want to mention my fondness for ice-rink organ medleys, an underrated musical form.)

Arthur Godfrey. I liked him better before he was recycled as an ecologist, when it took some courage to tune him in and risk being marked for life as a little old lady; however, all lovers of corn are at least 50 percent little old lady (indeed, I have an unnatural appetite for tearooms and cafeterias and will take a first-rate cafeteria over a French restaurant any day).

Godfrey is now an elder statesman of broadcasting and eminently revered, but there was a time when Serious People just did *not* listen to Arthur Godfrey on the radio. Of course, your hardcore crowd found Godfrey too highbrow; their taste ran more to Don McNeil's "Breakfast Club."

Paintings, posters, postcards and calendars depicting autumn leaves, snowy barns and crashing surf. If they're well done (or even if they're not particularly), I'm a terrible sucker for nature scenes. You can try disguising this fact by buying prints of the same stuff by Monet or Hopper, but you may as well recognize the fact that you have an innate taste for—well, pure corn oil.

The whole point is, there's nothing wrong with corn if only people would face it squarely instead of shuffling around and apologizing and changing the subject, or, even worse, giggling and saying, "I love Lawrence Welk's show—it's so awful," which is a very corny thing to say, by the way. If you think he's awful, don't go around liking him. I hate to see an accordionist patronized like that. When it comes to corn, it would be nice to see people holding their heads high as an elephant's eye rather than jabbing a toe in the ground and shucking their responsibilities.

So I'm going in now to put on some Eddie Fisher records while I thumb through this week's *People,* after which I may drop by Woolworth's to see if they have any new Peanuts dolls in or autumn scenes, then I'll probably just grab a bite at the House of Pancakes and finish this article on Billy Graham in the *Reader's Digest* or perhaps catch a little good uninterrupted Muzak, but I want to leave in time to get home for a Steve and Eydie special with Roy Rogers and Jerry Vale (with any luck, he'll do "You Don't Know Me").

And to hell with Carmen Miranda.

WHY JOHNNY CAN'T GRADUATE

IN THE LATEST Gallup news survey, U.S. teenagers are up to their old tricks—"displaying a startling lack of knowledge of some of the most important dates, events and personalities in history." Only 51 percent, it seems, knew when Columbus discovered America (or was it Armenia?).

Not a week goes by that U.S. youth doesn't reveal its ignorance of some new obscure field. One week it's English, then it's arithmetic, and if it isn't grammar it's geography. I found this hard to accept until I took a survey myself and learned that things are worse than even Gallup suspected.

Many teenagers, when asked to respond to questions, had no idea what a "question" was, and the few that did grasp the meaning were unable to grasp a pencil and mark "x" in a box. Many, in fact, had never made an "x" before, except on their report cards.

It's somewhat discouraging, but here are the results of the first Basic Incompetency (or How Stupid Can You Get?) Test:

—Two thirds of the teenagers polled didn't know the difference between Christopher Columbus and Columbus, Ohio, and those who did thought that he was a detective in a shabby raincoat who landed at Columbo Circle.

—Forty-six percent of those queried said that America was discovered in 1942, and 38 percent thought the event occurred the year they were born. The remainder had "no opinion" and asked to be excused from further questions on account of illness.

—Over half of all the teens surveyed said that Alex Haley freed the slaves and that Halley's Comet is thus named for him. Thirty-two percent thought that Abraham Lincoln was Moses' son.

—Fifty-six percent of the boys and girls said that "the father of our country" is Walter Cronkite (18 percent named Washington Irving). Only 29 percent had ever heard of George Washington and half of those said that he played tight end for the San Francisco 49ers.

—Forty-seven percent of all high-schoolers said that the capital of Texas is Oklahoma City, but 22 percent did not know what "Texas" is and identified it as the cause of the Boston Tea Party. (To quote one typical student: "It was Texas without representation.")

—Twenty-three percent of the teenagers told pollsters that America won its independence from England in World War I, and 81 percent named Canada as the fiftieth state. Only 29 percent could explain the difference between Winston Churchill, Napoleon and Gandhi.

—Forty-eight percent of American teens could name the national anthem, but 83 percent said it was written by Jose Feliciano.

—Fifty-two percent of those questioned realized that World War I came before World War II, but 77 percent went on to say that the Civil War was fought over the gold standard. Thirty-eight percent said that the war in Vietnam was caused by the Watergate break-in.

—Twenty-one percent were able to identify Harry Truman from a photograph; 57 percent said he was played by James Whitmore. Thirty-eight percent said "the buck stops here" was a Beatles hit.

—Twelve percent of the youths knew that Ronald Reagan is President, but 27 percent said he is "president of California" or "the West." Twenty-two percent didn't know where "the West" is; 14 percent said it was "out West somewhere."

—In the grammar area, 67 percent of U.S. teens were unable to name any parts of speech except "words." Many did not know the distinction between a paragraph and a parenthesis, and 26 percent confused the letters "o" and "e," causing some confusion in the essay portion of the test. Many of these students were later recommended for a brush-up course in remedial alphabet.

—Forty-four percent of the students were unsure of the

difference between a question mark and a giraffe, referring to the latter as "a tall leopard." Asked to define "adjective," 63 percent said it is "a large body of water surrounded on three sides."

—In the final section of the quiz, 87 percent of the teenagers questioned said they would rather be watching "M*A*S*H" than taking a test, 67 percent were unable to give the name of their school, and 98 percent listed their favorite subjects as European Film Making, Introduction to Death, Drug Science and the History of American Sex.

A MILD CASE OF ESTHETE'S FOOT

THE OLDER I GET, the more I'm confounded by certain art forms I don't much like but wish I did and feel guilty for not enjoying more—scat singing, say.

Anyone who knows a thing about jazz (and often many who don't) go crazy when a singer begins scooby-dooing, especially if it happens to be Ella. I like Ella as much as the next guy, except when she scats. I'm never going to appreciate singers who sound like trumpets, no matter who they are.

Elizabethan singers are right up there with scatters as practitioners of an art I feel no kinship with whatever, even though Elizabethan folk songs are probably very nice.

I might like them more if the singers didn't feel an obligation to dress up in Elizabethan costumes that don't quite fit and proceed to sing their tunes a foot away from me, but that appears to be part and parcel of Elizabethan folk singing.

Of course, I'm not even that fond of listening to Elizabethan songs on records, and leading the list of my least favorite seventeenth-century folk songs is "Greensleeves," the "Stardust" of Elizabethan standards.

I suppose it's pretty—in an Elizabethan sort of way—but it

sounds to me like a dirge. However, I'll take a dirge any day over the merriest of Elizabethan folk songs.

Another cultural expression I feel crummy about for not liking is chamber music concerts. Now, I've given string quartets about as good a shot as anything, but I'm not up to that rarefied level of concentration. After ten minutes, I'm ready for a thirty-minute break.

My gut feeling is that string quartet concerts are enjoyed primarily by the participants and were never intended to be played outside their homes. I'm talking about so-called "live" chamber music concerts. A string quartet heard on the radio, or a record, sounds like quite a rousing affair, but when you have to be there in person something just goes out of it.

It's not the music I mind—it's the actual sitting-there-motionless part that gets me. In no time at all, I'm so busy trying to find something to keep my eyes occupied (i.e., open) that I'm not paying attention at all to Mozart. Instead, I'm wondering if the violist is dating the cute violinist and whether the cellist has a hairpiece.

A third refined taste I've given up all hope of ever acquiring is an enthusiasm for mobiles. I'm simply not a mobile fan, and I don't care if Calder himself did them. They're still mobiles in my book, and there's no way around it.

It would help if I could just get over the fact that mobiles remind me of tinkly door chimes in cheap curio shops or those twirly things they hang over babies' cribs to keep them quiet.

I realize that mobiles "express the childlike exuberance of life" and are "a joyous use of space," but I still feel silly standing underneath one and watching it spin like a little toy windmill while I try to think of a more cogent comment than "Hey, look at it go around!"

Running close behind mobiles as a mode of artistic expression I feel uneasy with are tapestries. I never quite know how to approach a tapestry except with a routine pseudo-awe that I don't honestly feel for rugs. Perhaps if a tapestry were on the floor it'd be easier to know how I felt toward it.

I make the expected gasps of astonishment at the number of peasant women it took to weave, and I marvel at its antiquity and the fact that it looks as if it were woven yesterday, and I shake my head at what it would cost to produce one today—but basically I'm unimpressed. I'm always dubious of artistic marvels that try to wow you with statistics.

A literary equivalent of tapestries and chamber music is *The Atlantic,* a fine magazine I'm periodically ashamed of not reading avidly, but I can't get past thinking of it less as a worthwhile magazine than a worthy cause.

This really isn't *The Atlantic*'s fault so much as it is that of a high school forensics teacher who had us all read the magazine at knifepoint and prepare speeches on some of its interesting and informative articles about UN peace-keeping efforts in Africa and the rise of post-war industrial Germany, two topics *The Atlantic* used to have a corner on.

The Atlantic has since been spruced up, yet I'm sure if I opened any issue at random there would be an article about the rise of modern industrial Germany, although lately the emphasis seems to be more on modern industrial Japan and Alger Hiss.

I'm also allergic to articles about Alger Hiss and Whittaker Chambers, largely because I can't ever keep straight who's the good one and who's the bad one. I feel about the Alger Hiss case much as I do about "Greensleeves."

OUR OVERWORKED MEN ON THE STREET

AFTER LISTENING TO television man-on-the-street interviews, it's hard to know whether to feel sorrier for television or men on the street. (By men, I'm afraid I must also include women, children and talking dogs.)

For years, I thought this poor showing was limited to local men on the street. I figured: Well, maybe New York City streets just don't lend themselves to enlightened points of view. They certainly don't lend themselves to driving.

Then I noticed that even on network newscasts men on the streets of Detroit, Houston, Chicago, Boston, Los Angeles and, no doubt, Paris or Bombay are every bit as disappointing on camera as our own good old bumbling New York versions. I felt a little better after that, but not much.

So now I've adopted a general view that people on street corners (a) should not be stopped and (b) are not thinking hard enough about the issues—nuclear waste, Caspar Weinberger, resuming diplomatic ties with East Germany, things like that. What they're contemplating is whether to grab a hot dog or wait for supper.

A man waylaid on his way to the dentist shouldn't be held responsible for what he says about détente or people who fly motorcycles. When a TV reporter asks the one question he's memorized ("What do you think about all this?"), there's a dead pause as color drains from the lady's cheeks, she eyes the mike warily and says, "Well, I . . . I, ah . . . think it's . . . fine."

All of which is painstakingly filmed by a polished highly paid crew and transmitted to the nation as the collective opinion of mankind. It seems like a pretty low trick to pull on mankind.

Assuming it wouldn't bring TV news to a standstill, maybe they ought to reconsider this man-on-the-street stuff. After twenty-five years, however, TV news directors still cling to a hope that one of these days somebody in the street will master the form.

Last week, a reporter on a network newscast was querying people in Buffalo or somewhere to see how they felt about inflation. To a woman, everyone agreed it was bad, all right. Not one housewife came out in favor of high prices. (If she had, I'm sure it would have been quickly edited out.)

The reporter had been combing the city all day getting folks from all walks of life to say they disliked inflation. When Hank Aaron broke Ruth's record, people by the hundreds were found who approved of it.

A seasoned TV inquisitor can sense, however, if someone on the street is going to let him down, so often he'll sort of nudge them along a bit: Q. "Ma'am, what do you think of this awesome event in space?" A. "I think it's an awesome event." . . . Q. "Did it move you much?" A. "It moved me much."

A while ago, someone told a TV newsman, "It's none of your business." That shook things up for a second and was the first hint that, after years of naïvely playing along, men on the street may be asserting themselves. Well, TV won't; someone has to.

It's time people told TV reporters, "What sort of a goofy question is that?" or "Let's see if we can't rephrase that better."

Maybe I'm upset because *I'm* never stopped and solicited for my views on current events. I'm sure I could come up with some interesting remarks to amuse and inform the home viewers. If a reporter asked me what I think of inflation, I'd never get off a lame answer like "It's awful." After taking a few minutes to ponder it, I'd shoot back a zippy reply:

"If you mean, do I have any easy overnight cure-alls for our frustrating economic woes, the answer of course is no. If, on the other hand, you wonder how I'm personally affected by the monetary crisis, here are a few telling anecdotes . . ."

NIETZSCHE INKS TV PACT; PROUST REPLACES COSELL

"NBC-TV is upstaging CBS by skedding an hour-long Leonardo da Vinci special on June 20, beating CBS's five-parter on Leonardo which debuts Aug. 13 . . ." —Variety

NETWORK TALENT SCOUTS are scouring Europe for new fall series packages hurriedly being wrapped up since the dawn of "Civilisation"—not to mention "Elizabeth R.," "The Forsyte Saga," "Search for the Nile," "The Six Wives of Henry VIII" and "Masterpiece Theater."

Below, as leaked to me, is an exchange of cables between a

vice-president in charge of programming in Hollywood and his man in Europe.

"Murray: Have swung major deal for 26-parter on 'Finnegans Wake' sure to knock out NBC's 'Balzac Anthology.' Tried landing show with French angle, but CBS has tied up 'Best of Victor Hugo.' Off to London to nab 'Six Wives of Henry VIII' sequel—'Eight Wives of Henry VI.' As ever, Leo."

"Dear Leo: Nix 'Finnegans' in fall sked. Censors here uptight since recent Chaucer special. Need something heavier for Tues. at 8 as lead-in to 'Plutarch's Lives.' Any way to team Cicero & Pliny as weekly regulars on new 'Homer Hour'? Await word. Best, Murray."

"Mur: Cicero-Pliny packet locked up for '83 by BBC, but hope to ink J. Gielgud and Kenny Clark to co-host variety show on Socrates, 'Thursday Night at the Forum.' Also, can get Plato for a song. Yours, Leo."

"Leo: Not sure Plato will play well on Mon., but 7:30 spot is soft so willing to risk it. Moving 'Dallas' to Sun. at 11 A.M. Need property with girl, two guys. Any bid yet on D. H. Lawrence scripts? As ever, Murray."

"Dear Murray: Socrates set, but Plato holding out. Hear rumor 'Taxi!' being replaced by 'Forsyte Saga Revisited.' Now awaiting go-ahead on comedy series, with Congreve & Wycherley, à la 'Saturday Night Live.' Reviews here good. Advise. —Leo."

"Leo: Who Wycherley? Fall sked shapes up sweet, but need more sitcoms. NBC going with 'Capt. Brassbound's Conversion' and ABC with 'Lady Windermere's Fan.' Understand Thackeray still available. Can do? As ever, Mur."

"Dear Murray: Bad news. Thackeray nailed down by ABC. No loss. 'Vanity Fair' pulled good Nielsens but other stuff lacks boffo factor. Any interest in Henry James series, 'Love, Early American Style'? —Leo."

"Leo: James too light for Mon. at 9 slot. Word is ABC may yank Mon. football for 39-week Proust series with Dick Chamberlain. We want to counter with another soap, but need violence appeal. Any chance to snap up 'Oedipus Rex' for serialization? As ever, Murray."

"Dear Mur: Re violence: Gogol people asking too much, but am off to Moscow to view Tolstoy pilot. Has nifty war-and-peace combo. Can be cut. Have oppty. to snag Chekhov family show about three sisters. Please advise. –Leo."

"Leo: Skip Tolstoy for now. Am handling Chekhov deal from here. More important you fly to Germany and firm up 'Wide World of Goethe' ahead of CBS. Got raves from *Variety* man in Munich. Would make nice lead-in to Wed. night's 'Here's Nietzsche!' Best, Murray."

"Murray: Goethe set for Sept. premiere but producer insists we take package of four Thomas Mann shows. CBS dangling cash. Need O.K. fast. –Leo."

"Dear Leo: If Goethe's hot, grab him. Can always syndicate Mann episodes . . . . H'wood agog over fall series with Jack Klugman as Galileo. Have penciled in science show opposite 'Civilisation Reborn,' with Orson Welles narrating. Need releases from Pasteur, Newton, Freud agents. Going for Oct. air date with kickoff show, 'Marcus Aurelius, Ph.D.', followed by 'Benjamin Cardoza, Counselor at Law.' As ever, Murray."

"Murray: Am back in N.Y. and working on game show–'More Concentration'–with Günter Grass, Sue Sontag and Solzhenitsyn hosting. Could be a gas. –Leo."

"Dear Leo: Like game concept, but urgently need new talk show man. Rumor here PBS finally bouncing Cavett–too lightweight–and may sign Bucky Fuller, with Noam Chomsky as sidekick. Also just heard Ralph Nader replacing Rich Little on 'You Asked for It' . . ."

THE MALE LANGUAGE BARRIER

AFTER LISTENING TO fifty-two hours of taped conversations, a doctoral sociology student has concluded that men dominate women when they're alone together talking.

The sociologist is Pamela Fishman, who sounds suspiciously female. If so, this could bias her findings—but then I'm a man, which could influence my own conclusions, though I doubt it. Aside from being tall and trim, I'm very fair-minded.

According to Ms. Fishman, women raise twice as many topics of conversation as do men, since "many of these topics fail to elicit any response" beyond grunts and long silences. "Men," she says, "control topics by veto as well as by positive efforts."

If I can get a word in edgewise, I'd like to enter a major defense on behalf of both the grunt and the long silence, which appear to be causing so much of the trouble. All through history, grunts and silences have come under constant, unfair attack by wives and other organized women's groups.

Ms. Fishman claims women talk a lot because men don't talk enough. This is only because men are thinking of something worthwhile to say, busily winnowing out many of the very topics a woman will bring up later and take credit for.

Behind their silences and grunts, men are grinding away like beavers to come up with fascinating stuff to delight the girls. Women do all of this work in public, which is termed "saying what's on their minds." Men find it hard to think and talk at the same time.

My own research reveals that 67.4 percent of all topics mentioned by women can be dealt with nicely with a grunt or two and some silence. (It seems to me that if your best material isn't going over, you should try a new approach—juggling duckpins, say, or dancing the hornpipe.)

Women, reports Ms. Fishman, ask three times as many questions as men, often in the form of "Do you know what?" or "This is interesting." Sometimes a long silence or grunt is a generous response to topics that easily could be welcomed by "You call that interesting, do you?" or "Oh, everybody knows *that*."

If women would just give grunts and silences a reasonable trial, they might not be so upset by them. Most women have never put a silence or grunt to real use. They don't understand the first thing about lulls and mumbling. They fail to appreciate the subtle shadings behind an eloquent "brmph."

You have your slow, even, drawn-out grunt, a sort of "*Hm-m-m-m* . . ." (which means "Not real interesting but noted"). Then there's the routine medium grunt, more like "*Uh-huh*" (this means "Semi-interesting, but not worth further discourse"). Finally, we come to the fast, snappy grunt of "*Hm?*" (which means "No fooling!" and is closer to what the ladies want to hear).

Women should not be afraid of the grunt or silence, a concise form of communication perfected by males over centuries of classic use. The Greeks and Latins were incessant grunters.

Before women arrived, you couldn't shut men up. They gabbled ten times as much as women do now. Gradually, by the Middle Ages, men slowly had begun to clam up. By the early 1500s, male conversation had slowed to a low rumble and then a murmur.

(The grunt itself was introduced along about 1748–in Eastern Europe–but the silence did not evolve until 1796.)

By 1803, 16 percent of all men had given up talking to women and another 11.4 percent had stopped speaking entirely, except to themselves. There was a slight revival in male-female chitchat around the turn of the century, which persisted until 1927, when conversations between men and women slid into decline. The "long silence" was first developed in the U.S. in 1939.

My research shows that the reason for all this quiet is that when men do pipe up they usually get into serious trouble of some kind almost immediately. Either they don't say quite the right thing, or they reveal they weren't listening an hour ago. Or–if they're feeling very reckless–they may even take issue. Most men, however, would rather be accused of "silence" than risk being cuffed about.

I hate to be so blunt, but that's how it looks from this side, Ms. Fishman, and studies like yours are not helping to bridge the gap at all. In fact, who asked you to bring this up in the first place?

LAY OFF THE PRINCESS

"LAST YEAR," REPORTS *Time,* "Princess Margaret attended only 86 of the civic, cultural or charitable functions that protocol required, compared with an average of 115 in the years before her marriage crumbled"—by royal standards, a fairly steep decline.

If you ask me, Margaret did extremely well to have got around to eighty-six affairs while trying to conduct one of her own with a rock musician. It must be demanding enough to carry on a romance with a rock singer even if you're *not* a princess.

I'm pretty impressed with those eighty-six events she attended, which by my reckoning is fully seventeen more than any other member of a major monarchy in a similar position. Good show, Meg!

Princess Grace, by comparison, only managed to attend seventy-eight ceremonies last year, and she was happily married. Princess Beatrix of the Netherlands chalked up a measly forty-three regal events in '77, lowest of all European princesses under fifty years of age.

As *Time* notes, that 115 figure for Margaret during her marriage to Antony Armstrong-Jones is merely an "average." The princess's best year, royal-functionwise, was 1968, when she hit 204 events out of a possible 319, not counting 63 walks, a passed (masked) ball and 19 garden parties called on account of rain.

This may all sound trivial to you, but when it comes to estimating a princess's performance the only way to judge if she's worth a raise is to compare her work record with that of her royal colleagues.

By any reasonable standard, Margaret is worth the proposed $10,000-a-year wage hike that caused an uproar in England. She now pulls down 100 big ones a year, but three out of four

News of the World readers claim it's all she's worth. They don't feel the princess is "giving them value for money."

There is even talk they may take away her perks, such as reducing her allotment of ladies-in-waiting to twelve and letting all her footmen go.

Numbers are very deceiving, of course, so perhaps we'd better look behind that "86," quoted by *Time,* to see just what those civic, cultural and charity events consisted of. It is all too easy to juggle the books at Buckingham Palace.

Your typical modern princess should be able to cut 75 ribbons a year, sip 8,000 cups of tea, christen 40 ships and attend 200 charity balls, fashion shows, private parties and shopping-mall openings.

Princess Anne, despite her youth, stable home life and lack of injuries to her handshaking arm, only got to 37 royal events last year, a dismal showing by any standard, yet nobody is raising a fuss over Princess Anne's salary.

Clearly, the issue is not "Events Attended Per Annum" but whether it's proper for a princess to fall in love with a rock singer and sometime disco owner. Once more, I'm going out on a limb and taking the princess's side.

It's obvious that the English people have it in for Princess Margaret and always did. Nobody there much likes her taste in men.

She brings home a charming group captain and the British turn up their noses; she marries a magazine photographer and everybody squirms and says he's not good enough for her, or he hasn't got enough money, or something; she meets an ambitious up-and-coming rock singer and they thumb their noses again. So just what *do* they want? The English public doesn't seem to appreciate how difficult it is nowadays for a woman of Princess Margaret's age and standing to meet interesting single men.

Few in Britain know it, but she went out of her way to meet a fellow they would approve of by signing up with a very ritzy computer dating firm, Crown-a-Mate, which attempts to find suitable escorts for European royalty.

It didn't quite work out as hoped, however. The first man Margaret was fixed up with turned out to be a Swedish count, but he was ninety-two years old and didn't share the princess's interest in rock music. The next man, a Venezuelan baron, seemed to have everything, including a castle, but he was already married and was just looking for girls in London.

"We try to screen our applicants closely," explains Crown-a-Mate's London manager, "but sometimes a ringer slips through."

Indeed, after a couple of blind dates with an Egyptian shah and a wild weekend in Ankara with a Turkish pretender to the throne, Princess Margaret made one final attempt and the result was Roddy Llewellyn, who had listed his occupation as "Crown Prince of Rock."

The computer misread it and—BINGO!—the next thing you know Meg and Roddy were out discoing together and having a swell time. Well, as Henry the Eighth liked to say, "love is blind."

BABIES, IT'S COLD OUTSIDE

DUE TO THE NATIONWIDE decline in childbearing (now a misdemeanor in seventeen states), it has been necessary to open up homes for wed mothers and wayward wives who have decided to have babies after being married at least a year.

I went out to talk to the administrator of one such home, a matronly woman of seventy-three who told me that all of the wives in her care had been cast aside by society and forgotten about. People want nothing more to do with these women, she said. Many mothers-to-be are now made to feel "filthy," even after they have been brave enough to come forth and admit their mistake.

One mother, she confided, had to drop out of her NOW chapter in order to have a baby. "All the single women had made her feel uncomfortable at meetings and the younger girls were whispering some pretty nasty remarks behind her back, things like 'buggy bouncer' and 'baby machine.'"

One wife who ran an abortion clinic realized that the only thing to do when she got pregnant was to "visit her aunt in Ohio."

Another woman, who waited six years before having a child in wedlock, went to Europe for three months; when she got home, she simply explained that the new baby was left on her doorstep in Paris.

These homes for wed mothers try to rid women of guilt and get them to see that giving birth is a perfectly normal function which needn't ruin them for life. Wives are shown movies like *Cheaper by the Dozen, I Remember Mama* and *Life with Father.*

Many couples now claim that their babies are adopted. "We were afraid to admit we wanted to have our very own child," explains one twenty-four-year-old mother, Wilma G., who said that, while she finds life difficult since the birth of her son, she plans to raise him as her own. "We want him to feel wanted, just like our oldest dog," she says.

According to the head of the wed mothers' home, "It's very tough on the children when they go to school and all of the big kids who were born in the pre-Zero Population Growth era make fun of them."

She adds, "All the other children ask the new kids where they came from and they're ashamed to say. They don't want to get beat up."

These new legitimate children, she also pointed out, are forced to mix with many of the illegitimate kids whose parents just live together, and it's tough for them to feel a part of the group; they try to keep their fathers from showing up at PTA meetings and humiliating them.

Husbands have an equally touchy problem explaining to their childless men friends why they decided to become a father, what with the pill and all.

The single men tell these guys what heels they are to get their wives pregnant when the least they could do–to make honest women of them–would be to have a vasectomy.

Today's new fathers, I learned, are extremely nervous when

their first baby is due to arrive. They're terrified that somebody may find out. If that happens, the husband has no choice but to pass out cigars reading "It's a Mistake!" Otherwise, people are bound to talk.

Animal Urges

FISHING FOR A STORY

"Here are these animals, much like us, their brains larger than ours. Imagine being able to ask a question and learn from them." —Mike Nichols, director of *The Day of the Dolphin.*

AS AN OLD reporter, I don't just "imagine." Indeed, I've managed to corner two of the lead dolphins in Nichols' film who have agreed to answer a few questions in an interview arranged through their agent, a rather brash blowfish.

The interview took place on a private beach in East Hampton where the dolphins were Nichols' house guests. They sat sunning themselves in canvas chairs while studying new scripts and licking the salt off their margaritas. They wore dark glasses, yachting caps and the usual smug look of most big-time dolphins.

GN: Before we start, which of you is which? No offense, but it's pretty hard to tell one dolphin from another. And by the way, is there any difference between a dolphin and a porpoise?

First Dolphin: Must we go into all *that* again? Didn't you get a press kit? It's all in there. Max, give the man a bio.

GN: It's just that I've heard several conflicting opinions.

First Dolphin (*sighs*): Well, O.K. I'm Adolph and this is Gwen. We're living together but we're just good friends. I'm third-generation dolphin but Gwen has porpoise blood on her dad's side. Dolphins are smarter and cuter than porpoises, or even water spaniels. We're terribly sophisticated mammals. I take *The New Yorker* and Gwen is fluent in Italian. We're Algonquin regulars.

GN: How'd you two get involved in this particular film?

Adolph: It's weird how it all happened. I'd been knocking around the Pacific Ocean for years looking for work, or just anything to occupy my mind. It's pretty boring out there. I'm not really into swimming. It all seems so—well, aimless. Gwen's a pretty fair body surfer, though. Anyway, I got this call from Max here to report to Avco-Embassy for an audition with Mike Nichols. I couldn't believe it! I'd always been a huge fan of Mike's. It blew my mind.

Gwen: I tagged along for fun, but when Mike saw us together he said, "You're perfect!" We were just the type he'd been looking for—green, not too slick. He didn't even have us read.

Adolph: We beat out several veteran porpoises from Marine World, a humpback whale with a hit record and two performing seals trying to pass as dolphins. Boy, did they need the work.

GN: I've read that you're both natural, if not classical, actors. But Nichols says most of the dolphins did a lot of horsing around —moving the underwater lights, etc. When the cameras rolled, he claims you'd start stalling. "Their life is play," to quote him.

Adolph: Let me say that Mike was a pleasure to work with at all times. Oh, sure, we had a few artistic differences, but we got on fine. We like a good time but we're serious about our craft. Porpoises are the *silly* ones. If we cut up, it was just to relax the crew. Mike started it. He was always after us to play one of his word games and he got kind of miffed when the dolphins began trouncing him and Buck Henry; they're not so quick.

GN: Mike says you were so temperamental that when George C. Scott and Trish VanDevere had a spat you couldn't work. Is there any truth to that or to the rumor that one of the dolphins was seeing a lot of Trish?

Adolph: No, but Gwen and Jacques Cousteau were an item.

GN: What other directors would you like to work with?

Gwen: I'd *love* to do a Robert Altman film; he allows actors such freedom. Dolph is dying to work with Spielberg.

GN: What's your next project?

Adolph: There's been talk of remaking *Green Dolphin Street* but nothing definite. I've always wanted to do *Moby Dick*. Why must it always be played by a white whale? Even *The Old Man and the Sea* can be done with a dolphin—at least the stunt work. There's not any really talented marlin around to play it—except Brando; he can do anything.

GN: Is *The Day of the Dolphin* faithful to the ocean?

Adolph: Well, it beats "Flipper."

GN: One last question. Would either of you do a scene fully dressed?

Gwen: Only if clothes were integral to the plot.

LEAVE IT TO BEAVERS

OREGONIANS ARE VISIBLY upset over the prospect of New York State naming a beaver as official state animal after everything beavers have done for Oregon, and I can't say as I blame them.

My solution is that New York should let Oregon keep their beaver and try to locate an equally nice animal of its own. Are New Yorkers so dull and unimaginative that they're forced to filch another state's best animal? I should hope not.

There must be plenty of native creatures left in the woods who'd give their right foreleg to represent a first-class state like New York. I'll bet Governor Carey could sign up an otter, say, for half the price of a beaver; we might get the weasel for a song ("Pop Goes the Weasel").

I don't know if New York State taxpayers are willing to go all out and hire a fancy raccoon, terrific as it would be to have one on hand for ceremonial occasions. Raccoons can run into real money.

If I were a beaver, I'd probably side with Oregon, although according to New York State Assemblyman Rolland Kidder, "beavers were important to this state long before anyone had ever heard of Oregon." And I needn't remind New Yorkers how vital beavers have been to the state; they're second only to Robert Moses.

Assemblyman Kidder claims that back in the seventeenth century the Dutch settlement in Albany was called "Beverwyck." I'll have to take Kidder's word on this, as I'm a little weak on my seventeenth-century Dutch colonial history, but it sounds pretty contrived to me.

Maybe one way to settle the beaver controversy, short of civil war between Albany and Salem, would be to interview some of our four-footed friends for the post of Official State Animal—and whichever one submits the lowest bid for the job will be appointed Chief Animal. If it turns out to be a beaver—well, to hell with Oregon!

As Mr. Kidder writes in a letter to the *Times,* there's no reason why two states can't share the beaver as head animal. He points out: Have not Missouri and New York both designated the bluebird as their highest-ranking state fowl? Indeed they have—and Missouri and New York are all the closer for it too.

Plenty of other examples can be trotted—or flown—out.

Seven eastern states claim the cardinal as state bird, which Kidder says has "caused no interstate friction." Not so. Three of these states are barely talking to each other and two have asked the cardinal to leave quietly. Cardinals everywhere suffer from severe identity crises; many in St. Louis undergo breakdowns.

Kidder claims the beaver is "big enough for both states," but opinion in Beaver Valley is divided. Your typical mainstream beaver feels any state should have a chance to prove itself worthy. A leading Eugene, Ore., beaver writes: "This might be our only opportunity to crack the big time."

Beavers in upstate New York would just as soon be in Oregon. "The quality of life is so much better out there, and you can't beat those firs," remarks one toothy contractor of a large Adirondack dam. "I know if I leave, though, I'll sure miss the seasons."

Speaking for myself, I'd like to look over a beaver résumé to see what their credentials are, what they've done lately for New York and how they plan to fulfill the duties of First Animal. This isn't just figurehead positions like Lieutenant Governor.

Will beavers bring in more tourism? What are their ideas on ecology? Why even have a state animal if we're not going to make use of his talents? There are too many fur-lined state jobs as it is.

WHAT'S UP, PUSSYCAT?

BARELY A WEEK passes that I don't read about somebody who owns six or eight or twelve cats. This week it was Gloria Swanson.

Although I am decidedly pro-cat, I've never understood the exact point in owning more than one cat at a time—or at the very outside, two. When I was a boy, we always kept a cat handy; however, one cat at a time seemed to serve the bill nicely. That still strikes me as a sound philosophy of cat owning.

I am willing to meet cat lovers halfway and excuse them a couple of cats, but anything beyond this seems redundant and slightly sloppy. Cats numbering nine or ten is just plain silly. With cats, as with most things, quality, not quantity, is what counts.

Nonetheless, the rule appears to be that people who own more than one cat are unable to hold it down to two. People who go in seriously for cats don't merely own them—they crave them, the way other people crave jelly beans or dill pickles.

I don't care who it is—Gloria Swanson or the weird lady on the corner who won't open her front door—there is something funny about folks who refuse to be satisfied with less than fourteen cats. It may be the reverse of ailurophobia (fear of cats): the fear of not owning enough cats.

Sandy Dennis is a celebrated cat collector. She admits to fifteen or twenty cats (perhaps there are several more she won't reveal). You would have to love someone very, very much to agree to share your life with her and twenty-three cats.

It always seems that eccentrics are attracted to cats in hordes, but maybe the cats are the eccentric ones, and they seek out the people. Well, whoever starts it, cats have a bad reputation for being surrounded by kooky actresses and odd old ladies.

If I were a cat, I'd prefer to be owned singly than en masse. I wouldn't want a lot of other cats padding around cluttering up the place, mewing up a storm and spilling milk all over my nice kitchen floor. I'd want to be the No. 1 cat, loved for me and me alone. It's not ego; it's just a question of self-esteem.

I raise this issue only because cats are making a major comeback and getting a lot of nice publicity lately. If you're a cat, it's a wonderful time to be alive. Cats are back in style after several thousand years of maintaining an extremely low profile. They were big in Egypt, I'm told, but ever since Cleopatra it has been pretty much downhill for cats.

While cats have always been plentiful, they have never clamored for such attention before, and frankly I'm a little worried. I wonder if it's a healthy thing for cats to be in the limelight like this. In the past, they've remained aloof to anything that smacked of curiosity. I just don't know if they can handle an overnight renaissance.

Very few cats have made it in show business, let alone literature and the arts, so all of this sudden fame may go to their furry little heads. Cats could lose their hard-earned identity as indifferent, even uppity, animals who couldn't care less what people think about them.

It would be a disgusting sight indeed to see pussycats jumping up and down in pet-shop windows like common ordinary puppies. Should cats become popular, in the sentimental manner of dogs and budgies, it would spell their demise. Nobody wants a cat who wags his tail and compromises himself in public.

I'd like to think that the cat world is above the dazzle of celebrityhood, but when the offers start rolling in from New York and Hollywood, it's probably hard to resist.

Cats pretend to have no interest in such matters as talk shows and celebrity roasts, but deep down I'm sure they love having people slobber all over them for a change.

THE WOODPECKING ORDER

A STUDY BY UCLA researchers reveals that woodpeckers are protected from concussion and headaches due to a spongy bone in their skulls, but one man has written in to ask the scientists, "How do you know woodpeckers *don't* get headaches?"

A recent news story says that "Dr. Philip R. May and his colleagues are preparing a reply." I trust that Dr. May won't try to duck the issue now raised, one of many he failed to consider before rushing into print with his woodpecker study.

All of the woodpeckers I studied tell me that, yes indeed, they do get headaches–lots of them, bad ones that really throb–but "it's all part of the woodpecker game," in the words of one longtime bird. "It comes with the territory, Mac. What am I gonna do at my age? Become a bluebird?"

Dr. May wanted to learn why woodpeckers can withstand repeated jarring impacts in the hope of designing a safer crash helmet for test pilots, athletes, workers and perhaps cormorants.

The woodpecker community greeted Dr. May's report with understandable suspicion. "When they get one of them fancy helmets designed," said a woodpecker on a lunch break at UCLA, "I hope they build a model small enough for me to wear." Woodpeckers now work without a hard hat of any kind.

For years, woodpeckers have complained to environmentalists that they get splitting headaches from all this pecking, often forcing them to lie down for long periods inside a dark tree with ice cubes on their little foreheads.

Some birds report nasty bruises and many woodpeckers end up, after years of tapping, dazed victims of an occupational hazard, "bark shock." They must leave the forest for some other line of work or go batty; many woodpeckers wander around the woods with double vision, unable to fly straight.

"Do you think anyone in the lumber industry gives a damn?"

asks a prominent woodpecker leader who, like his colleagues, works with cotton stuffed in his ears to keep out the racket of surrounding woodpeckers.

Woodpeckers don't get headaches, says Dr. May, because evolution would not permit the woodpecker to perform his function and suffer from it at the same time. When you've lived as long as I have, Dr. May, you lose faith in evolution.

What about secretaries and other people who type for a living—tap, tap, tap, veritable office woodpeckers—and after millions of years still have sore fingers, chipped nails and battered thumbs? That's evolution for you, my good fellow!

"Simple reasoning," adds Dr. May, "would dictate that if woodpeckers got headaches, they'd stop pecking." That's easy enough for a scientist in a cushy job to say. He gets to loll around UCLA, gazing out his window at woodpeckers all day. If you're a woodpecker—or a clerk-typist—there is not much else you can do to scrape by these days.

Dr. May might as well claim that hummingbirds don't get dizzy spells, when in fact many suffer from vertigo if they hum too high too fast; or that larks don't get laryngitis, but they do—also strep throat and, the day before spring, opening-night jitters.

You don't hear the birds complaining, though, because they realize they're here to perform a function, with little or no compensation, often at great personal risk to life and limb. Evolution has failed them, but they have a job to do and they do it—quite well, too, if I do say so.

If only more of us were as selfless and dedicated as our little woodpecker chums, we'd never again whine about a headache. Instead of studying any more woodpeckers, Dr. May should figure how to get a few million aspirin out to them; I wouldn't wait around for evolution any longer, gang.

Days Off

MY COMPLIMENTS TO THE CHIEF

EVERYONE KNOWS what the first Thanksgiving meal consisted of, but–until now–nobody's revealed how it was critically received.

So, somewhat belatedly, here is a review of that famed feast of 354 Thanksgiving Days ago by the most prominent Pilgrim food critic of the period, Prudence Sheraton:

"As is my wont, I reserved a seat for the 4 P.M. sitting under an anonymous name at the most elegant wigwam in Plymouth, Mass., Le Maison Maize, long famous among Indians in the area for its bountiful banquets, attentive service by friendly, efficient squaws and authentic late-autumn ambiance (gray skies, barren trees, crisp air and fresh haystacks at every table).

"I noted that the restaurant had been awarded an unprecedented four arrowheads by the Michelin guides and, in all my months of dining out in the Massachusetts Bay Colony, I can't recall a more sumptuous repast: twenty-one side dishes, nine varieties of apple cider and five desserts.

"My companion and I began our dinner to end all dinners with a vintage cider, a rare 1587 Winesap known for its tart dryness. It was a fair test of the cellar and quickly cleansed our palate for the meal just ahead.

"Our host, Chief Squanto, welcomed us with a serving of garden tidbits, or 'canapés,' consisting of carrot curls, raw cauliflower, miniature tomatoes and a kind of brittle stale bark, known as 'corn chips,' that we dipped into thick sauces tasting ever so faintly of onion, blue cheese and clam.

"We deliberated at length before choosing an appetizer–a fruited compote, or 'cocktail,' in which citrus slices are blended with diced pineapple and melon balls and then allowed to marinate overnight in a sweet syrup.

"My partner, more adventurous than I, ordered a pâté of finely chopped liver, hard-boiled eggs and chicken fat, and pronounced it quite unlike anything he had ever sampled in the English colonies or, for that matter, France.

"For our entrée, we were advised by the chief to try either a succulent roasted turkey (a specialty of the wigwam) or veal parmigiana. I chose turkey, a rather overgrown goose-like fowl stuffed with a peculiar mixture of dry toast, celery and chestnuts. The mushy substance is then shoved inside the turkey and cooked; see recipe below for 'Stuffed Indian Bird.'

"While this may sound like a repugnant way to prepare game, in fact it tasted quite divine and I asked for seconds.

"Meanwhile, M. Squanto dazzled us with an array of 'trimmings' that ranged from lime aspic (called 'jell-o mold' by the Indians) and jellied cranberries to a casserole made from green beans, almonds and cream-of-mushroom soup, a staple of Indian cuisine.

"My own favorite delicacy was an exotic 'sweet' potato, a sort of orange squash coated with brown sugar and topped with puffy white squares, called 'marshmallows'; my partner found it too sticky to digest. To clear our palate, we sipped a very dark cider that our host identified as a recent 1614 McIntosh.

"Chief Squanto suggested that, before the dessert course, we take a walk around the reservation so as to (in his words) 'make room for what's coming.' Half an hour later, we sat down again and M. Squanto wheeled out a dessert cart loaded with baked pies made from apples, minced meat, even pumpkins!

"My friend settled for Indian pudding, but I selected something less mundane, the pumpkin pastry, which the chief insisted on serving 'à la Plymouth Rock'–i.e., with a mound of iced custard on top that smacked of vanilla. A triumph!

"Our perfect meal ended with a serving of a hot black brew that M. Squanto called 'java' (my companion ordered the customary tea), after which the men adjourned to a front room to smoke their pipes in peace while the ladies stayed behind to rinse the dishes. 'It won't take but a minute,' they said.

"As we left, Chief Squanto thrust into our hands several small packages in aluminum foil—'leftovers,' he called them. 'You'll eat it for a midnight snack,' our host smiled, hustling us out of the tepee. It was typical of the hospitality to be found at chez Squanto, an authentic native Indian dining experience."

IS YOUR TREE ON TIME?

LAST WEEK, THE first Christmas cards arrived, mocking reminders that already my holiday season is well out of hand.

People who mail their cards on December 8 just do it to make everybody else jumpy, knowing full well I haven't quite decided whether to send any cards, let alone how many or what kind. I haven't even figured out exactly where to hang the ones I get—that's how far behind I really am.

Early card-senders are the same show-offs who order their holiday greetings in August at half price, buy gifts on their summer vacations ("It's such a nice feeling to have it all done!") and generally make you out to be a real Christmas loafer.

It might not seem so hard to take if the people who insist on organizing Christmas would lay off reminding me how efficient they are. I feel increasingly guilty watching them swing into full gear.

By December 10, all their presents are sent or wrapped and neatly stacked in closets; by December 15, their Christmas dinner is bought and in the freezer (maybe the oven); by December 20, I assume they've got all their Christmas carols sung and put away.

These are the people who crack the whip on Christmas morning by announcing that all wrappings and ribbons are to go into a large box and immediately burned (to avoid anything that might look like a spontaneous burst of merriment).

Members of the holiday Mafia have this whole season well under control, down to the very last Christmas cookie. If the eggnog is running a few minutes late, or the department store choirs are not all in place, they get very cranky. I admire these people; I just don't want them around me during the holidays.

Any minute now, they'll be chiming, "Well, we went out last night and picked out the tree! Got yours yet?" This is normally said about twenty minutes after the Thanksgiving dishes have been washed.

While normal people are pondering what size tree to buy, if any, your Christmas efficiency expert is busily trimming away like crazy, stringing lights and hanging tinsel and possibly even throwing a tree-trimming party, proclaiming smugly:

"Well, the tree's all trimmed! It looks so pretty. I just love having a tree up all month, don't you?" (You, meanwhile, hope you'll manage to tack up a piece of holly in time for New Year's.)

Actually, people who turn Christmas into a time-motion study are the ones who years ago gave up buying live trees. "Oh, they're *so* messy and expensive," they frown, adding how much more collapsible their bright blue aluminum job is.

"It's so simple to pack away once Christmas is over," they maintain, as if a Christmas tree is a card table and the season itself a sort of party game. They love Christmas, all right, but mostly they love clocking it in and out.

People who insist on streamlining Christmas are inclined to herd everyone into caroling parties or put stuffed camels out on the front lawn in a serious effort to outdo the Radio City Music Hall pageant; if it were possible, they would hire Peter Gennaro to choreograph the neighbors.

On the other hand, if it wasn't for these holiday militants, I would undoubtedly be picking out my own half-price cards on Christmas Eve and nothing around here would ever get celebrated.

HELLO! I'M BUTTON GWINNETT

The following dispatch—dated June 27, 1776—was filed by a correspondent for Colonial Press International, who was sent out from the Philadelphia bureau to cover a big convention downtown:

PHILADELPHIA, PA. (CPI) – Nearly 200 excited conventioneers, representing some 13 Original Colonies, gathered here last night in order to "form a more perfect Union" at a weeklong conclave slated to end Sunday, July 4, with the signing of a controversial new declaration.

Independence Week Committee Chairman Jack Hancock hosted an opening-night delegate mixer party in the hospitality suite at the New World Statler, site of the conference, and announced that a seminar on "The Pursuit of Happiness" had been switched from the King George Suite to the Nathan Hale Room off the mezzanine.

Tomorrow's 10 A.M. panel, kicking off a busy week of events, will be devoted to "Life & Liberty: Do We Really Need It?" Moderated by Patrick C. Henry, the outspoken activist, a panel of experts will debate the sensitive preamble to the proposed upcoming agreement with Great Britain.

Other workshops include "Self-Evident Truths and How to Recognize Them," "Equality in the Changing '70s," "After Ratification, What?" and "Fomenting Revolution at Home." (A combined panel on "Lives," "Fortunes" and "Sacred Honor" has been canceled.)

Guest speaker Benny Franklin, a popular local merchant much in demand by service clubs and women's groups on the Pennsylvania lecture circuit, will deliver the keynote address next Sunday on "Making Capitalism Work for You."

Franklin, known throughout the Colonies for his pithy sayings, was the center of attention at a no-host suckling pig barbecue held yesterday, following registration. The raconteur was cornered by delegates' wives and, at one point, told Mrs. Jim Oglethorpe of Georgia: "A penny saved is a penny earned!" The crack was greeted with roars of delight.

This evening's distinguished speaker, Thomas H. Jefferson of Virginia—the sometime writer, educator and architect of freedom—will reveal how he came to create the so-called "declaration of independence" and explain some of the problems involved in drafting a major historical document. A question-and-answer session and refreshments will follow.

A few disgruntled guests, however, report that they have been unable to get seats on the floor to the big ceremony at Independence Hall.

"They want us to sit in the balcony and I wrote ahead two months ago for seats downstairs," said an unhappy Mrs. Eldridge Gerry of Massachusetts. "I mean, if this is how they treat the family of an original signer, what is the country already coming to? You can carry this democracy business a little too far."

Various companies have set up booths at the hotel to demonstrate their wares: Franklin's Poor Richard, Inc., firm has taken an entire wing to display his latest inventions; Paul Revere's silversmith factory is selling commemorative dinner plates; and Thomas Paine is in the lobby autographing copies of his best-selling *Common Sense*.

The big disappointment of the convention so far is the news that General George Washington, who was slated to make the official welcoming remarks tonight, won't be able to attend the signing. He sent a telegram that was read to the delegates last night:

REGRET WAR KEEPS ME FROM BEING IN PHILLY WITH THE OLD GANG. AM SURE COUNTRY IS IN GOOD HANDS. HOPE TO SEE YOU ALL SOON AT FIRST CONSTITUTIONAL CONVENTION. BEHAVE YOURSELVES! —GEORGE ("FATHER") WASHINGTON

JUST BROWSING, YOUR HIGHNESS?

OUR JOLLY TRADITION of last-minute Christmas shopping began with the first Christmas, when the Three Wise Men were as tardy as we are now—although, of course, they didn't know until quite late that there would even *be* a Christmas. When they stopped off to shop on the way to Bethlehem, this scene ensued:

First Wise Man: Pardon me, clerk, do you have anything unusual for a most joyous occasion?

Shopkeeper: No problem. I got a very lovely selection of swaddling clothes over here. A nice sheepskin coat maybe?

Second Wise Man: What do you have in the way of jewelry?

Shopkeeper: How about something in gold? We have some cute charms, a lovely pendant by Noel of Jerusalem . . . Uh, while you gentlemen are thinking, I'll just be over here helping this shepherd. . . . Yes, m'friend, what'll it be today?

Shepherd: Say, do you have any of those new fold-up crooks?

(*Wise Men confer in whispers.*) Third Wise Man: Gosh, I'm not sure. Gold seems a bit—I don't know—ostentatious. These are very simple people. I think they're abiding in a stable.

First Wise Man: Well, gold does denote royalty. We can't be too choosy on Christmas Eve. This place is about to close.

Second Wise Man: Did you two happen to see the nice display of frankincense in the window? That might be sort of original.

Shopkeeper (*smiles*): Well, have you gentlemen finally decided?

First Wise Man: We're curious about the frankincense . . .

Shopkeeper: It makes an awfully nice house gift—very tasteful. Here, *smell*. It says on the box that frankincense signifies divinity. It's something you can always use.

First Wise Man: Do you think it's . . . enough? I still lean toward something a little more exciting. I just love gold.

Shopkeeper: Gold is forever, but frankincense is very popular now. It seems to be "in" with the young crowd.

Second Wise Man: If we take it, I'm sure it can be exchanged.

Shopkeeper: Certainly! I have a full line of fragrances. Say, do you mind if I ask what you all do? Those crowns caught my eye when you came in—and such fancy camels parked outside!

First Wise Man: Oh, just three kings from Orient are, bearing gifts we travel afar. We're spending the New Year in Bethlehem. Maybe you know somewhere we can stay. All of the inns seem to be filled. Is there a nearby Holiday or Ramada Inn?

Shopkeeper: I don't know where everyone's headed, but the roads are jammed with people. Must be something important going on in town. These can't *all* be last-minute taxpayers . . .

Third Wise Man: Y'know, I was just noticing this weird-looking stuff on the counter. Pardon me, clerk—what's "myrrh"?

Shopkeeper: It's a new rare exotic aroma. Here, *smell*. It's very big with the occult set; they say it denotes death.

Third Wise Man: We're kind of amateur magicians ourselves. Let's take a chance on the myrrh. It's certainly *different*.

Shopkeeper: Myrrh is something you'd never buy for yourself.

Second Wise Man: Oh, let's splurge and get one of each! We can afford it and this is no time to stint.

Third Wise Man: It's settled then. Wrap up a gold bauble, a handful of the incense and—oh, two pounds of your best house myrrh.

Shopkeeper: Is this cash or charge—and should I send it?

First Wise Man: Uh, do you take MagiCard? We'd better take these with us; they have to arrive by Christmas.

Shopkeeper: Do you have any identification?

First Wise Man: We're from the East, but I have a valid out-of-kingdom Oasis Oil credit card.

Shopkeeper: Hmmm. Why don't you just give me your name?

First Wise Man: Well, actually I'm a Wise Man . . .

Shopkeeper: "Wiseman?" O.K.—first name and initials?

First Wise Man: I'm Melchior, he's Kaspar and that's Balthazar. We're fairly well known at home. Like I say, we're, you know, kings.

Shopkeeper: Uh, sure. Say, suppose we just make it cash. . . . Thanks. You can't be any too careful these days. You'd be amazed at some of the characters we get in here around the holidays . . . Well, gentlemen, I'd say you've made three *very* wise choices.

THE FROST IS ON THE CANAPÉS

AS WE PULL further away from 1620, it becomes more of a struggle to keep Thanksgiving traditional. Everywhere, little liberties are being taken as modernists gnaw away at the ancient feast.

Everybody has his own sacred notion of what Thanksgiving should be. Since it's one of our dearest holidays, based wholly on food, people are easily annoyed if anyone fiddles with the menu; it's like tampering with the Constitution itself.

Even before anyone sits down to eat, a debate arises: What time *do* you sit down? Conservatives view 4 P.M. as the proper time; reformed celebrants claim the forefathers obviously intended turkey to be downed at 6 P.M., like any other meal; the orthodox insist on 5 P.M., standard Indian dinnertime.

It jolts traditionalists in big cities to wander into the Midwest and be confronted with a full-course dinner at 3 P.M., which seems almost decadent until one learns the wise reason behind such a presumably pagan hour: Dining early allows one to eat again that same day. (Somewhere in the middle of a turkey sandwich at 10 P.M. in Ann Arbor, Mich., in 1965, I was converted to an earlier starting time; I became a staunch believer in warmed-over stuffing.)

I am still against the ritual of going to strangers' homes, where there is no way to control the menu. If you break the family bond at Thanksgiving, you have only yourself to blame when a hostess announces that the minestrone's on.

Radicals are always trying to improve on Thanksgiving, a practice the Pilgrims would frown upon. Many of the faithful have strayed so far from the old ways that they eat steak, ham and fish. This year, revisionist food editors are even suggesting chicken. No wonder the young ask: Is Thanksgiving dead?

As for trimmings, think twice before asking guests to "bring something," which is open to heretical interpretations. Somebody is bound to offer oyster dressing, or a creamed zucchini casserole. I say: We put the yams back in Thanksgiving!

Certain simple dietary laws must be obeyed. Introducing cranberry relish (instead of sauce) into the observance can disrupt the day's original meaning; baked rather than sweet potatoes should mean banishment from next year's table; any dessert besides pumpkin, mince or apple pie calls for stoning.

One way to deal with an overambitious aunt who tries contributing some odd-smelling, inedible, often indefinable vegetable is to dutifully pass it around, admire it and pass over any so-called "new recipes for curried squash." Blasphemy.

There is mixed opinion among Thanksgiving scholars as to whether a buffet endangers the mood of the meal. Reformers believe a buffet retains the essential spirit of the occasion while hardliners hew to the sit-down dinner, claiming a buffet is invariably chaotic, clumsy and lukewarm.

At the 364th meeting of the Plymouth Council of 1982, the matter of hors d'oeuvres was discussed and tabled. "Did the Indians serve little sausages in sweet-and-sour sauce?" asked an enraged elder.

"Sure," said a young wife, munching on celery stuffed with Brie, "it takes the edge off your appetite so you don't overeat." To this day, the validity of hors d'oeuvres at Thanksgiving is a source of heated controversy. Compromising, the Council recommended: "Well, just a snitch before supper."

Another issue argued at length—Is it irreverent to eat out on Thanksgiving?—found scholars unanimous in their belief that sage dressing prepared in restaurants is the devil's work and refused to consider the question any further.

Before adjourning, the Plymouth panel brought up the age-old problem of Leftovers. As members put on their coats to go, small bags were thrust into their hands. "No, really, I had plenty," they cried, edging away. "Please—we won't ever eat it," a hostess insisted. "Sam hates turkey. It'll just go to waste."

Over pleas of "No-no, I won't hear of it!" tinfoil packets were jammed inside guests' pockets. "Just do me a favor and take a drumstick, a piece of pie. It'll only get thrown out! Eat it for lunch next week. . . . Have it tonight before bed—it makes a nice snack . . ."

THE HUNDRED HARDIEST CASES

A MAN CAME to the door the other day asking if I'd like to donate a little something to the newly founded St. Shepherd's Yuletide Relative Relief Fund, and I invited him in to tell me more about it.

"St. Shepherd," he explained, sitting down, "is the patron saint of black sheep. He was known for bringing together family outcasts of all kinds—the dull and peculiar, mostly—but primarily relatives who never appear at any other time of the year but the holidays."

He said that most of the people are just plain boring, but many are downright strange, not to mention those who simply get on everybody's nerves. "At St. Shepherd's, however, we welcome them all," he added, "and they feel right at home among their own kind."

"Why, that's wonderful!" I said. "What fine work you're doing, taking weird relatives off people's hands and giving them somewhere to go over Christmas, rather than pester their own families."

He went on, "Every Yuletide, the dining hall at old St. Shep's is filled to overflowing with the sound of relatives driving each other up the wall."

"It must be a merry pandemonium to hear," I said.

"Ah, it is, it is," he smiled. "Many of these folks would otherwise be making the holidays miserable for hosts and hostesses around the country."

"This sounds like an extremely popular cause," I said.

"We bring in more people every year than the Salvation Army and the New York *Times* put together."

"How does it all work?" I wondered.

"Along with your check, you contribute specific relatives you'd rather not have to deal with. We do the rest."

"It must be very rewarding to be involved in such a noble cause."

"Best of all, it gets me out of the house and away from my own zany family, because I'm over at St. Shepherd's playing host to the scads of silly and unsavory cousins, aunts, nephews, nieces and brothers-in-law from all over . . . Would you care to contribute anybody?"

"Well, I've got an Uncle Irv you might be interested in."

"Sure—what's his problem?"

"He spends the entire dinner discussing the route he took to get there and how much traffic there was on the new interchange."

"He'll be right at home."

"Well, as long as you're here," I went on, "perhaps you'd also take Uncle Al off our hands—just this once."

"We'd love to—what's wrong with Uncle Al?"

"Oh, he reminisces something terrible."

"Yes, we've got plenty of those, but there's always room for a hundred more. Talks endlessly about the colorful old days, does he?"

"Yes, except we've all heard the stories six hundred times and much of the initial impact has sort of worn off."

"Anyone else you'd like to donate? It's only once a year."

"Uh, do you take in kids?"

"Certainly, but no orphans. We'll only take a youngster if he's unusually spoiled or unruly, or tears up the house and drives the adults bonkers. Many parents contribute their own kids–using false names, of course."

"I got about seventeen of those I'd like to contribute."

"You're a warmhearted soul, I can see that," he smiled, making a note of their names and ages. "Anyone else, before I go?"

"Well, I didn't want to bother you with dirty old Uncle Walt, who drinks too much and makes passes at his teenage nieces."

"No bother," he said. "We have a special dining room for lecherous uncles, well away from all the tender young nieces."

"And then there's cousin Eddie, who's newly single and arrives wearing a purple suede jumpsuit with chains around his neck."

"Sure, send cousin Eddie over. Love to have him!"

"While you have your pen out, let me donate just one more–a right-wing brother-in-law, Vic, who spends the evening blasting minorities, liberal judges and 'gay Commie schoolteachers.'"

"Gosh, I think that's about all we can handle," said the man from St. Shepherd's. "We have a limit of twenty to a family. You've been very generous, but I'm afraid you won't have enough relatives for your own Christmas dinner."

"Don't worry," I said. "There's lots more where they came from."

FEAR OF PACKING

AFTER TWENTY-FIVE years, I still make the same mistakes in packing, only today I'm a lot faster at it. What I've done is refined my technique in such a way that it now takes me only half as long to bring too many neckties, sweaters I won't wear and the wrong shoes.

The whole thing has become a perverse charade in which I naïvely attempt to outmaneuver my wardrobe. But in the end my clothes always get their way. Every last thing I own, it seems, is pleading to come along with me.

I've loaded up luggage with irrelevant stuff long enough by now to know what I'm doing, yet I can't stop myself from cramming it all in anyway. This is not packing—it's portable masochism. For some reason, I just refuse to travel anywhere without bringing my old blunders with me.

What I do first is hold a brief packing rehearsal the night before, when I calmly scan the drawers and closets, efficiently weeding out what I won't ever need on the trip. These are the things I pack at the very last minute, on my way out the door. Even as I'm putting in my necessary clothes, mentally I'm leaving little soft spots and holes here and there in the suitcase for sneakers I vowed I would not take, undershirts I won't need in a hundred years and an extra jacket I told myself there simply isn't room for this time.

Well, replies myself, you never know (but you know, all right). In fact, I once met a man who went on a dig to Guatemala and packed a pistol, in case of marauding bandits. "You never know," he explained.

"You never know" are the three most lethal words in a traveler's lexicon. Just because you're leaving town, you presume something horrible is certain to befall you, for which you must be prepared. Suppose somebody steals your underwear at the airport coffee shop in Rio? What if customs asks you to hand over your good brown shoes in Paris because they're out of style? Maybe you'll spill shoe polish on your socks in Madrid and the stores will be shut for some big Spanish holiday? Suppose they don't sell Crest in Tokyo?

It is this paranoid crisis mentality that does in many otherwise sane, rational people when they go to pack a suitcase. Someplace in your mind, as you throw in 108 pairs of socks, you are envisioning a blizzard in Miami, one of many likely cataclysms that are bound to occur if you dare to travel light.

You never know: You could fall in the Seine while wearing your nice tan suit, so you'll need a backup suit. You might be hijacked to Uganda and held hostage for a week more than you'd planned. In such an eventuality, you'd best bring plenty of extra

T-shirts and maybe an emergency pair of drip-dry slacks. Suppose you meet a wealthy couple in London who invite you back to their castle in Scotland for a fancy-dress ball? Better bring that black bow tie and dark shoes after all (you can probably pick up a cummerbund over there).

Underlying many foolish romantic packing fantasies is the hope that, with any luck at all, you'll meet some fabulous dark-eyed stranger and be clean out of fresh slacks. This is why you must squeeze in as many emergency pants as will fit. One can't very well carry on a mad affair in Venice in rumpled gray trousers.

It is only in the quiet of your bedroom at home that all of these silly exotic notions occur. On the trip itself, it never matters what you have on. Nobody else in Europe knows you've been traipsing around wearing that same blue coat and gray slacks for two weeks. Much to your surprise, in fact, no one in Italy has ever come up to you and said: "So sorry, signore, but you will have to change immediately. We have been notified that you were seen in this same outfit for the last nine days."

One of the nice things about traveling is that you *can* get away with wearing the same ensemble for six months if you just remember to change cities often enough. (Indeed, the First Law of Luggage states that it is twice as easy to pack for a month in Moscow than a weekend at Lake Tahoe; you are less likely to run into anyone you know in Russia.)

My main problem in packing is the Dark Suit Syndrome. If I'm even going to Honduras for the day, during the hot season, I'm unable to leave without bringing a good dark suit. I have a sort of dummy pinstripe black suit that I take along to make me feel secure; it has never been out of my overnight bag. Well, you never know. Someday, if I'm invited to a funeral in Honolulu, I'll be all set.

In practice, it wouldn't work out anyway. I used to wear my dark security suit on the plane, in the hope that this would keep it from wrinkling; when I got to the hotel it was always neatly folded into a permanent sitting position. The crease was O.K., but the rest of the suit needed about a week's vacation in the mountains. Trying to steam it out in the bathroom simply presents you with the choice of a suit that is clean but baggy versus one that is nicely pressed but gamy.

The Second Law of Luggage is: Know thyself. This applies to other facets of life as well, but in packing it is particularly important to know ahead of time which two of six potential shirts you will in fact wear everywhere. It is a hardheaded decision, requiring someone of great personal courage and self-knowledge. The unexamined suitcase is not worth taking. In brief, you must face up to some plain facts about yourself—namely, that you are not going to cut any more dashing figure abroad than you do at home.

It is tempting to kid yourself into thinking that, once out of the country, you will finally put on that crazy red and yellow tie you haven't had the guts to wear to the office in five years. If that is the case, the odds are at least 500 to 1 that you will *not* be seen in your crazy necktie in Calcutta or Prague. You will rely, as always, on the dark green tie that hangs funny.

Another precept of packing, or the Third Law of Luggage, is that, no matter how logically you organize a suitcase, you will use only what is lying on the top layer. Whether this is due to inherent laziness or the hubbub of travel, nobody knows, but it can't be prevented. It's not until your last night on a trip that you suddenly uncover a vast treasure trove of laundered shirts in the bottom pouch of your bag, after a week of trying to make one badly rumpled shirt last the final three days.

For the novice, or even veteran, packer, here is a partial list of items not to stuff in your suitcase under any circumstances:

1. *The Collected Letters of Henry James*. Despite your noblest intentions, you won't look at this (or any) book on the entire trip except while pawing around it in desperate search for a clean hankie.

2. Cutaway suit. If you should find yourself at a formal affair you'll simply have to apologize to Princess Diana that all of your cutaways were lost en route when you had to abandon ship in the middle of the Atlantic.

3. Surgical kit. Most of the standard operations for major illnesses and injuries are available in Europe, or even Vermont, so forceps, splints, IVs, oxygen masks, pacemakers, scalpels and

plasma will most likely be unnecessary and only get mislaid in your hotel room. If you happen to be struck with a rare disease in, say, Marrakesh, it's only a short flight to the nearest hospital.

4. Raccoon coat. It isn't a bad idea to plan ahead for those chilly autumn evenings, especially if you're in the vicinity of the Harvard-Yale game, but in most instances a raccoon coat tends to get in the way and doesn't pack too well. A pea jacket should be plenty.

5. Scuba-diving outfit. Although there's a 50-50 chance you'll be asked to join a shark-hunting expedition off the coast of Acapulco, you can rent all the necessary underwater gear from the concierge.

POSTCARD MORTEMS

PEOPLE WHO SWORE OFF writing postcards in the summer of 1922 are still at it today, leading me to wonder if anyone really *wants* to quit writing postcards, deep down.

Those who claim to despise the postcard habit love nothing more than to receive them, belittling each one as it arrives. They're terribly hurt if anybody forgets. "Well," they huff, "at least the Zergs might have dropped us a card!"

If they do, we just make fun of it behind their backs, sneering, "She calls this a card? It doesn't say a darn thing!" We know very well that a postcard is not supposed to say a darn thing—a classic case of "the medium, not the message."

The main point of a card is to remind people at home that *they* are not on vacation, best achieved by scribbling meanly across the photo of an azure lake, *"Eat your hearts out!!!"*

Note the overuse of exclamation points, always the mark of a good postcard; the idea is to make up for a lack of words with a wild burst of punctuation. In writing postcards, I often find myself taking on a totally new and rather giddy personality, suddenly using terms like "cute," "fun place" and "adorable."

As near as I can piece it together, postcards began as a way to prove that (1) you are, indeed, where you said you would be; (2) you are, to be sure, having the time of your life; and (3) you will return as promised, on the stated date.

Any variation from this standard form is frowned upon by postal authorities. They claim it only confuses mailmen who have to deliver postcards with a bunch of writing all over them. Each summer, several postcards wind up in the dead-letter office due to insufficient white space in the area marked "Message Goes Here."

Postcard makers have come to grips with the writer's burden by printing 500-word descriptive captions and leaving only enough writing area to scrawl, "See ya soon!"

Every June, I vow before a notary public not to send any postcards, but forty-five minutes into the trip guess who is greedily snatching up cards by the dozen at the first coffee shop? I'm so conditioned to grabbing postcards that my desk is crammed with cards from diners in Reno and even places I've never been.

Postcard buying is not to be taken lightly. Choosing the best picture takes hours, as long as finding a funny birthday card. "Oh, *these* are nice—they show the big shade trees," one person points out. They probably are nice, but the question is: Are they any nicer than those in your hand depicting a rugged coastline? (or the ones with a good shot of the cabins off to one side?).

You hunt in vain for a postcard that will give a vague idea of what the spot looks like, not realizing that these cards were sold out in May. This leaves you with a shot of the downtown area taken in 1957, a close-up of the golf course, a photo of a bridle path you have not actually seen or a picture of the downtown area at night.

It's always necessary, therefore, to scrawl a disclaimer across the top of the photograph: "Where we're staying is prettier than this!"

Eventually, you must decide what to say on the card that will sound properly jaunty and holiday-like, something you can quickly mass-produce on twenty-five cards and yet will be personal and peppy.

You settle down by the pool with a stack of postcards from the front desk and a ball-point pen that runs out midway down the second card, followed almost immediately by your enthusiasm. Postcard-writer's block has now set in. "Oh, I'll do these cards later," you sigh.

Meanwhile mailboxes at home are being emptied and people are muttering, "There's no reason they couldn't at least have sent a *card.*"

VOTE "NO" ON AUGUST

EASILY THE BEST thing about Labor Day is that it signifies the end of August.

There should be a law against August. It is, by any measure at all, the worst month in the year. No really first-class calendar would tolerate it. The year should go directly from July to September (not that July 5 through 31 is all that terrific).

At the very least, August ought to be reduced to the shortest month. Four days strikes me as about right, just long enough to make us appreciate all the other months. At its present insufferable length, it seems to have no other purpose but to prolong summer with a kind of vengeance.

There are no holidays in August, which reveals the month for what it is—a complete loser, a scandal of major proportions, a national embarrassment. Do you want to know what there is to celebrate in August? Colorado Day, that's what.

Here is what happens in August: The Little League world series, subway and forest fires, back-to-school sales, meteor showers, the Hall of Fame game at Cooperstown, the bluefish run and Hawaiian Admission Day. You call this a month?

August is so far out ahead for the title of "Worst All-Around

Moon Phase" there's not even a second-place contender. January, maybe, but just when you've given up on January along comes my birthday to pull it out of oblivion. August hasn't a single saving grace; I vote we shelve it.

All that August has going for it is that it means September is around the next heat wave if you can just sit it out. Plenty of people don't make it. They vanish during the last week of August, never to be heard from again.

Studies will show that more drinking, fighting, kicking and overall crabbiness occur during August than at any other time. Children turn sullen; mothers collapse; men leave home in droves.

There is, of course, a good reason why August is such a terrible time. It's a false month, tacked onto the calendar for political reasons by Caesar Augustus, who wanted a month of his very own, just like Julius Caesar (a typical Roman boondoggle). He then insisted it have as many days as July, so to even the score with Julius he swiped one from February and—well, the year has never been quite the same.

If August were abolished, very few people would even notice except die-hard fans of Emperor Augustus. Along about September 12, someone might say, "Hey, whatever happened to August?" Everybody else would just shrug and walk away.

Anyone born during August should be glad to be rid of it. I feel sorry for people born in August. Who wants to come to a birthday party on, say, August 23? No good parties have been held in August since 104 B.C., when Caesar Augustus died.

Even the very word "August" has a dreary ring—more of a thud, really. It sounds stuffy and clogged and hay-feverish. I get so depressed just thinking about August that, when I type the word "August," all the keys get stuck.

August is universally loathed. In Paris and New York, they close all the good restaurants and dry cleaners. It's such a bad time nobody wants to be seen in public and leaves town to avoid it. To confess you were around during August is a clear defeat.

There is only one problem: What to replace August with? Anything would be a big improvement. Since Pope Gregory, calendar reform has never got off the ground. People are afraid to monkey around with the months. Pope Gregory, to round things off, simply lopped ten days off the year. No one whined.

That's the spirit we need today. Everybody fears something horrible might happen if Congress, the UN or the Pope suddenly canceled August on account of worldwide disgust. What could be any worse fate than an infinity of Augusts?

LITTLE INNS AND OUTS

IF YOU WANT to be entertained away from home, you must lower your sights. Inns are great fun until 8 P.M., when you find yourself confronted by a quaint room and no TV. (I never miss TV until I don't have one to turn off.)

Those quaint old inns could hide a quaint old TV in the closet under the spare blankets in case of acute cabin fever. A small radio would do it.

My favorite amusement when stuck in a resort town is watching local news reports of awful events that can't get me, since I'm checking out tomorrow—tornado warnings, property tax increases, herpes outbreaks.

Most inns and hideaway vacation homes give you a choice of a stack of 1980 *Time* magazines and last week's copy of a local entertainment guide ("The Hank Hawkins Trio Plays Nitely at the Toddle Room on Rte. 83. Gourmet Food").

There is always a shelf with dog-eared games—Chinese checkers, pick-up sticks, Parcheesi, and some version of Scrabble that came out at Christmas time in 1975 and failed to catch on—plus my favorite holiday reading, the guest book.

I can spend hours poring over guest books dating back to 1928. It's amazing to find that fifty years ago people were writing the same stuff: "Mr. and Mrs. Howard Gunz, Paso Robles, Calif.—We loved the view and can't wait to return! It's so *quiet!*" . . .

"Mimi and Les Martle, Roseville, Ore.–Everything was heavenly. Great veal!"

Once you've exhausted the games, the guest book, a cover story on the Iranian hostages, and have reread the checkout time, you wander into the lobby, where there's a choice of Watching the Fire Go Out or Staring at Stars.

If I'm feeling especially giddy, I may do both. You can only look at a fire so long before nodding off, itself a major source of vacation fun. If you should luck out and have an unusually nice fire, you can postpone bedtime a half hour. There's something depressing about turning in at nine o'clock on a vacation. If you've been relaxing all day, you feel guilty turning in before ten. By brushing your teeth a lot, you can drag out bedtime fifteen more minutes.

Another vacation diversion is Going into Town, but I like to save that for a late afternoon. I delay Going into Town as long as possible, not wanting to do everything the first day.

Day One is spent Getting a Tan, or the equivalent of two tans. I may Take a Nap, to get up the strength to Make Dinner Reservations. Reading bound menus of seafood restaurants can kill a deadly hour or two in midafternoon.

Going to dinner will eat up five hours, if you: (1) Sip a Drink on the Porch and Gaze at the Sunset and/or Ocean for a Long Time; (2) Slowly Drive a Mile to *Another* Adorable Inn (don't eat where you're staying, or you're stuck); (3) Linger over Coffee and Engage the Waiter in a Discussion on the History of the Inn; about 9 P.M., (4) Wander into the Parlor for a Glass of Port and Sit by the Fire to (5) Watch Other People Watching the Fire and Sipping Port, everyone waiting until the clock strikes ten.

At 10:12 precisely, the first bold couple will stand up, make a pretense of yawning and announce they're going to turn in. This is the signal that it's O.K. now for everyone else to Go to Bed. The night is finally, officially *over*.

Reluctantly, everyone strolls out, stopping in the corridor to peer in the showcase and read fading *Holiday* articles on the joys of a weekend at this very inn, which somehow always sounds a wee bit peppier in old travel columns.

The Editorial Me

SQUEAK UP!

I WONDER WHAT happens when somebody who has read *Winning Through Intimidation* sits next to someone at a party who just finished *Power: How to Get It, How to Use It* and Mr. Power tells Mr. Intimidation to put out his cigar and make it snappy.

Assuming Mr. I. doesn't say yes when he means no, it could end up with somebody in tears, or possibly dead, but I doubt it—not if I know my fellow mice.

No matter how many advice-to-the-hatelorn books they've read, people who hope to learn a little harmless Fascism to use around the office are sure to slip when shove comes to push. If you try doing Charles Bronson numbers on everyone when, underneath, you're still Charles Nelson Reilly, you are bound to (a) look pretty silly and (b) mess things up even worse as a semipro bully.

All the self-assertiveness best sellers claim that once you stand up for your rights, maître d's will step aside with a flourish and say, "Yes, *sir,* Mr. Mitty, your table is ready!" Bosses will be so deeply moved by your sudden table-thumping skills they'll boost your salary that afternoon with a hearty "By Jove, Milquetoast, I can see now you're a man on the move, whereas just two days ago I took you for a total nerd!"

In my own spotty experiences of standing up for my rights, statistics show that about 83 percent of the time I'm wrong—a cruel blow to your up-and-coming Machiavelli. Whenever I call a waiter over to growl that the bill is $2.35 too high, he growls back that I forgot to add the onion soup. Exit scampering.

If, by some quirk, it turns out I'm right, I have to wait around for the manager to get back from lunch or fill out a twelve-page complaint form. Standing up for your rights involves a lot of standing up.

When you *can* force someone to bend to your demands, they make it doubly rough on you. To quote the Mouse Manual: "Leave bad enough alone." In the classic case of sending back an undercooked steak, the chef always sends it right back out with sixth-degree burns, just to let you know who's really in control. (Most of the people who've benefited from aggression books seem to be waiters, chefs, desk clerks, etc.)

If you ask a hotel clerk for a nicer room, say with a view, you'll get your lousy room with a view all right, but it will also have cold and cold running water. As the Mouse Manual notes: "You can't win."

All serious attempts to get my way are treated like crackpot ravings. A Manhattan bakery that advertises "San Francisco sourdough French rolls" invites you to call the company president with any complaints. When I phoned him to say that his rolls would get him arrested in San Francisco for bread pollution, a secretary told me, "Gosh, nobody ever complained before."

In any given disaster, I'm always the "only one" to fuss. If I told the manager of the Leaning Tower of Pisa that his building appeared to be teetering, and I'd like to check out, he would just chuckle and say, "Funny, you're the first person to complain."

Conditions are never ideal for asserting myself. If my stereo breaks a week after it's been fixed, the man who did the job is in Lapland for a year. If I demand my way, I'm suddenly "causing a scene" and now everyone is mad at *me;* the mouse suddenly dwindles to pest.

Recently, I swaggered into Nathan's with free passes for two hot dogs and the henchperson said, "Ain't no good here. Next." After I'd illustrated the sound logic (more sound than logic) that it plainly states "Good at any Nathan's," the manager grudgingly agreed to fork over the wieners. I felt I'd won my first clear-cut intimidation victory, good for at least a Gold Cluster from awed bystanders, but I'd somehow lost again, shot down from behind by an ex-ally: "Boy," said my wife, "were *you* obnoxious."

Look who's talking–little Ms. Power Grabber herself, a born self-asserter who simply assumes she's always right and if not–well, she deserves it anyway. No matter how often I watch her in action in the ring, and hold her coat, I can't seem to get that attitude to rub off. Advises the Mouse Manual: "Marry into power."

Whereas I was born looking over one shoulder, she's always on the lookout for holes in the defensive line. One summer, we went to Clint Eastwood's outdoor restaurant in Carmel, Calif., but it was 3 P.M.–Patio Closing Time–and we were told to eat our avocadoburgers inside.

They hadn't figured on my wife, who pointed out that her watch showed 2:59, that we'd come clear from Egypt and that if we were not seated outside she would "take it up with Mr. Eastwood, an old family friend." It was a fistful of intimidation that Dirty Harry would have loved. We got a pretty patio table, overlooking a two-inch-high manager.

Now, if I'd tried this gambit (as if I can think that fast on my feet; mice tend to think best in the tub a day later), I'd have been arrested for inciting a riot.

Not that we macho mice don't have our own cute little power plays–none of which works, but they make us feel lots better, and that's what counts. I settle for moral defeats.

One of my favorite tactics is WALKING OUT IN A HUFF, a swell way to assert yourself without risking a scar. When things get hot, I can be counted on to clench my fists and snort, "O.K.: if they don't serve us in *five* more minutes, we leave." (If anybody ever noticed us leave, they'd be destroyed.)

Another pet ploy is known as GLARING. I have perfected an arsenal of withering scowls and whammies that wear me out but that noisy people behind me at the movies just take to be my normal scrunched-up expression.

Then there is my famed HEAVY SIGH OF DISGUST. This must be done with great melodramatic exhaling, enough so that outsiders can tell you're burned up as hell but not so extreme that people think you're having an asthma attack.

My last-ditch technique is LEAVING A NASTY NOTE. I used to live in an apartment under a man who liked to see how loud he could yell at 2 A.M. It was a hobby and he got awfully good at it. I could have marched upstairs and simply beat him up, but I preferred to write a violent note that read "QUIET!!," slip it under his door, push the bell and run like crazy.

I don't recall if it worked, for I was so flushed with joy at my own ingenuity that I didn't care. And I was so tired from sitting up all night thinking of what I *might* do to him that I fell fast asleep.

PEOPLE WHO GO BUMP IN THE NIGHT

WHEN PRESIDENT FORD whacked his head coming off a plane years ago—not a week after getting into an auto wreck by mistake and a week before nearly being poked in the eye by a boy waving a flag—the nation's accident-prone citizens were glad to know that one of their own was in the White House.

Mrs. Ford was quoted as saying, "He's not clumsy—he just gets involved that way," which is how it is with people like Ford and myself, who are not clumsy, exactly, but who nonetheless end up mysteriously "involved" in mishaps.

Within one week, a while ago, I sprained an ankle stepping off a curb that suddenly dropped two feet; inflicted a nasty gash on my wrist when a wastebasket I tried to empty took a nip out of my arm; and, as always, I cracked my knees the normal number of times on coffee tables that are out to maim me. (Maybe someday I'll find out what I ever did to coffee tables that they should want to launch a nationwide attack on me.)

Now none of this is strictly "accident-prone" in the scientific sense of the term, which refers more to klutzes who go out of their way to fall down stairs; with me, it's the stairs that move. I could stand still in a barren room and come out badly bruised in an hour.

Indeed, I wake up once a week with unexplained wounds all over my body. "You must have done it in your sleep," people say, dismissing it lightly. I'm not so easily satisfied. Things don't just happen to you while you're fast asleep unless somebody is coming in during the night and beating you up in bed.

No–people like me and Gerald Ford are sort of object-prone. Presumably dormant objects–usually angular pieces of furniture with sharp edges–simply hurl themselves in our paths, actually moving sideways across a room from their usual spot. Maybe I should just have a good exorcist come in twice a week and spray; perhaps that would rid the house of all these bedeviled chairs and tables that won't sit still.

At home, shoes creep along the floor to trip me up; desk drawers jump out and grab my fingers; the freezer door is forever roughing me up and all the kitchen-cabinet doors mug me at will (they see their favorite head coming and swing open on their own, taking deadly aim at my forehead).

I have another theory, equally plausible, that *I* am not accident-prone at all, actually–my knees, thumbs and feet are.

As a kid, I left a trail of broken silverware, torn sofas, busted chair backs and stained tablecloths, and yet I was–and still am–considered a nice, quiet, well-behaved boy. It's just that ordinary objects give way at my gentlest touch.

Even now, I'm so afraid of demolishing people's apartments that I just sit there, arms folded, until it's time to leave. If I so much as reach for an hors d'oeuvre, the air is instantly filled with flying corn chips and guacamole.

Much of my property damage is done in public. At parties, I'm the first one to drop a drink on the rug. I'm so dependable at it, in fact, that I'm in constant demand from hostesses to stop by and spill a drink or two; it's a great little icebreaker.

THE VOICE OF THE TURTLE

THE LATEST MECHANICAL device that has me in its clutches is the telephone recording that asks you to leave your name and number when the beeper sounds. If you like, you can also do a few bars of "Body and Soul."

At least in my case, the human being at the unrecorded end is at a disadvantage. What happens is, the mechanical voice sounds quite real and animated while my own little voice sounds more like a recording, one made under duress.

One reason, of course, is that the machine has had a chance to rehearse its lines until it has the wording just right, but the unwary caller is caught without a script and has to respond on cue. Under such circumstances, I wonder if Lawrence Olivier could do more than squeak out his name and number.

It's a paralyzing experience in which the throat tightens, the pulse quickens, the mouth dries out and the mind turns to tapioca. In a split second–poised breathlessly for the beep–you must decide: (1) how much you want to say, (2) the exact wording and (3) the proper tone to use, which is the trickiest of all.

It's a mistake to adjust your tone to fit the disembodied voice at the machine's end. When you hear, "Hi! Janie Jumpup here! Sorry I'm out but I'll be back real soon and call you when I get home! Bye now!" you're tempted to be equally chirpy, which is often wrong: "Hi, there, Miss Jumpup! Monroe Frumpkin of Metro Savings! You're $768 overdrawn!"

How does a lover, say, respond to one of these recordings? "Hello, Janie? I adore you and can't live without you another moment. This is Leonard Gravitch speaking. I can be reached at MI 4-8791 between six and seven tonight. Thanks."

If someone has a funny recording, I want to match wits, with disastrous results. Or if the voice is sincere and businesslike, I try to equal it with a John Chancellor attack–but it all tends to come out sounding the same:

"Yes. Oh! This is. Um. Well. My name is. Mr. Nachman calling. Jerry. I wonder if you. That is, if you get home. I mean, *when* you get home. Sorry. You can just call me at. Oh, I'll call back later . . ."

I want to erase the tape, gargle and begin again, or just call up and take it from the top, briskly and with more feeling. My voice begins to fail the moment I realize it's being recorded. The voice sounds as if I just learned how to use it and am trying it out publicly for the first time. Even with live people present, it's barely audible. As I hang up, I realize that nobody hearing a feeble croak like this is going to call back. I think what I need is somebody to come in and dub my phone calls.

I have a sort of science fiction vision in which the recording device calls back and chews me out for having such a ridiculous voice: "Hey, frog!" it says. "This is 555-8791. I'll thank you not to dial this number again until you have a voice worth listening to."

I'm afraid my voice isn't ever going to make good on the telephone, which just is not my medium. Perhaps it might go over better in small intimate supper clubs.

TOOTH AND NAIL

IF ONLY PEOPLE had told me how much fun it is to talk about afterward, I'd have seen a dentist years ago.

Considering the joy you feel upon leaving the office, it's well worth the minor inconvenience of wracking pain and a few lost teeth. Indeed, discussing one's visit to the dentist beats recalling a trip to Mexico City or an affair fifteen years ago.

That is, it doesn't matter a whit if anybody cares to hear about the experience–I'm determined to talk about it anyway. That is my reward for being such a good boy and not even crying. (The reason I've not gone in fifteen years is that I was waiting for painless dentistry to be reduced to a pill at bedtime.)

For years, I refused to discuss teeth (my own had been "neglected" to the point of desertion), yet I remained in thrall to people who casually referred to their "new caps." How I longed to say nonchalantly, "I'm having some dental work done . . ."

It's now possible for me to drop the phrase "dental work" into any conversation. Last week, without even trying, I was able to sneak "root canal" into a discussion of the Panama Canal. Or I'll say, "Oh, speaking of Harry Bridges . . ."

If the other person refuses to request more details, I'm forced to take out my X rays and pass them around like snapshots of the kids. "Now this li'l fella here," I explain, holding an X ray up to the light, "can probably be saved, since the gum is healthy . . ."

What is nicest of all, though, is when someone else is impressed that *I'm* seeing a dentist. "Oh, gosh, I haven't been in so long," I love to hear them say, looking good and guilty about it. That's my cue to reply, with a big bright grin: "Oh, I was the same way, but it's not as bad as you think. Really, it's nothing at *all*."

When people would tell *me* this, of course, I didn't swallow a word of it. I rightly suspected they were just delighted with themselves for going to a dentist and were acting as a shill for the American Dental Association.

What happens is, after you tell somebody about your terrific teeth, they make an appointment on the sly and then brag how brave they were to *their* friends. This is the only way dentistry could ever have lasted so long; the profession is based entirely on gloating.

That and smiling. You do about 600 percent more smiling than usual, mostly at yourself as you pass store windows and rearview mirrors, practicing up on your new roguish grin. You become so generally giddy, in fact, that a man with a few new fillings is easily mistaken for a Moonie.

During this period, the dentist and hygienist become your nearest, dearest chums. Once someone has rummaged about inside your mouth for several hours, it seems like nothing at all to unburden your most secret fears and desires.

If you were able to speak, how easy it would be to say to some gentle blue-eyed blond hygienist: "Gee, if you think those back molars are bad, honey, wait till you hear what I've been going through at the office." I'm sure she would put down her little pick and say, "Oh, you poor sweetheart—now you tell Miss Prettikins *everything!*"

In no time at all, a very solid friendship—perhaps even a marriage—could be founded on fixing your back teeth. Many a lifelong relationship has been cemented with far less.

After you've been freed from the dentist's chair, the man is a friend forever. There is *nothing* you wouldn't do for good old Dr. Tarter, if he were in a jam or needed more money. Why, the fellow is by far the most decent, charming chap you ever met, a man among men, and both of you must have lunch one day soon and discuss new flossing techniques.

TOOTH AND NAIL (PART II)

IN A RECENT ISSUE of *Cosmopolitan,* I noticed an article entitled "The Fabulous World of Fingernails!" presumably aimed at readers who still have at least five functioning fingernails.

My own nails—or whatever they are—haven't been much help to me in the last twenty-five years, ever since I took up full-time nail biting. It's a pleasant pastime, cheaper than smoking, and the death rate is lower.

I'm not even interested in having "fabulous-looking nails," if only they worked. At any given time, however, I have no more than three out of ten fingernails in fully operational shape. Most of the time, they're neatly trimmed to just below the second knuckle.

There's a good reason for this, obviously. A man in a rough occupation like writing, who must bang away at a hot typewriter eighteen hours a day, can't be expected to have long, lovely, well-kept nails. That's for sissies. Fellas like me—loggers, longshoremen, catchers, male secretaries—can't do our job properly with pretty nails.

It is, to be sure, a severe handicap trying to get along in the world without fingernails. There are all sorts of simple basic tasks most people take for granted that those of us without nails find ourselves helpless to perform.

Picking up spare change, for instance, becomes a nightmarish experience. I make a pathetic attempt to scoop it up while the people behind me (all with elegant nails, no doubt) sigh and look at their watches. Often, it's also necessary to fish a credit card out of my wallet, another impossible chore for the stubby-fingered.

People without a full complement of nails who drop a coin on the sidewalk will just let it roll away rather than suffer the humiliation of being unable to pry it free of the cement. Onlookers stare as you try to scrape a nickel off the ground, like some poor derelict, even though it's your very own rightful nickel.

Or just try sometime to jimmy open a carton of milk without the usual-size fingernails, as the milk burbles out the side of the spout after you've finished tugging at it. I must allow an extra ten minutes every morning to pick at cartons and puncture cellophane bread wrappers. If you really want to torture a person with no nails, by the way, hand him an orange to peel.

Folks with fingernails are able to open envelopes without even thinking about it while I have to use an entire finger, often gashing the tip on the flap, finally ripping the envelope open at one end and tearing the letter in half. A mature fingernail person slits it open calmly, smoothly, efficiently.

If you try to grope through life without regulation-length nails, it takes you twice as long to read a paper or magazine, because you can't separate the pages as a person with normal fingers might. You sort of pinch the pages together, or you can wet your thumb if you're old-fashioned and don't mind eating a little ink. They ought to equip magazines with thumb indexes.

A person with blunt fingernails is also handicapped when it comes to Scotch tape, bandages or new license tags. We're unable to wedge a nail under the tape where it sticks to the spool or peel off adhesive backing without making a real mess of everything.

If you have fingernails, there are all sorts of extra little tasks you can perform that make life so much more worth living–things like inserting your thumbnail in a screw and unloosening it when you don't have a dime handy. Or like being able to unsnarl a knotted shoelace without breaking into a childish tantrum and heaving a shoe through the bedroom window. (You can always tell if a person has no fingernails just by looking at his shoelaces.)

A person with normal nails can pick up almost anything off a table without clawing at it forever, ending up with a fistful of splinters. I am like some primitive beast when confronted by, say, a toothpick, a paper clip, a pin or–God forbid–a piece of paper that has fallen on the floor.

In my youth, I'd simply wait until the paper had hit the floor, then lean over and pick it up, or maybe make a grab for it in midair. Lately, I'm forced to get down there on all fours and crawl around until I find an edge with a bent corner.

It's enough to make a person give up fingernail biting and take up something harmless, like smoking.

THE CUSTOMER IS ALWAYS DOPEY

IT MAY JUST BE my old paranoia kicking up again, but I detect a distinct anti-consumer crusade on the part of clerks and repairmen who take an unusual delight in telling me how wrong-headed or outdated my living habits are.

I am afraid to try on a new pair of shoes now for fear the salesman will berate me for my present shoes.

Recently, I had high hopes of taking home a comfy pair of loafers, but I hadn't counted on a salesman who skillfully talked me out of it and into a state of depression about the things I've been wearing on my feet for thirty-five years.

The shoes I liked were too narrow, he said, and would crack at the toes, making me quite unhappy. Then he felt duty-bound to add: "How long have you been buying shoes this size?" He seemed ready to hand me over to the manager for buying loafers without a state license.

When I try to buy anything at all unusual–tires, say–the salesman quickly assures me (1) I know nothing about tires, (2) I should not be allowed to purchase tires in my present stupid state and (3) I need a good stern lecture on the lousy state of my tires plus a brief statement on "The American Tire Industry Today."

Perhaps the idea is to discredit the customer and take any fight out of him so he won't cause further trouble. The customer is, if not always wrong, ridiculously uninformed, possibly illiterate. Moreover, he has no idea what he really wants in life.

About a year ago, my regular barber suddenly told me, "They aren't wearing their hair that way anymore," and then attempted to sell me on a splendid hair-shaping program that, he implied, would make me look much less clownish than usual.

It's not that these people hope to sell me something more expensive, which I wouldn't mind if it didn't include slurs on my personal habits. Their real purpose, it appears, is to make me feel unworthy of some item I naïvely plan to purchase.

I nearly got talked out of buying a brand of pen I've used since 1962, but resisted. The salesgirl shrugged hopelessly and rang up the sale with a fine look of disgust. She did not care to transact any business with somebody who has so little knowledge of 59-cent ball-point pens.

Clerks can smell an amateur shopper on the premises, all right. When I wander into a place that is obviously out of bounds for me —hardware store, jewelry shop, florist—the clerk just grins, crosses his arms and flashes a look that says: "Well, well—and who do we have here?"

Optometrists are practiced consumer guilt-inducers. They slip off my spectacles and peer through them with thinly disguised disdain, which I interpret as "You call these things eyeglasses?" They then add: "Say, it's lucky you got in here when you did. Two more days and this left lens would have just fallen right out."

Of course, people who repair anything—autos, stereos, wristwatches—enjoy making you feel that you've let them down rather badly. They want to be sure you're aware just what a miserable embarrassment of an owner you've been.

"This speaker is in dreadful shape," the stereo man says, gravely shaking his head at my reckless and slovenly way of life.

"Tsk-tsk! I don't know why folks let these things fall to pieces like this. I doubt if I can be much help. It's beyond saving."

This is to set you up for an estimate that could rock the European economy, during which time they take you aside and make comparisons between a turntable (or a Chevy engine, a clock, etc.) and the human body.

Doctors, thankfully, are willing to let you alone, but any day now I expect to confront a physician who holds up an X ray and says: "Well, I've seen a lot of bad backs in my day, but this spine you have is a joke. Why, you should be ashamed to walk around town with a lower lumbar region in such abysmal shape! Where did you get a skeletal system like this?"

SHIRTS IN TODAY, RUBBED OUT BY TUESDAY

WHEN I WENT in to ask the man at the laundry why some of my shirts had been returned torn off at the elbows, he told me this is how they do them now.

"I didn't say anything when you began stapling the belt loops to my pants," I said, "and I kept still during all those years when my collars came back fuzzed up, and I was even silent when my shirts were folded in twenty places, but ripping off the sleeves does seem unnecessary."

The guy at the laundry shrugged but held his ground; he is not an easy man to bully. "Look, mister, if you want your shirts cleaned, you got to take 'em the way they do 'em, no questions asked. Them are the rules."

"But can't you just clean and return my shirts in more or less their original shape?" I asked. His attack dog began to growl, sensing an unfriendly customer on the premises.

"If you want your shirts laundered, pressed and wearable, you shoulda said so. That's extra."

"How much more does it run?" I asked.

"It's $4.50 a shirt, but that guarantees they'll come back in good enough condition to use."

"It sounds like a new form of 'protection,'" I grumbled.

"For that price, they won't stick any staples in the pants pockets," he said. "Your collars will be left alone, no cuff buttons will be split or crushed, and you'll get the shirt back with or without starch, as you say."

"Since you mentioned it," I said, "what gives with this new starch racket anyway? If I stipulate 'medium starch' my shirts come back frozen stiff; if I ask for 'light starch' they have to be worn at home a week before I can move my neck."

The shirt man frowned. "You got to request *minus* starch, pal," he said. "It's only for our best customers. So next time you come in, tell 'em Louie sent you and they'll know to send your shirts to our special destarching plant in Jersey."

"There's something very strange going on here," I said. "Why can't just anybody get their shirts done without starch?"

"Are you kidding? The shirt syndicate won't stand for it. You seem like a straight guy, so I'll level with ya: all the laundries are run by Shirts, Inc., outta Chicago, where they purposely rough up men's shirts so you'll have to keep buyin' new shirts all the time. Naturally, they also own all the shirt shops."

The laundryman whispered that eventually Shirts, Inc., will force the entire laundry industry out of business, so that men will only be able to wear a shirt once, throw it out and buy another one the following week, like they've already done with razor blades and socks.

"That explains why my socks only last one cleaning," I said, "and why I only get back one pair of shorts for every two I send out. Obviously, Shirts, Inc., also controls the launderettes."

"You said it, I didn't," he shrugged.

"I felt something was going on when my shirts started coming back more soiled than when I took them in. I thought it was kind of odd, but by now I'm so happy to get them back at all that I figure, what's a little grime? I can use the cardboards, so it's worth sacrificing a few shirts."

"This ain't no fancy hand laundry. We do the best we can. You want to leave these shirts or not?"

"Well, all right," I said, "but this time please promise not to fold, staple or mutilate them. I got a family; give me a break. How soon can I get 'em back?"

"Next October 15, O.K.? It's the best I can do."

"Well, if you're sure. I'll need a clean shirt for the holidays."

"No problem," he said. "I'll just say 'Must Have by Fall.'"

"Don't I need a ticket or something?" I asked.

"Nah," said the laundry hit man. "I'll write your name on a tag and paste it inside the collar so it'll scratch the back of your neck all day and drive you crazy."

"Thanks," I said, and turned to go.

"Anytime," he smiled. "It's always a pleasure."

REST ROOMS THROW IN THE TOWEL

WHY THERE HAS been no public outcry, or even whimper, about the rest-room hand drier, I can't say, but it proves how mankind has learned to clam up in the name of progress.

The automatic hand drier, of course, isn't an advance in drying hands at all but a throwback to a time when man had not yet discovered paper towels and was forced to stand outside his cave shaking water off his hands and rubbing them together briskly.

Whoever manufactures mechanical hand driers knows nothing about either drying hands or human nature. Nobody wants to stand around a rest room with his hands hanging out to dry. Hand drying is a semi-private act, best done quickly and without fanfare.

Also, hand driers leave you helpless. If someone is trapped and needs you in a hurry, you must wait until your hands finish drying, forcing you to shout above the roar of the hand blower:

"Be with you in a jiffy! I only have six more fingers to go."

Then, too, while your hands are being dried, you don't know where to look or what to do; you can't even hold a paper. If you're like me you say, "To hell with it," and walk out wringing wet.

Hand driers are part of a movement to prevent the public from drying its hands and face. How else do you account for those grimy cloth towels that hang down limply on rollers, covered with ancient palm prints? Or metal boxes that make you crank until an arm falls off for one lousy section of towel, barely enough to dry a baby's hand.

Was there a sudden demand in the nation's rest rooms for more modern hand-drying equipment? Has science learned that paper towels are hazardous to your health? Who, in brief, decided that paper towels were just not doing the job?

The last time I was confronted by a hand drier, I read the instructions on the front, to pass the time while drying, and I realized that the makers of these machines go to great pains to get the public to use them correctly. Maybe if I'd cooperate and stop resisting recent innovations in civilized hand-drying methods, it would pay off in softer, lovelier, more caressable hands.

At the top it says, "Modern Sanitary Drier—Prevents Chapping," which I took to be an insult aimed at old-fashioned, presumably unsanitary—perhaps germ-infested—paper towels that leave one's hands rough, red and filthy (*paper* towels—*ugh!*).

Next, the drier goes on at some length to tell us what to do:

"1. Shake Excess Water from Hands."

The real issue is where to shake all this excess water—on the tile floor, causing slippage? On your shirtfront? On innocent passersby? It's easy enough to say, "Shake excess water from hands," but most people, in fact, do nothing of the kind. They just turn on the drier and right away they're off to a bad start. The drier simply can't handle two soaking-wet hands simultaneously, at least not like your old-time paper towels.

"2. Push Knob—Stops Automatically."

This is vital to a full understanding of hand driers. For years, I walked away from driers that were still blowing and always wondered if they ever went off. Now we know; this brief thoughtful note puts the novice hand-drier user at ease at once.

"3. Rub Hands Back and Forth Rapidly."

This line is in red, so it mustn't be skimmed or taken lightly. A lot of folks, I gather, are not rubbing hands back and forth rapidly; they expect the machine to do everything. Let me tell you, these driers are in no big hurry. The drier doesn't have to get back to the table, pay the check and make an 8:30 curtain.

"4. Turn Louver Upward to Dry Face."

This, of course, is patently absurd. Nobody plans to stand still and have his face dried for him by any louver. It's not just decadent, and silly, it's inefficient. The air doesn't get into all those nooks and creases; it neglects the neck and ears, and ignores the chin completely.

I've been in my share of rest rooms, and I can testify that people simply are not having their hands and faces dry-blown; they are not playing along. In fact, just to avoid the offensive task of machine drying, people have nearly given up washing altogether.

S-M ESKIMO DESIRES DELAWARE NYMPHO

PHENOMENA I SECRETLY do not believe actually exist:

BISEXUALS: Oh, there may be four or five in Morocco and Turkey, but you never heard of a bisexual until a few actresses boasted of "bisexual experiences" and it became a rather chic thing to whisper about. Then the men's magazines got into the act and made bisexuality as popular as Reuben sandwiches. Well, I'm not at all convinced. Listen—if this kind of stuff went on, I'd know about it; I get around.

THE CHICAGO CUBS: All my life, I've read about them, and I hear there's a ball park in Chicago with ivy where they're said to live—but I've yet to clap eyes on a Chicago Cub in person or know of anyone who's ever seen them en masse.

RUTABAGAS: If there truly is such a vegetable, why aren't they ever sold in grocery stores? Nope—this is just a funny word concocted by comedians to get a laugh. No such item exists and don't try to tell me it does.

ESKIMOS: I want very much to believe in Eskimos, but I just can't no matter how hard I try. I'm talking about Eskimos who live in so-called "igloos" (sure, sure), eat blubber and fish through holes in the ice—like the people depicted in my 1923 edition of the *Book of Knowledge*. All the sepia photos of Eskimos I've seen are as blurry as those of the Loch Ness Monster.

SALVADOR DALI: There is a man who *calls* himself "Salvador Dali," I grant you, the character you read about and see crazy photographs of and who claims to do all those surrealistic paintings. I insist this is just a man who is paid to go around promoting the wild canvases turned out by some wily Hollywood art dealer. Any rational human being knows that Salvador Dali could not exist all these years and still look exactly the same age as he did in 1943. The person known to us as "Salvador Dali" has, I submit, been enacted by various men over the years.

NYMPHOMANIACS: Here is a phenomenon that survives only in college boys' imaginations and dubious clinical studies (the main purpose of which is to enflame impressionable young men of forty and under). Nobody has ever met—let alone dated—a real live "nympho." If one will kindly step forward (or even send a small snapshot), I'd be much obliged; actual names and phone numbers will, of course, be kept in the strictest privacy.

DELAWARE: O.K.—name me one well-known, or even *un*known, fact about "Delaware" and I'll concede there is such a place. Name me a city, a celebrity from there, a famous bridge, anything at all. "Dover" is allegedly the capital, but you aren't going to sit there and tell me that "Dover, Del.," is an actual city, with people. *Come on!* It would be a good joke on Americans to learn, after 200 years, that no such state ever existed called "Delaware"—that it was once nothing more than a sort of Indian territory nobody could quite locate and that Washington was too sheepish to reveal he never crossed. If "Delaware" was one of the Original 13 Colonies, as rumored, it went out of business by 1904 at the very latest. When I grew up, all that remained was a grape drink called "Delaware punch," and even it had very little credibility.

GIGOLOS: This is another romantic fiction popularized by songwriters and silent films. There may be a few very *old* gigolos in Italy, but that's it. Just what is a "gigolo," anyway, and would you recognize one if you bumped into him at a party? I'd like to see the latest census figures on U.S. gigolos.

SADO-MASOCHISM: A similar body of literature exists on "S-M," and there's a lot of glib talk now about "leather bars" and "bondage" gear, but show me one sado-masochist in rubberwear and handcuffs who will identify himself without laughing.

TO OPEN SESAME, SHOVE HERE

AFTER WRESTLING WITH the top of an aspirin bottle for two hours, I located the office where they design all such devious bottle caps, tin-can tabs, cereal boxes, spice jars, flour sacks, tennis-ball cans, plastic seals and gum wrappers, and spoke with chief engineer Mark de Sade.

I told De Sade it was impossible to get anything open nowadays (except, of course, car locks and front doors) and he said he was happy to hear it. "That's why we're in business," he beamed. "Our job is to make it as tough on the old consumer as possible. Nader hasn't quite won yet."

"All right," I demanded, "why are medicine bottles so hard to open? By the time I get to the aspirin, my headache is gone. I thought the idea was to keep *kids* from unscrewing the bottle."

"That's what we tell adults, so they won't get angry," he chuckled.

I asked De Sade why beer and tennis-ball cans are so dangerous to open. "Look," he said, "we don't want any sissies buying beer or playing tennis. If you can't open a can of Bud without cutting yourself, maybe you shouldn't be buying beer."

"So why is a pull-tab necessary on soft-drink cans too?"

"Well," he said, "if you didn't have to toss out half a can of soda when it goes flat, due to the open top, they'd only sell half as much. So we designed what I call the 'rip-off' tab."

I asked him why I've never been able to open a sack of sugar, or flour, or a cereal box, by pressing along the dotted line that allegedly makes an "easy pouring spout." "It always caves in on me, and I end up tearing open the bag with both hands, spilling sugar all over the floor."

"Don't tell me you still take that dotted line stuff seriously!" he roared. "We *want* people to spill the stuff, then they'll buy more. Sugar and flour sacks are impossible to pierce with the human thumb; we tested 20,000 thumbs. It requires a pick-axe."

"Why must a gum wrapper also be so invincible? I can't ever pry loose the string that supposedly unravels the pack."

"I should hope not; it's soldered in place. The idea is to make you claw feverishly at the wrapper so it falls apart and sticks of gum fly all over. You lose half a pack that way."

"Which reminds me," I added, "bandages now seem twice as tough to get at as before, and they were never a picnic."

"That's because we hide that tiny red thread, forcing you to pick at the paper with the fingers of one hand while the other hand is covered with blood. Once open, the bandage is designed to curl back on itself and stick; then you have to throw it out and open a new one or bleed to death—usually from opening a can of cream soda. Clever, eh?"

I said, "I'm sure it was also your idea to pack potato chips in hermetically sealed plastic bags that have to be opened by standing on the package with both feet and tugging for twenty minutes." He merely winked.

"Why did you have to put frozen orange juice in a cardboard can that unwinds and—as you peel it open at 7 A.M. with your eyes half shut—drips orange guck all over your pajamas? I guess frozen orange juice in tin cans worked too well?"

"*Now* you're catching on," he beamed.

"So, what new baffling packages are you working on now?"

He unrolled a blueprint. "I'm devising a top that won't ever come off—or, once off, is impossible to get back on. It's sort of a push-in ketchup bottle with a string you unwind, all packed in plastic."

"Say, did you ever consider making things *easier* to open? Like, whatever happened to plain old lids?"

"Oh, they outlived their usefulness," he frowned. "People began figuring out how to open jars by running them under hot water or knocking them against the sink board. We nearly put ourselves out of business."

SOME AULD ACQUAINTANCES TO BE FORGOT

AT THIS TIME, the management would personally like to thank some of the people who make this column impossible:

Jeo Kodas: Joe Doaks is the printer who, week in and week out, in foul weather and sunshine, messes up words, drops lines, transposes letters and, all in all, does his utmost to rewrite me, with often entertaining results.

Recently, Jeo cleverly switched "machoism" to "masochism" and "grungy" came out "lumpy"—both in the very same column, an unusually good day for him. Another time, "Camp Dix" became "Camp Camp" (a gay army base?), "friends" turned into "fiends," "freeloading" turned out "freeholding" and somehow "orbit" lost gravity and ended up an "obit."

Leo Gliggs, Albert Smoof, Trudy Namkin, Norm Neebo (and others too numerous to mention):

These are just a few of the folks who keep me constantly supplied with funny ideas, free of charge, and never complain when they don't quite get into print.

Gladys Willowaw: A switchboard operator at the newspaper

who never heard of me and informs callers that no such person works here. (Her brother Delbert works in the Circulation Dept. and calls me every year to see if I'd like to subscribe to the paper.)

Walter Deagle: Walt is the fellow who says, "Hey, I see your picture in the paper all the time," never suspecting there is also a column right underneath it. (He thinks I'm a prominent politician.)

Marcia Budgely: Marcia is a jolly press agent who calls with a hot item about a new disco she's handling, or has the author of a book on human sexuality who would make a funny column. When I explain, feebly, that I'm not, nor have I ever been, Earl Wilson, she sighs in disgust. I often suggest she give the item to Art Buchwald.

Bert Stebbins (USN, Retired): Bert is the fellow with a lifetime supply of lined school paper, red pencils and American flag stickers who writes in regularly with news of various take-overs by a group of Communist Italian black Jewish lesbians who are trying to sell the Panama Canal down the river.

R. T. Gaffney, Jr.: Mrs. Gaffney, who just became a reader, doesn't yet realize I make all this stuff up.

Lila O'Lunny: Lila is the little old lady I meet at parties who titters, "Uh-oh! I better watch what I say or you'll go back and write a column about me!"

Dick Frunch: Frunch never fails to compliment me for some terrific column that Russell Baker did last week.

Gordon N. Cratchnik: Gordie, on the other hand, always asks: "What else do you do besides the column?" Since it only requires fifteen or twenty minutes (top) to knock out a new column, I also have a paper route that, happily, takes up most of the day.

Ed Klaxon, Betsy Overshift, Hal Noff, Hank O'Henry, others: These are but a few of the folks who say, "I like your column, but when are you going to get that awful picture changed?" They don't realize it took forty years to perfect that awful picture.

Clara Bemis: Clara invariably greets me at least once a week and points out the most recent sexist slur I've made in print.

Larry Nunckleman: He always goes out of his way to tell me,

"Pretty good column today—but not quite up to your usual caliber." Larry is such a flatterer.

Fran Pettiby: Fran reads a piece that took three days of sweat, plus twenty-seven rewrites, to finish, and says, "Very cute." (She's the same woman who, when Tolstoy showed her *War and Peace,* read it and told him, "How nice, Leo.")

Arnold Neubauer: It would be a thin year indeed without a visit from ol' Arnie, a friend from school who never fails to ask me when I'm going to start writing something serious.

Norma Foote: Norma invariably inquires if I happened to read a terribly clever column Erma Bombeck did yesterday on a subject I finished writing myself only an hour ago.

CONFESSIONS OF AN INTERSTATE INCOMPETENT

I AM A victim of a disease not unlike agoraphobia, a fear of leaving the house. I can leave the house all right—I just can't get where I'm going afterward. I'm plagued by a malady that causes cold sweats, sudden fits of swearing and unimagined trembling, a psychic illness called "geographobia," the unreasoning fear of off ramps.

Whoever designs maps and road signs assumes too much expertise on my part, such as a working knowledge of east and south. What they need is a wrong-way consultant, a person like myself who instinctively turns the wrong way coming out of an elevator; who has difficulty translating highway sign language made up largely of such pidgin Indian as "Ohio Traffic Left"; who loses his house if he approaches it from a strange angle; who can't read an arrow.

In my opinion, road signs tell you much more than you need to know, pointing out every teensy hamlet, creek bed and private airport. In Highwayland, each town is treated with equal significance.

You'll be chugging along looking for, say, Boston, but all you see for miles upon miles are signs reading "Saugus 72" or "Braintree 108."

What confuses things is that "Braintree" appears to get as much play as "Boston," maybe more. What they should do, of course, is print the names of little towns in littler letters, to prevent you from shouting, "Hey, wait—this looks like something important up ahead! . . . No, just another sign to Saugus."

In brief, highways should learn to focus their efforts more on those places where most of the customers are going. True, it may slightly inconvenience the fifteen or twenty folks who are actually bound for Braintree or Saugus, but in this country the majority rules, and it seems to me that if you're going to Saugus you must be willing to search for it awhile.

People who put up road signs feel they've done their job after telling you, a mile out of San Francisco, that Los Angeles is 380 miles south. What you really want to know is: If I take this funny little road here, will I still be pointed more or less toward L.A.? And, if I go through Fresno via the truck route, will I miss Fresno altogether? Which exit should I take if I'd like to see just a smidgen of Fresno and yet not get snarled in rush-hour traffic?

A common misunderstanding is the familiar "North Flummox" or "South Flummox" quandary. Rather than make you guess which way to turn, why can't the signs say "North Flummox (Nice Section)" and "South Flummox (Crummy Section)"?

Road signs should be more specific. It does nobody any good to be told "Downtown Dallas Next 38 Exits." What we need to know is which exit goes to the cute part, which one to the boring part, which one to a charming coffee shop and which exit leads directly to six miles of auto dealers, garages and used-car lots?

It also seems that highways might be much more encouraging along the way. Every ten miles or so, I would like to see signs reading, "Chicago-Bound Travelers Doing Just Fine," rather than drifting aimlessly for an hour, wondering if I'm still on the same road even though it seems to have deliberately changed names when I wasn't watching.

It really should be against federal law for any highway to switch names simply because it's been rebuilt or a politician has died. This only leads to directions like: ". . . Then you'll see a sign that says 'Old Ox Road'—well, just ignore it. That's a continuation of the Major Kickback Causeway, which later turns into the Admiral Curmudgeon Turnpike, but after you come into town it's simply called Bayside Boulevard . . ."

Many major arteries, you may have noticed, don't have names that correspond to what's on your map. Very often, they're known modestly in life as just plain old "318," but you'll never know once you're on it. There is no sign that will say, boldly and unequivocally: "Curmudgeon Turnpike, Alias Major Kickback Causeway and Bayside Boulevard, Affectionately Known Around Town as 'The Old Ox Road' (or on map as 'U.S. 318')."

Likewise, there's no logical way to explain how to cope with spiral off ramps that tend to deposit you in some remote Spanish fishing village twelve miles down the highway, heading in the reverse direction, traveling down a lonely, dusty, deserted "access road." The problem with these "access roads," as far as I can tell, is that they isolate all the drivers who don't know where the heck they are—motorists meandering back and forth next to the main highway wondering how to get back on it while staying out of the ocean to their immediate right.

Even quite sincere drivers end up here, having been neatly seduced into taking turnoffs by signs that suddenly loom up ahead screaming "THRU TRAFFIC MERGE LEFT." I'm never sure exactly how *thru* I am, so I often merge anyway just to be on the safe side —especially if everyone else is merging with great confidence. I assume that any car in front of me knows precisely where *it's* going, and if I happen to be very lucky it may even be going my way.

At least a third of all "merge" warnings seem to be false alarms, thrown in to keep drivers awake. I break my neck swiveling around to switch four lanes in 3.5 seconds, endangering the lives of hundreds, only to learn a moment later that if I hadn't merged I'd still be in good shape.

Many such near disasters are caused by people who use fuzzy terms like "bear to your left," a meaningless instruction to me. To take care of intersections with varying degrees of leftness, I want people to specify Regular Left, Medium Left, etc.; no more of this "bear left" business.

Sooner or later, somebody is certain to inquire innocently of me, "Could you take a peek at the map and see where we are?" You don't just "peek" at a map. For me, anyway, a map only means more trouble; maps are for people who know exactly where they're going and merely like to test themselves. We need beginner maps, intermediate maps and advanced maps.

The beginners' map would explain the difference, if any, between "underpass" and "overpass," the purpose and meaning of "alternate routes" and the exact relationship between, say, "Route 11" and "Route 11-W." (Just what is that tantalizing "W" all about anyway? Does it stand for "West"—and if so, why won't it come out and say "11-West"? Why all this cloak-and-dagger stuff?)

I have sat alone many times in the front seat of a car fighting back tears when I could not relate the road in front of me to a little red line on my map. First of all, I'm never sure if the map is aimed in the same direction as the car. Secondly, I rarely have a map with me that depicts my entire route; the roads I'm on always seem to run off the edge of the paper.

When lost, most people rely on their instincts. I have no instincts, except to pull over and call a taxi. I'm too easily upset by any new off ramp or forks in the road I haven't been carefully warned about. I have no geographical memory, let alone anything as fancy as a sense of direction. If taken two miles beyond my neighborhood and spun around once, I may as well be in North Korea.

If somebody says, "Say, you know that narrow road just before you get to the old high school?" I immediately give up, although it may very well be that I used to walk that same road to school for four years. My answer is more likely to be "What old high school is that?"

Maps are no more unreliable than people, however. The problem is that people who try to give me directions take far too much for granted. Usually, they start at a point several steps ahead of what I consider starting out, by which I mean the front door.

What they must learn to tell me is: "When you come out of the garage, you drive to the corner and turn right . . ."

Instead, they'll say: "As soon as you get off the bridge . . ." without taking into account my inability to get *on* the bridge. Probably, I'm not even sure just which bridge they're talking about, or I'm too ashamed to admit I don't plan to use any bridge at all, since I always go the long way around because, even though it takes thirty minutes more, that's how I first learned my way seventeen years ago.

If I have to find a restaurant on a new street, rather than follow explicit directions, I'll just go to a corner in the area I understand and begin asking strangers. It cuts my time in half.

I take directions almost as poorly as I follow them. For one thing, I take them literally. I like no room at all for any interpretation. If someone says, "Turn left at the first street after the stoplight," I'll swerve sharply left at the first hint of a path, even if it leads into a backyard. When people mean the first *major* street, they must say so.

Everybody always gives me twice as many directions as I can handle, clouding my brain with all sorts of useless geographical data, negative information about what turnoffs *not* to take, which churches to ignore and all the dead ends to keep away from. Being geographically perverse, as well as backward, I memorize everything I'm not supposed to do.

Then, too, other people's sense of distance is at wild variance with mine. They'll say, "You drive two miles up the road until you see a big oak tree . . ." So I get 100 feet up the road and spy a semi-large tree. "Is this the tree he means?" I wonder. "Will there be an even bigger tree further ahead?" I ask. "Is that an oak tree?"

It would help if I could keep my mind on highway directions as they're being told me. I *appear* to be taking it all in—nodding brightly, listening perkily—when in fact I'm not hearing a word being said. If I decide to write it all down, the person laughs, "Oh, it's not all that complicated. You just go six miles, take a pair of lefts, then you make a quick jog right and keep driving until you see a big Gulf station. Or maybe it's Mobil. Anyway, just go as far as you can, follow your nose and you can't miss it!"

The above instruction is, of course, riddled with pitfalls and Mobil stations. "A quick jog right" isn't my idea of a direction; it sounds like a golfing term. "Go as far as you can" is the sort of thing I love to hear, but it's sure to involve a couple of cul-de-sacs, a blind alley and perhaps a cliff. People assume I'm bright enough to maneuver around such hazards and resume going in the same direction.

"Just follow your nose" is so reassuring-sounding you don't realize that in practice it's open to several hundred interpretations. One man's straight-ahead is another man's hook left. Always ask what is meant by "nose." "You can't miss it" is a reckless thing to tell anybody like me, who can miss the World Trade Center if I forget to look up. Everyone thinks that their homes or restaurants are big as life when, in fact, they are usually nestled behind shrubbery twenty feet high or resemble old abandoned garages.

Even the most detailed directions neglect some life-or-death fact, which you learn only after arriving forty minutes late, all hot and mussed. "Oh, of course!" the host says, slapping his forehead. "I totally forgot they're putting in that new shopping mall where the interchange used to be, so I guess you had to detour across the railroad tracks and around the ball park . . ."

There is only one direction I truly comprehend: "Stop! Turn Around. You Are Going the Wrong Way." It's the first sign that somebody really cares.

SIX SEMI-DEADLY SINS

DEPRAVITY IS SO commonplace today that a fellow hardly knows what to do anymore if he wants to feel especially evil—hence, new taboos must be found to make the ordinary man feel as crummy and low-down as he used to when the seven deadly sins were less dull.

Murder, rape, torture, terrorism—they've all been done to death.

After discussing the problem with some master criminals, I came up with a few suggested vices for the modern citizen who desires to feel properly wretched, reprehensible acts highly recommended by professional big-time sinners.

Watching a Rerun of "Love Boat" on a Monday Afternoon:

This is unusually wicked, since Monday is the one day not to be squandered on major silliness. Simply switching on a TV set at 3:30 P.M. creates immediate intense feelings of guilt, which are then multiplied by purposely tuning in to the shabbiest third-rate show available at an hour when all decent, law-abiding people are busily engaged in meaningful pursuits.

Going Out at Midnight, Buying a Large Pepperoni Pizza, Bringing It Home and Wolfing It Down All by Yourself:

To achieve this state of exquisite squalor, you have to be at an extremely low point in your life; if not, this will hurry it along. The very thought of such a despicable act makes one writhe with self-loathing. Many experienced evildoers, asked if they'd ever performed such a rotten deed, could scarcely hide their disgust. "It's unthinkable and inexcusable," said one man on death row. "I mean, it's repulsive enough to consume a pizza all alone, but in your very own living room? How gross!"

Going to a Horrible Movie on Your Lunch Hour:

Businessmen were once able to feel fairly scummy by attending an X-rated film at noontime, but even this old thrill has now sadly degenerated into accepted practice. Rather than ducking into a porno house, therefore, today's ne'er-do-well might consider seeing just a plain lousy G-rated movie—*Herbie Goes to Monte Carlo,* say. To increase his feelings of filth tenfold, he must lunch on a large sack of popcorn, a giant Coke and a big Baby Ruth bar. (Once, I snuck off by myself to a Wednesday matinee of a Broadway musical and felt unclean for weeks. I didn't dare confess to it, but my wife eventually pulled the truth out of me.)

Passing Through a Town You Once Lived in and Stopping at a Telephone Booth to Look Up the Number of an Old Girlfriend: You need not actually call her at home—and probably won't—to be overcome by waves of wickedness. It's quite degenerate enough merely to thumb through the phone book as devious little fantasies race around your mind. Among 218 death row thugs, only two would own up to ever having committed this ghastly perversion.

Checking into a Ritzy Hotel and Immediately Dialing Room Service: This is a decadent binge favored by people on expense accounts and junkets, but that takes all of the indecency out of it, alas. If you really want to feel guilt pangs, the thing to do is dial room service when *you're* paying the bill and order a sirloin steak and strawberry shortcake the minute you check in.

Fixing Yourself a Dinner Consisting Entirely of 283 Crackers with Butter and Jam, Topped Off by a Dozen or So Hostess Chocolate Donuts and a Side of Cool Whip: If you plan to try anything as naughty as this—a dieter's descent into hell—you must first shut all the doors tightly and pull the shades so nobody can witness the senseless carnage going on inside your kitchen.

LIES OF COMMUNICATION

FAMOUS LINES which nobody believes:

"I was just going to call you."

"Your money cheerfully refunded."

"I find pornography basically boring."

"New shoes are supposed to pinch a little at first, but they'll feel comfortable after you wear them a few times."

"Except for documentaries, I never watch television."

"Mr. Leemish is in a meeting right now."

"I don't know what's wrong with little Timmy tonight–he's usually *so* good with strangers."

"I tried to call you on Christmas (Mother's Day, Easter, your birthday, Halloween, Arbor Day), but it was impossible to get through."

"If you leave a porch light on, the burglars will think somebody's home."

"I'm just looking for a friend."

"Mr. Leemish just stepped out of the office."

"I'd like to buy it but I want my wife to see it first."

"I don't know what got into Queenie–she never bites anybody."

"I've found some great bargains at flea markets."

"Office romances are a bad idea."

"Mr. Leemish is away from his desk right now."

"Museums are a great place to meet girls."

"A grizzly bear (rattlesnake, shark, etc.) is twice as afraid of you as you are of it."

"Good music is coming back."

"I loathe cocktail parties."

"I'd estimate this repair job shouldn't run you more than–oh, $30."

"Waiter, we'd just like to look at the dessert menu."

"Mr. Leemish is out to lunch, and may not be back today."

"He's actually very nice once you get to know him."

"The best French cooking isn't at all rich."

"We'd better be getting home–the painters are coming tomorrow."

"There's no reason we still can't be good friends."

"When you're on the highway, the best place to eat is where all the truck drivers stop."

"Mr. Leemish left word he'll be in conference all afternoon."

"Sorry for the delay, folks, but everyone on our staff seems to be out sick."

"Sir, that's a *very* flattering style for you."

"I was only in town for the day or I really would have called."

"Press Here to Release Oxygen Mask."

"If you can stick with the plot for the first 100 pages, it gets much better."

"Mr. Leemish left early today and won't return until Tuesday."

"I can't understand why you didn't get my postcard–I sent it soon as we got there."

"It only takes me forty minutes, tops, to get from my front door to the office."

"Every vote counts."

"The line seems to be moving very quickly."

"My alarm didn't go off."

"I'll need some identification, not that we don't trust you."

"Mr. Leemish will call you as soon as he returns from Europe."

"I really don't eat that much but my body retains a lot of fluid."

"Getting there is half the fun."

"Your Comments on Our Food and Service Will Help Us Serve You Better in the Future."

THE CUBBYHOLE PRINCIPLE

BACK IN THE old days, I would jeer at people who kept sloppy desks, but the jokes have finally come home to roost: I now have a sloppy desk all my own.

With age comes understanding, if not tidiness. I know why people own messy desks, and it's nothing to laugh at either. It's not that they have messy minds, or sloppy lives, as I once thought when I was young and naïve and neat. It isn't the person's fault at all–it's the desk's fault.

Basically, I am an orderly, organized man, and all I need is a few more desks to prove it. I am simply severely under-desked. Nobody can be expected to cram an entire career into six little drawers; I need a desk just to store all of my empty pens.

Don't talk filing cabinets to me. They don't work after a week. I've had filing cabinets and all they do is become sideways desks. The phrase "filing cabinet" *sounds* efficient and reassuring, I grant you, but don't be misled for a moment that it's the answer to basic disarray.

The tough issue here–the nub of this universal problem–is that the real world refuses to be organized and alphabetized. Put something into a desk drawer and, in no time at all, it reverts to its normal chaotic state.

Possibly, Murphy's Law covers this complex matter of messy office drawers and how they get that way, but here is Nachman's Law of Cubbyholes governing unruly desks: "Any item to be filed and assigned a category instantly overlaps into a new category."

Let us say you have a swell cubbyhole set aside to store Letters to Answer, a common category that seems harmless enough on the surface until you realize that all letters break down into Business and Personal, plus a more prevalent all-inclusive third category called Sort of Business, or Business/Personal.

Business letters, of course, immediately split into Reply and No Reply, but it doesn't end there. Your Reply pile quickly subdivides into Old and New Letters–or in my own sorry case, This Year and Last Year. Meanwhile, No Reply has quietly subdivided into Keep and Throw Away.

For instance, where should I file envelopes that have been addressed and never sent? I mean, there is no known label for this silly bastardized category. I can't just devote an entire pigeonhole to Used Envelopes, so I stash them in there with the Unused ones and it's the start of a nice new mess. They don't even qualify for Miscellaneous.

Miscellaneous itself is a bad joke, a trash pile pretending to be an orderly area. In fact, I have several Miscellaneous areas. Now that I think of it, my entire desk—my whole world—is a big Miscellaneous box.

The things that destroy any semblance of a "system" are those items that resist filing, such as negatives from a Mother's Day brunch in 1968. Or what of all these old Christmas cards? It seems almost sacrilegious to throw them away, they're so pretty, yet they take up valuable room that might be used for something important, such as old diets.

There are nearly enough Old Diets to warrant their very own drawer, and the same goes for Old Invitations, Napkins with Phone Numbers but No Names, 1975–78 Calendars, Coupons Granting 10 Cents Off on a Can of Maxwell House Coffee, Dental Insurance Forms, and Subscription Cards to Magazines I May or May Not Order Someday.

In brief, there is nothing in, on or around my desk that may either be filed or thrown away, so it all gets mixed up together in what is politely referred to as "the rolltop desk." This is how an otherwise tidy person, like myself, gets a scandalous reputation for harboring a sloppy desk. There is no way out of it, except arson.

In the meantime, if you ever want to find me, I'm somewhere in the middle of the desk, beneath the empty matchbooks and half-canceled stamps, filed under Hopeless.

THEY'RE ALL OUT OF ME

NOBODY WILL SAY why, but everything I like eventually is "discontinued." If I want it, they don't make it anymore. After fifty years, a certain sort of something I've been using (or more likely, just discovered) suddenly will go off the market for no discernible reason. Well, no, there *is* a discernible reason: They want to watch me whimper.

This is especially true of some item I have been eyeing timidly for months, mustering the nerve to buy. When I finally make a bold decision to get one, the manufacturer in Texas simultaneously will decide to discontinue it.

There is something willful about it, if you ask me (for one thing, why is it always a factory in Dallas?), but I doubt if Ralph Nader has the manpower or the guts to get to the bottom of it.

Here is my personal analysis of what happens down in Texas, if anybody's interested:

The Dallas manufacturer takes a look at his entire line, notices that something is appealing to people exactly like me and quickly orders it junked. This will be tough to prove, but I know it's done on purpose and somehow aimed specifically at me. It happens far too often for this to be mere "coincidence."

For years, I scoured the country for a very thin make of owlish tortoiseshell spectacles, and wherever I went to ask about them the salesman would say (trying very hard not to snicker), "Oh, they were discontinued," often adding with a small snicker in his voice: "They haven't made those in *years!*"

His implication was all too clear: Anyone who wanted frames like that was just silly, or maybe unpatriotic. For, as the clerk would always explain, "The kind you have in mind are only made in Europe; they haven't been available over here in–oh, gosh, thirty years." If he felt like rubbing it in good, he would say, "They don't seem to be wearing those kind any more"–and the sooner I was out of his store, the better.

Here's the snapper: A month after I give up and grudgingly buy something I don't quite like, the exact item I've been pounding the streets for since 1974 becomes a national craze. (I was ten years ahead of hippies with "granny glasses," but I knuckled under to a barrage of Harry Truman jokes.)

Or if I should stroll into a bakery where I haven't been in a while and innocently request a dozen of "those delicious pumpkin muffins," the lady behind the counter will smile sweetly and say, "Oh, my, we haven't had *them* in some time. How about the blueberry–they're very nice."

I try to show her she's wrong: "No, no, you always sold them on Tuesdays–the ones with the cinnamon on top?" She fends me off with another kindly smile: "Oh, I know just what you mean, but we don't have them now."

"Do you know when you *might* have them?" I ask, but the pumpkin muffins have vanished without a trace. "No telling," she says. "Come to think of it, they've been discontinued."

It's futile to demand details, but I do it anyway just to make myself miserable and cause a scene: "Why won't they make the pumpkin ones anymore? They were superb—perhaps the finest muffins known to man!"

Then, to really burn me up, the little lady shrugs and says, "We didn't have much call for them . . ."

My impulse is to take her aside, sit her down and say: "My good woman, don't you realize you have a moral obligation, a duty to society, to keep those pumpkin muffins coming?" (By "society," of course, I mean me.)

In a furniture store, I'm afraid to say if I especially like a certain piece, for I already know the reply: "I have a hunch they've discontinued that style," the clerk says, "but let me check."

"Don't bother," I tell him. "I'm sure they have. If it's a design I particularly admire, the company is forced to stop making it under terms of the Geneva Convention."

Once in a while, an item is merely "being discontinued," meaning I can still order it, special, at twice the price if I don't mind waiting nine months for delivery.

I've grown so fatalistic about it all by now that if I don't instantly see what I want, I slip out very quietly without waiting to get the bad news. It's too depressing to keep hearing how my little world is being phased out. Usually, the clerk is a teenage girl and utterly heartless: "If you don't see it, sir, we don't have it."

When this used to happen, I would merely throttle the salesgirl and, in a crazed voice, shriek: "But don't you see, you silly goose, if you had a decent, sensitive, cultivated bone in your body, you *would* have it!"

A few moments later, the store would call for an ambulance and carry me away to the Discontinued Customer Ward.

MUDDLING ABOUT THE MIDDLE EAST

THOSE OF US with only the flimsiest working knowledge of what is loosely termed "the Arab world" are well in over our heads in sand.

Now that Dior and Saint Laurent have opened boutiques in Arabia ("Arab sheik"?), we all ought to know the plural of "burnoose," the titles of at least two volumes in *The Alexandria Quartet* or one Omar Sharif film, which Arab states are "oil-rich" and which "beset by drought," and where to find a decent place to eat in Beirut.

It's necessary to know the difference between Iran and Iraq, Gaza and Giza, the Jordan and the Nile, the Red Sea and the Dead Sea, Princes Fahd, Saud and/or Said, King Hussein and Faisal and El Sadat, El Fatam, El Kwadaffi and El Al.

If somebody asks, "Hey, Pete, what d'ya think of Syria?" Pete should have a reply ready, plus an inkling where it is. It won't work anymore to speak of this whole glob as "the Arab world," "the Middle East" or "that place over by Israel."

A major stumbling block to comprehending the Middle East is its geography, which for centuries has kept the rest of the world at home—hence the phrase "mysterious Middle East." If only we could figure out where, say, Egypt and Jordan go, maybe the Middle East would be no more mysterious than the Midwest.

Also, the Arab world is a sort of "region," and nothing on earth is more fuzzy than a "region" (unless it's a "landmass"). An area should be either an actual country or nothing; none of this "region" business. No place called a "region"—or a "zone" or a "nation-state"—ever amounts to much. Look at "Lapland," "the Gold Coast" or "the Netherlands," all haphazard "regions" well beyond definitions or maps; they're as bad as "British Columbia."

To get down to cases, what exactly *is* "Arabia"? Is it the same as "Saudi Arabia" and "the Arab nation"? What does "Egypt" really mean? Is "Egypt" just a catchall term people recklessly throw around without the vaguest notion what it entails?

I have a hunch Egypt is the root cause of all this confusion, that "Egypt" is the only name anyone can ever remember and when we say "Egypt" we in fact may mean Jordan, or even Africa. (Someone just broke the news to me that Egypt is in *Africa*—imagine that!) And where does all this leave Kuwait?

What makes it so hard to fathom dispatches from the Middle East is trying to visualize the lay of the land. A map is useless: no two artists are able to agree which end is up. It took me twenty-five years to get a fairly firm handle on Europe and I'm still not sure where Wales is.

It doesn't even help to have visited the Middle East. After four days in Tunis, I still wasn't able to pinpoint which continent we were on (I finally narrowed it down to Europe, Africa or Asia). It's all this indistinguishable desert terrain that causes so many Middle East wars; a king has no idea where *his* sand ends.

What's needed is a way to translate Arab nations into American terms—for instance: How far is it by car from Cairo to Haifa? (Can you make it in a day or do you have to stay over in the Golan Heights?) Does Damascus look more like Miami Beach, Salt Lake City or Portland? Is the Sinai Peninsula anything at all on the order of Palo Alto, on the San Francisco peninsula?

I wouldn't be surprised to hear that even Middle East natives can't tell where they're at half the time. Iran is probably twice as baffling as the Bronx. A man from Teheran who hops an express camel train may well end up in Yemen and not realize it for hours.

Finally, he turns to a lady next to him and says, "Um, excuse me—is this Lebanon or Libya or what? I'm afraid I've gone right past my dune."

Stage Stricken

THE RIGHT LINE OF WORK

THE MAIN ADVANTAGE in being a critic is not, as I was led to believe, my choice of chorus girls but, rather, the many-splendored delight of no longer waiting in line for movies. It's worth more than getting in free—or for all I know, chorus girls.

I would make a lousy Russian. After twenty minutes of waiting in line for potatoes or shoes in Minsk, I'd be forced to defect to some country where the lines are shorter.

Sitting in line for gasoline was a breeze compared with standing in line for a movie. Inside your cozy car, you're sheltered from the elements and, best of all, protected from all of those intense movie-line conversations so neatly parodied in *Annie Hall*.

Before, I would beg off seeing movies by pleading overwork, or weekend visitors, when it was just my slippery way of avoiding the lines outside *Jaws* or *Superman* or any other worthwhile movie; as a result, I went to plenty of awful movies. The lines were better.

Due to this pathological aversion to long lines (or even to medium-size ones—e.g., anything more than twelve people, or twenty feet, whichever is longer), I've had to skip some modern classics, but it's well worth it. By the time I get inside, I'm in no frame of mind for any classic. Either I can go to a movie or I can stand in a line, but I just can't do both late at night at my age (ninety-one).

Standing in line is grueling, backbreaking work, rougher than breaking up rocks. For one thing, there's nothing to do but stand there, whereas on a chain gang at least they have all those nice big boulders to keep you busy.

Your truly ace line-standers are able to bury themselves in *Anna Karenina* or catch up on their crocheting, but I can't concentrate on anything except how rapidly the line is not moving.

There is almost no event I would deem of sufficient cultural—or even prurient—interest to wait in line for, including King Tut. Standing in line to see Tut itself became a cultural pastime. While waiting in line for Tut tickets, people met, dated and agreed to move in together. Outside the museum, they settled down, married and raised kids. Once inside, waiting to examine the actual artifacts, they grew old and crotchety, or died while standing in line at the gift shop.

Curiously enough, I'll gladly wait in line for a hot dog at a ball game, whereas I won't for King Tut, which is a fairly damning comment on the state of Egyptology today.

In New York, I made three honest attempts to see *Manhattan*, but the first-week lines extended all the way to Scarsdale. Standing in line is a finely developed form of masochism at Upper East Side movie houses, where the ushers are specially trained in crowd control by a tac squad. During the run of certain sensitive French films, the use of cattle prods on Saturday nights is not uncommon.

Last week, I threw caution to the wind and got in line for *Manhattan*, mixing with the common folk, none of whom seemed to mind standing in line the least little bit. They reveled in it. People knew each other from previous movie lines, and it was a veritable block party—lots of hugging and giggling and horseplay. These must be the people who drive all day to wait in line at rock concerts, Disneyland, the World Series and Horowitz recitals.

Where there used to be only one line at movies, there are now two—for the haves and have-nots. No greater joy in life compares to telling some poor wretch, clutching an anxious five-dollar bill, that he's been standing in the wrong line.

By now, of course, I'm spoiled rotten and rebel at waiting in line for anything, even behind six people. One weekend, I found myself standing in line for free tickets—and grousing about it.

At a recent wedding, I ducked the receiving line and kissed the bride later, on my own. If you want the truth, I was rather annoyed at not being rushed to the front of the line by a press agent, ahead of some of those third cousins and minor uncles.

OVERBITE SUCCESSES

FILM QUARTERLY has yet to deal with this matter of Overbite in the Cinema. Sexiness on screen—as perhaps in life—depends to a surprising degree on a woman's overbite. It's what makes Bo Derek less interesting than Bonnie Franklin: Bo is sex whereas Bonnie is sexy, and all because of her overbite.

My theory is that certain actresses' entire movie careers can be traced directly to a dental problem, what the dictionary calls "faulty occlusion," whereby "the upper incisors and canines project over the lower to an abnormal extent." Abnormal? You bet. Faulty? Never.

Few men realized at the time that Raquel Welch's appeal was based largely on her overbite. Really. (Also Dracula, but that's another story.) Another sensual overbiter is Catherine Deneuve, whose teeth you probably never considered before. A great beauty, sure, but an even greater occlusion.

Without her endearing overbite, you can be sure Woody Allen never would have even noticed Diane Keaton, nor would we. One of filmdom's classic overbite figures is Tuesday Weld. Even if she *wasn't* called "Tuesday," she'd have hooked us with those perky little incisors.

As for Valerie Perrine—well, she proves the point perfectly, not to mention Faye Dunaway and, for my dough, the Queen of the Great Overbiters, Lee Remick. I once thought Remick's sexiness was based on how her eyelids pull back at the inside corners, but I've decided that, no, it's primarily the Overbite Factor.

An actress has what is termed Nifty Occlusion if her teeth peek out even when her mouth is in the "closed position." Look at most so-called sexy actresses and you'll observe that they don't look like much until they smile. An overbite star, however, looks sensuous even while *frowning,* the prime examples being Jane Fonda and Jeanne Moreau.

Fonda is an interesting case, students. You can't actually see her overbite, but you know it's there because the upper lip stretches seductively over those upper incisors and canines in what we in cinematic circles term "interior overbite."

I was watching Liza Minnelli being interviewed on TV a few weeks ago, and what she said was far less interesting than how the words sort of fought their way past her front teeth, an extreme case of star-bite; see also Goldie Hawn.

Both women have lots of nice teeth, but what makes them major stars is the degree to which their uppers protrude so prettily.

There's a subtle difference between overbite and just plain old buck teeth. Shelley Duvall, for instance, has buck teeth—and very cute they are too—but it's a clear case of buck, not overbite; same with Mackenzie Phillips.

Even such a great international beauty as Sophia Loren owes her success less to her talent and her body than to her little-discussed but ever so crucial faulty occlusion. Remove those front teeth and where would she be?

I would guess that fully 85 percent of the world's beauties are possessed of overbite.

Jacqueline Onassis would scarcely rate a second look on the street were it not for her toothsome quality. Many stars who undergo plastic surgery after forty probably aren't having their eyes tucked or their chins lifted—they're having their incisors pushed.

Or look at Liv Ullmann, a superb overbiter if ever there was. Ingmar Bergman, in an interview he once gave to *Cahiers du Cinéma,* said he didn't care a fig for Liv's brooding Scandinavian sensitivity and ethereal nature. Nosiree, said Ingmar, what captivated him was "du overbite."

The list of overbite stars is endless, ranging from Ali MacGraw, Bernadette Peters and Cybill Shepherd to Barbara Walters, Diahann Carroll and Sally Kellerman.

Believe it or not, gentlemen, it was never Sally's legs, or even her lips. Nope, it was all in the teeth. In "M*A*S*H," she really should've been called "Hot Occlusion Houlihan."

Every so often, a sex symbol slips by without overbite, such as Liz Taylor or Marilyn Monroe, though if you look *very* closely, I do believe you'll find that Monroe had just the weentsiest millimeter of overbite. It doesn't take much.

OFF THE ROCKER

UNLIKELY AS IT may seem today, underground pockets of people still fail to grasp the essence of rock music, so in an effort to open them up to the experience, I went to a Graham Parker concert and can now offer an in-depth analysis of the British New Wave singer:

When Graham Parker first arrived on the pop scene, many rock fans wondered, "Why?" Others asked, "What?" Some people insisted there was no need for another English rock singer at this time, with the British pound being in such sorry shape and all.

Parker, of course, is not just another noisy rock singer—as a cursory listen might suggest, and as some people over sixteen have insinuated. No—his rock roots go much deeper into the American pop tradition, extending well into early Buddy Holly, middle Platters and late Spike Jones, with perhaps just a dash of Oregano (the now-defunct Italian rock band).

There's no doubt that Parker not only has been influenced by recent rockers but has, in turn, adopted many of the traits of earlier pop-culture heroes, in and out of rock. Dagwood Bumstead comes to mind, as do Huntz Hall, Tiny Tim and Krazy Kat.

Is Graham Parker an undiscovered lyric genius, as some have indicated? There are those who compare him, not unfavorably, with Browning. His poetry, though inaudible at first, second and even third hearing, is as witty—in its unintelligible way—as much of T. S. Eliot's best stuff. His oblique literary references and Greek puns are especially dazzling.

When Parker was just emerging as a force in English rock, one of his sturdiest supporters was Noël Coward, who found in him certain traces of Ivor Novello, William Schwenk Gilbert and Tommy Steele.

So Parker is not just "loud," as some claim. He is visceral in a way that makes the listener want to leap from his seat and bolt the auditorium. It's precisely this sort of spontaneous gut-level reaction that one experiences in many New Wave rock performers.

No matter that Parker's words cannot be totally absorbed by the inner ear. No matter that certain clever lines are repeated 36 times when the point might be more succinctly made after only 15 or 20 times.

What matters is Parker's music, a direct descendant of the Funky Blues School of Rock, founded in Manchester in 1976 by the Kidney Stones and popularized by its veteran PA system player, Wes Hager-Smith, who went on to become lead engineer for the New Ripoff Band, which introduced the sound known as "working-class rock."

Working-class rock (or WCR), which Parker so typifies, features 48,000 more amps per guitar than the so-called middle-income rock and is primarily distinguished by a tendency of the musicians to fall asleep at their instruments.

Parker has been with his current backup group, The Rumour, two years—years that have not been wasted by any means, years that have, in fact, seen the tremendous growth of Graham Parker's sound system and groupie collection.

Their sound is a subtle blend of Hard Metal Rock (with a 17 percent aluminum alloy), Little Rock and, to be sure, Pop Rock, with its somewhat more explosive (and yet strangely sweeter) sound than even the old Tootsie Pop groups of the mid-1960s.

Nothing about Graham Parker is merely for effect; everything has its artistic purpose, however obscure.

His indoor sunglasses are a wry comment not only on sunglasses generally but also on Sunglass Rock, best exemplified by the Miami Beach New Wave. The T-shirt beneath his dark suit is a devastating put-down of straight society (and the "Hart Schaffner & Marx mentality"). Finally, the black shoes—a Parker trademark–are an obvious inside reference to Elvis Costello, if not Abbott & Costello.

To depart a Graham Parker concert after only six songs is not a criticism, per se. It is a personal statement, a way of telling the performer (to borrow from one of his best-known lines): "I say 'sayonara' but it doesn't mean goodbye."

RABID FANS

LEO HUBRIS, president of Formerly Taboo Pictures–which makes films on incest, rape and child prostitution–announced that his firm had begun production on a picture in which a St. Bernard encounters a small girl on a lonely ski path and, after toying with her affections, sexually molests her.

It is the first such film to deal with the formerly taboo topic of "dogomy"–or defilement by a rabid beast, usually a dog or raccoon. The crime is so hideous that it's even considered repulsive by primitive cultures.

"Look," explains Hubris, "we've handled the subject in an adult, sensitive manner. We could have shown the grisly details, like a close-up of the dog's face as he undresses the girl, but decided that was going too far."

Hubris adds: "We decided to wait until the sequel to go too far. People weren't quite ready for it. This is strong stuff, sure, but thank God we didn't compromise our integrity."

Accused of exploiting a formerly taboo topic, Hubris argues: "Taboo is the name of the game, pal. Themes that might have sent shock waves through audiences fifteen years ago are now freely discussed in homes and offices everywhere. The nation has matured."

"That's progress, all right," I nodded. "We openly discuss rape and incest around the water cooler all the time."

Hubris went on: "We're gratified that, instead of hiding behind a veneer of gentility, society has reached a point where we may now frankly confront subjects that once made people throw up—and sell a few tickets to boot."

I told him, "Some might say that, in dealing with dogomy, you're just fanning the flames, perhaps pushing certain deranged dogs over the edge, so they'll want to commit similar acts."

"Anyone who would say that would burn books and destroy the First Amendment. We live in an open society, where, to paraphrase Judge Learned Hand, 'Anything goes, kiddo.'"

I asked, "But isn't this an incredibly disgusting topic, even for a frank film?"

"Life is disgusting, may I remind you," smiled Hubris. "We're only reflecting what goes on around us. Don't be naïve. It's no use sticking your head in the sand. Sometimes, yes, it takes courage."

"Well, you've certainly got oodles of that," I said. "There hasn't been a film maker with your courage since Sergei Eisenstein. It must have been hard to treat this taboo topic with restraint."

"Where others might have pulled out all the stops, we've held back," he replied. "For instance, we decided against actually showing a scene where the dog asks the little girl to dance. That seemed too much, even for today's enlightened filmgoer."

"Good for you for exercising restraint," I said. "At least some producers have a sense of propriety."

"Propriety is my middle name, Jack. As I've said before, we only made *Dog on the Run* so people would have a better understanding of this horrible crime and know how to deal with it, as well as learning some of its root causes."

"Oh, root causes for sure," I nodded. "I love root causes!"

"By showing *exactly* what occurs during a vicious act of dogomy, we can better cope with it and perhaps curb it. Many people have but a faint glimmering of what truly goes on between sex-crazed St. Bernards and women—or, in this case, a sensuous twelve-year-old."

Hubris added: "I make movies to enlighten, to educate and, if possible, to amuse. If some animals get off on these films, that's their problem. Our main concern is frank depiction, no matter how offensive or 'obscene.' Obscenity is in the eye of the camera. To some, dog food itself is obscene, but I would be the last to outlaw it."

I asked Hubris, "How do you feel about the twenty-seven other studios who are also making films and TV shows dealing with dogomy?"

"I'm appalled, naturally. It sounds like they're just leaping on our bandwagon. Before we made *Dog on the Run,* we did plenty of soul-searching—we soul-search every day between two and two-fifteen—and decided this film *had* to be made. We didn't flinch from our responsibility."

"It's nice to see somebody's not flinching these days," I said.

SEND IN THE LIONS

THE CIRCUS HAS COME to town and I'm afraid that means clowns.

I am pro-circus but definitely, unreservedly and chronically anti-clown. I knew something was seriously wrong with me as a kid when I was unable to laugh at clowns, as one is obliged to; in all my childhood, I couldn't work up so much as a smile. (It was about here that my future as a critic was sealed.)

Clowns remain my least favorite part of a circus, even though they symbolize The Circus. They're O.K. as a symbol, I guess, as part of the publicity, but in person their act collapses. It's very simple: There's nothing funny about a clown. Strange but true.

At a circus, I can't wait for the clowns to get off so we can move on to the really good stuff involving possible death. Even a train of sad-eyed elephants is more amusing than a pack of clowns laboring feverishly for laughs.

Clowns frighten small kids and make them cry, as they do me. I still fear that a clown is going to accost me in the stands and attempt to get clowny right in my lap.

Tots who wail when confronted by a live clown, grinning hideously, may be less scared than depressed and merely expressing a critical opinion: *get this joker out of here.* (Public opinion could be changing; the words "clown" and "bozo" now mean jerk, with clear-cut pain-in-the-neck overtones.)

Elephants are amusing for the same reason clowns are not—they don't try too hard. The trouble with clowns, first off, is that they look "funny," an immediate downer. Nobody looks like a clown except a clown trying to look funny, or maybe a man with a lampshade on his head. Clowns are sort of professional lampshade wearers.

What made the late Emmett Kelly a genius is that he realized, in his truly comic soul, that acting clown-like was (a) silly and (b) boring, even to certain kids. If I had a kid who laughed at clowns, I'd worry that he might grow up to giggle at Barbra Streisand comedies and buy clown paintings. Kelly went the other way, playing against the cliché—a Flatbush Pagliacci who laughed on the inside and wept on the outside.

A clown can impress me by walking on stilts, or falling off a high wire, but then he usually goes and ruins everything by wearing official clown regalia. Why not a clown in a three-piece suit, or is that in violation of union clown rules?

I suspect clowns rely on props and auto horns to get your attention. They sense that, despite the yellow lips and goofy clothes, they still don't quite make it as comic figures per se.

Is it even *possible* to be funny while wearing a big red nose, baggy pants and a ruffle collar? I doubt it. Clarabelle worked for years to pry a grin out of me, and never succeeded, klaxon and all. Deep down, I felt Clarabelle was a kiddie rip-off of Harpo.

Even so, the clown industry is booming. I sympathize with would-be clowns, however, since they seem to have so much working against them and must realize, sooner or later, that people are laughing at them largely because they're wearing long, floppy shoes.

Only one thing is more sobering than a Bozo the Clown, and

that's an animal dressed up to appear comical (i.e., human), such as monkeys and poodles in tutus and other winsome little outfits.

This is unfair to dogs and chimps who may harbor a mistaken notion that they're funny as hell when, of course, they're just sad-looking clowns, albeit four-legged. It's a mean joke to play on any creature born without an innate sense of showmanship.

If a poodle or monkey ever learned what was going on, he'd immediately throw off his tutu and demand to be given a lot zippier material. The crummiest trick of all is putting hula skirts on elephants—an affront to their essential elephantness.

I feel fairly certain that no veteran elephant, left to his own devices, would be hokey enough to try for a cheap laugh by wearing a grass skirt and shaking his rear end to the tune of "Sweet Leilani." Elephants are cleverer than that; you can see it in their faces. That's a distinctly man-made type laugh—and a pretty stale one it is too, something only a clown would cook up.

THE SOUND OF JARGON

AT THE OPENING OF the new symphony hall, I met the man in charge of acoustical double-talk, who told me that the new concert hall has a natural live resonance but too much aural clutter.

" 'Aural clutter'?" I said. "What's that?"

"You mean you can't *hear* it?" he frowned. "It's so *obvious*. Mainly, it's the woodwinds."

"What's wrong with the woodwinds?"

"They're not aiming their notes high enough to reverberate off the plastic disks. As a result, the middle C's, glissandos and double entendres are going over the heads of the audience—by as much as two feet—and right out the window."

"I trust you can fix it," I said.

"Either we'll have the clarinetists aim higher, or lower the ceiling by twenty feet. But if the clarinets point up in the air, they're going to look like the Tommy Dorsey band."

"What else is wrong with the sound?"

"You didn't hear any 'tuba bounce'?"

"Can't say as I did."

"'Tuba bounce'—or the Crumpacker Effect—happens when the tuba is played so loudly that the notes end up inside the trumpets, producing choking noises from the brass section."

"How embarrassing," I said.

"Not only that, it distorts the composer's original intent if the trumpeters are unable to inhale."

"Are the acoustics too 'dry,' as they say?"

"Too moist—and wrinkled. Also, the flutes can't be heard over the card-playing in the orchestra."

"Not to seem an acoustical dodo, but what do you mean?"

"In the first tier, you can hear cards being shuffled by the percussionist—beautifully, to be sure, but disturbing. Unless, of course, the piece *calls* for 'the sound of shuffling cards.'"

"Can it be cured?"

"Oh, yes. The sound of card-playing, not to mention critics in the rafters, is very common. At the new hall in Pittsburgh, they had to knock off the top half of the building and attach interior 'earmuffs.' This allows for sound to be absorbed if there are too few mink coats in the dress circle."

"How can we be sure of enough fur coats to muffle the tubas?"

"You up the ticket prices so nobody can be seated downstairs in a cloth coat. Otherwise, you create what we call 'warp-over.' What happens is, the notes from the French horns slide off the cloth coats at a 37-degree angle, bounce off the ushers and ricochet into the ladies' room."

"I presume this will be adjusted."

"In time. Sound must be allowed to 'age.'"

"In any new hall, we allow from twenty to thirty years for the sound to cure, as it were. The prestressed concrete becomes 'mellow' and assumes the general properties of old hiking boots. In your newer halls, they're using presoaked pickle barrels. This enables the notes to 'bend' with the curvature of the hall, so the music isn't just heard, but actually appreciated."

"One critic called the hall 'bass-deficient.'"

"That's when one of the bass players fails to show up on time. It happens in even the best of halls. Opening night, we were only deficient by one viola, so nobody could tell."

"Doesn't 'tonality' depend on where you sit?"

"Definitely. For Mozart, I suggest the grand tier. Mahler is best heard in the balcony, rows 11 through 18. Nothing written after 1925 should be heard above the orchestra, if at all."

"Where are the best seats in the hall?"

"I'd say E-43 and E-45 in the top balcony. You can't hear much, but what you get has incredible aural integrity and moral commitment. It's best to sit in a new seat for each movement. That's why they're called 'movements.'"

"Well, it sounds like, for now, we won't be hearing quite the music we *think* we're hearing."

"I'm afraid not. What sounds like Brahms will, by the time the notes finally strike your ears, be closer to 'The Muskrat Ramble.'"

ASK DR. SHOWMAN

TO DISCUSS TODAY'S complex subject–Entertainment Etiquette–I've called on Dr. Nathan Showman, an expert on show business behavior, who will reply to many uncommonly asked questions:

Q. I saw a show in which a singer tried to get the crowd to clap along in unison. I felt silly, childish and yet guilty for not joining in. My wife calls me a "spoil sport." Am I? And if so, how do I get over my nightclub inhibitions?

A. Don't give in. This is simply a shabby showbiz tactic to coax a little easy applause, unbeknownst to the audience. Asking people to "join in" anything soon descends into tawdry pandering to the mob's worst instincts, persuading people they're having a great time when, in fact, they're having nothing of the sort. (Many singers subtly induce applause by clapping on the beat.) In its ugliest form, they will ask half the audience to "compete" against the other half, telling part of the house to chant "da-da-da" while the other side goes "bah-boo-bah." On such occasions, it is perfectly acceptable to hurl pencils, forks and other sharp objects at the performer.

Q. Whenever I see a big star, there's always a dummy who yells, "We love you, Liza!" At a recent performance by Ella Fitzgerald, a man made a short speech: "On behalf of everyone, Ella, may I just say it's a great honor to have you here." Who are these people and why can't the police do something about them?

A. These thwarted, often twisted individuals are unable to express themselves in the normal way, or are just looking for some free exposure at the performer's expense. A glass of ice water usually subdues them, or else a quick, smart blow behind the knees.

Q. Why does everybody who plays a town feel a compulsion to say San Francisco (New Orleans, Chicago, etc.) is his or her favorite city? I'm told that performers go on to Bangor, Maine, and say exactly the same thing. Is this so?

A. I fear it is. In Bangor, however, they take it with a grain of salt. Some people go to shows only *to hear their city lauded. One singer played San Francisco in 1961 and said: "This is among my favorite cities!" She was, of course, never asked back.*

Q. Why do comics always say, "Hey, you're a great audience!" before they begin? For all they know, we're a mediocre audience.

A. Audiences need encouragement. Many spectators are shy and unsure of themselves. An audience likes to know how well it's going over.

Q. Why do so many female singers hold microphones over their heads, tilted down, and sing up into them? Lately, I find I'm more intrigued by mike than singing technique. Is this normal?

A. Quite. Many people have become rabid mike fans. I myself am a devoted admirer of those real slender microphones with the little knob at the end. Any singer who uses one of those has got me in his or her hip pocket.

Q. Why do singers say, "If I *may,* I'd now like to . . . ?" Has any audience ever yelled back, "Like hell you will!"?

A. Oddly enough, yes. There is historical precedent for this odd custom: In the early days of pop singing (1883–1909), people just came out and sang whatever they wanted, without fawning all over the audience. This incensed the public, and in 1909 the whole thing came to blows when a crooner was roughed up for singing "My Old Kentucky Home." Ever since, singers have been afraid to utter a peep without first saying: "With your very *kind permission,* if *you'll allow me, I'd like to* attempt *a song I* hope *you all enjoy . . ."*

Q. Why do singers (Italians, usually) invariably loosen their ties, remove their coats and mop their brows with someone's napkin in the middle of the act? Is it union rules or what?

A. No, it's to show the audience that they're really knocking themselves out, so people will shake their heads on the way out and say, "Hoo-boy, Sammy sure gives one helluva *performance!"*

Q. Why do singers claim every song is their "personal favorite"? Wouldn't we eventually pick this up on our own? Has anybody ever done a song he or she personally despised?

A. All the time. You certainly don't think anyone actually enjoyed singing "Feelings," do you?

CUTTING REMARKS

UNBEKNOWNST TO HOLLYWOOD, there's an easy way to make any movie better than ever—merely by removing some of those scenes that, no matter how nicely done, hold things up. Moments such as these cry out for the cutting-room floor:

Storms at Sea: All that splashing and banging and creaking, with sailors yelling "Lash that batten to the mainmast!" just isn't worth the time and water. One quick shot of a ship in distress could get the point over in a jiffy—plus saving a fortune in pea-coats.

Therapy Sessions: All group therapy scenes, but especially those between psychopath and psychiatrist ("I suddenly felt I was another person"). Even in fine films—*David and Lisa, The Three Faces of Eve*—a few therapy sessions can drive you crazy.

People Traveling from Place to Place: Fifteen minutes of every movie shows characters getting on planes, out of cars, off buses—or, worse, checking into airports, hotels, etc. This is tedious enough in real life. Please, everybody, just *get* there.

Prisoner Talking to Visitor: "You look real good, Frank." . . . "You too, Ellen . . . How's Dad?" Nearly anything involving prisoners is pretty slow going (except daring escapes): filing into the mess hall, meeting the parole board, jogging in the exercise yard.

Fights Between Prehistoric Beasts: Of interest only to special-effects fanciers, or perhaps pterodactyl buffs. Of course, everything set in prehistoric times tends to dawdle, almost by definition.

People Shopping or Buying Groceries: This always looks like it's about to fade into a commercial. Also under the general heading of Whiling Away Time, I include: Walking Down Halls, Waiting in Offices, Holding Meetings, Climbing Stairs, Talking on Phones and Swimming.

Battle Scenes: My basic argument with all war films, up to and including *Apocalypse Now,* is that if you've seen one minefield, foxhole, tank, bazooka, strafing, you've seen enough. This takes in all military maneuvers—war games, drills, parachuting, air shows, etc.

Flashbacks: I kind of like swirly flashback devices, but flashbacks themselves steal time from the *real* movie, especially childhood flashbacks hinting at an early traumatic event ("Hey, you, Bonaparte—how come you're so puny?"). Most maddening are films consisting of one huge flashback: Just when you're all caught up in small-town life in 1908, the movie suddenly pops back to the present.

Fantasy Creatures: As far as I'm concerned, all Munchkin-like people, elves, robots and blobs from black lagoons can take a hike.

Pages from Books or Letters: I can't read at the same pace as the camera panning a page, and am usually so busy deciphering the handwriting that I miss the whole message. If it's a newspaper, I start reading adjoining stories, filler items and headlines, and studying the name of the paper (or some column), which always sounds slightly wrong (*The Daily Times,* "Broadway Chatter").

Prizefights and Horse Races: Even in good boxing films, the Big Fight is always the slowest part, rabid crowds notwithstanding. I can't wait for the match (or the race) to get over with—I don't even care who wins. Auto races, of course, are terminal ennui.

Nighttime: The whole first third of a film like *Yanks* takes place at night—in the dark, anyway—and it seems like morning will never arrive, when things can finally get *moving.*

Childbirth, Shock Treatment, Surgery of Any Kind: Even in terrific movies, say *Gone With the Wind,* childbirth scenes take forever, but pokiest of all are recovery scenes: "Wh-where . . . am . . . I?" "You'll be O.K. . . . Don't move." . . . "Wh-what happened?"

People Eating Dinner: Since you can't ever see *exactly* what they're eating, it detracts from the story, and all you can think about is what you'd like to be eating right now yourself. I suggest using subtitles: "Lester is having veal piccata; Bev is scarfing down banana split."

FEELTHY HISTORY

WITH RECENT LATE-BREAKING revelations about Eleanor Roosevelt, FDR, Joan Crawford, Thomas Jefferson, Babe Ruth, J. Edgar Hoover, Bill Tilden, Ike and JFK, none of our old heroes is safe from scandal. In fact, my own snooping into the past has paid off handsomely in some titillating tidbits I've put together into the first historical gossip column:

HEART AND SEOUL: What really went on at Panmunjom between **MacArthur** and **Truman?** In a recent memoir, the general's personal driver, **Harriet Petkin,** says she had her army cap set for "Mr. President," who was definitely wild about Harriet. HST, she adds, used Big Mac's decision to cross the 38th parallel as an excuse to humiliate MacArthur for stealing his girl. As he repeatedly told the general: "The WAC stops here!"

SWEETS FOR THE SWEET: **Mary Pickford,** America's Sweetheart, had more sweethearts around America than she could shake a hoop-and-stick at. Her longtime secretary, confidante and snitch, **Louise Snaffey,** reveals some letters in which the poor little rich girl tells how she would dress up in urchin's rags and pick up bums and winos on Sunset Boulevard. "It's sad, yes, but her fans have a right to know," says Snaffey, "and they'll find out in my new collected letters, to be published soon–$19.95 in fine bookshops everywhere."

CURRYING FAVORS?: Insiders in India now identify that skinny little guy who frequented Calcutta's red-light district in the 1950s as–**Mahatma Gandhi,** often seen chasing through the streets at four in the morning clad only in bed sheets. No sacred cow, he.

THANK HEAVEN FOR LITTLE GIRLS DEPT.: A British newspaper claims **Lewis Carroll** wasn't the only children's author fond of ten-year-old girls. Also caught hanging around London playgrounds, alleges the paper: **Hans Christian** (*Thumbelina*) **Andersen** and **A. A.** (*Now We Are Six*) **Milne,** both of whom, it sez here, "were into kiddie porn in a big way."

NEVER MET A MAN HE DIDN'T LIKE: **Will Rogers,** the old "poet lariat," had his pet use for ropes, whips and chains–or so **Jed Blinn,** ex-Rogers boot polisher, claims in his book, *Will of Iron.* Rogers, he says, would tie up congressmen and make fun of them to their faces. **President Coolidge,** especially, loved being humiliated publicly *and* privately.

REVERENCE FOR NIGHTLIFE: **Al Schweitzer,** our pick for all-time Top Doc, had a violent streak in his youth and, says a magazine article, once beat up a nurse during one of his bouts of beer-hall carousing. Dr. S. fled to Africa to escape the law and, while there, was sued twenty-seven times for malpractice. He always settled out of court—with his dukes.

INVENTIVE TOUCHES: **Alex Bell** (you know him best as "Mr. Telephone") and **Tom Edison** did plenty of tinkering with male lab assistants, a recent book maintains. Edison's "catnaps" involved more than dozing, and Bell's famed command to his aide, "Come here, **Mr. Watson**—I want you!," was a routine order to ring his chimes. Seems both Tom and Alex were heavily into sexual experiments too.

TRANSCENDENTAL DECAY: The Transcendentalist School of writers, consisting of **Emerson, Thoreau,** the **Alcotts,** etc., was long whispered to have practiced strange sexual rites in its intellectual circle. Thoreau, a known pansexual (one abnormally fond of all wildlife), often dressed up in bonnets like **Louisa Mae Alcott,** whose own random sexual partners included **Amy Lowell, Harriet Beecher Stowe** and **Emily Dickinson.** Concludes **Dr. Horace Wooten,** in a just-published re-evaluation of the Transcendentalist Movement: "Not unlike the Bloomsbury Group, it was dike city."

WHISTLING DIXIE: **Abe Lincoln** was kind to the South, states a new historical work, because he had a couple of Atlanta honeys on the string (one reportedly Creole). The author, **C. W. Vebbitch,** states that **John Wilkes Booth**'s true purpose in slaying Lincoln was to even an old score with the Great Emancipator when Abe began a dalliance with **Mrs. Robert E. Lee,** the belle of many a Northern ball.

INDIAN LOVE CALLS: **Priscilla Alden** (no puritan, this Pris!) wasn't just a casual friend of **Pocahontas** but, writes **Professor Loren Dabney,** they had a liaison that lasted until Alden's death. Accounts vary as to exactly what "went on," says Dabney, "but it was a good deal more than an exchange of Indian pudding recipes."

GRAND OLE BOGGLE

IF NOTHING ELSE, *Honeysuckle Rose* cleared up a question that had nagged at me for years, but which I was too ashamed at the time to ask anybody, namely: Who the heck was Willie Nelson?

I knew vaguely, as I know vaguely who Renata Tebaldi is, but not enough to get by. He wasn't Willie McCovey, I knew that much, nor was he quite Harry Nilsson, who, in turn, is not Harry Chapin.

It turns out that I have an acute case of Country-Western Befuddlement, which grows worse and worse with the almost hourly emergence of a new Country-Western star.

The same month I learned at last that Loretta Lynn is not Lynn Anderson (thanks, in large part, to *Coal Miner's Daughter*), it was time to figure out Emmylou Harris—who, by a stroke of luck, plays a small part in *Honeysuckle Rose,* nicely filling in *that* gap. Seems I'd slipped her into my Bobbie Gentry file.

Two people gave me Willie Nelson albums, but until two years ago I couldn't have picked him out of a lineup of hot new Country-Western singers. Once you fall behind on Country-Western stars, there's just no quick catching up. It was so nice when you only had to worry about Tex Ritter.

It took a TV commercial before I got a fix on Johnny Cash, who wasn't Johnny Nash, neither of whom was Johnny Paycheck, who I thought was the name of a song.

Cash, of course, is the one with the black shirts, the scar and the "family"—but just a minute! Willie Nelson *also* has a "family" he sings with—and, in fact, so does Willie Stargell of the Pittsburgh Pirates.

There should be only one "Willie" in baseball at a time, as well as a much stricter policing of all Country-Western names. This would prevent Kenny Rogers and Kenny Rankin from becoming one big fuzzy Kenny, keep Crystal Gayle and Gale Garnett from blurring and help us determine which is Charlie Rich and which is Charley Pride–aside from the fact that one is black (this should make it a lot easier, but no).

It all began to get out of hand with the basic Hank Williams–Hank Snow mix-up (one of these Hanks is dead, maybe two), and it's not being helped at all by Hank Williams, Jr., who, if you ask me, is purposely trying to create new chaos.

I still can't tell you how many Jimmy Rogerses there have been, one or two. Is the "late great Jimmy Rogers" the same one who sang "Honeycomb"? I have a feeling he's not, but don't bet on it; country singers are a slippery bunch.

Until *Five Easy Pieces,* I lumped Tammy Wynette and Tanya Tucker together; Tanya Tucker remains a ghostly presence to this day. All I can say for sure about Waylon Jennings is that he's definitely not Wayland Flowers, the gay puppeteer.

All the old-time *Grand Ole Opry* stalwarts merge into one singer named "Webb Tubb." I can't separate Merle Haggard from Eddy Arnold any more than I can pinpoint Chet Atkins and Roy Acuff or Roy Clark and Roy Orbison.

The only Country-Western singer I know, hands down, is Roger Miller, but he's almost disappeared, so knowing him is now worthless. What I need to know, desperately, is who Richie Havens is, and how Barbara Mandrell fits into all this.

I never learned the difference, if any, between Homer and Jethro and Flatt and Scruggs, and for some reason I keep mixing up Anne Murray with Phoebe Snow, maybe because Murray sang "Snowbird"–or was that "Yellow Bird"? Murray's the one with a lesbian following, if that helps any; it doesn't.

One of them *is* Canadian, however. It's always nice when someone is Canadian–or, in the case of Buffy Sainte-Marie, Indian, even though I never know if I'm looking at Buffy Sainte-Marie or Rita Coolidge, another Indian.

Country-Western stars I can tell at a glance are: Dolly Parton, John Denver and Glen Campbell. No big deal, I realize, but a start. My goal this year is to learn to distinguish between Kris Kristofferson and Leon Russell.

To help others, I'm devising an International Country-Western Identikit, whereby all the Johnnys must wear cowboy hats, the Hanks will be in neckerchiefs, the Roys all relegated to fringed jackets and the Willies will be the ones with the beards.

ROLE REVERSALS

THE IDEA OF Lucie Arnaz and her co-star/husband Laurence Luckinbill switching roles partway through the run of *Whose Life Is It Anyway?* has caused a complete turnabout in how shows themselves are now being cast.

Producers of the *My Fair Lady* revival are trying, without much initial success, to persuade Rex Harrison to assume the role of Eliza three weeks into the run, and to try Cheryl Kennedy in the part of Henrietta Higgins.

"Some rewriting may be necessary, but not much," says producer Monroe Slatkin, who calls the concept "refreshing."

Harrison, it seems, would prefer switching roles with George Rose, who plays Mr. Doolittle, but Rose's agent has balked, saying the actor is holding out for the role of Higgins' housekeeper, played by ninety-year-old Cathleen Nesbitt, who is actually content with her part. Cracked Miss Nesbitt: "Why can't a man be more like a man?"

Since Mary Tyler Moore took over Tom Conti's part of the paraplegic in "Who's Life?" audiences have taken to the idea of actors trading parts for the hell of it. Claims a producer: "People love coming to a show not knowing exactly who's going to be playing what–it adds to the excitement of live performance."

When *Camelot* opens, Richard Burton may or may not be portraying King Arthur. He could easily turn up at any matinee as Guinevere, or the psychiatrist in *Equus,* or even as King Lear, a role he's long coveted.

No longer need actors feel "locked into a part" for a long run.

Many stars even have it written into their contracts that they may, if the whim strikes them, switch roles during the actual course of an evening's performance.

"That *really* keeps the playgoer on his toes," says producer Manny Martin. "People who might otherwise go home can't wait to return after intermission to see if the star is still in the show."

On the road, especially, actors grow weary of doing the same lines night after night. In Boston, recently, Joel Grey left the part of *Gypsy* and the audience was none the wiser.

When critics learned of the switch, they complained that the public was duped, but the producer insisted it was up to the critics to prove that Grey was not on stage.

The only way to do this is for critics to attend every performance of a show during the run. The New York *Times* now stations stringers at all the big shows on Broadway where name actors may decide at any moment to swap roles. The stringer calls the *Times* drama desk immediately if the star should suddenly turn up in the part of, say, Third Policeman.

Some late-breaking cast changes:

At a recent performance of *Peter Pan,* the lead usually played by Sandy Duncan was taken over by a 280-pound bearded actor, who normally does the part of Nana, the sheep dog. Several playgoers who had paid $30 a seat were overheard to grumble their disappointment.

"Hey, listen, he's flyin', ain't he?" responded the producer when an irate couple demanded their money back. He argued that, since Peter Pan is a boy played by a thirty-five-year-old lady anyway, who cares if he's a fat middle-aged man?

In *42nd Street,* the musical based on the film classic about a chorus girl who goes on for the star, producer David Merrick (ever the sly one) thought it might be fun if now and then a *real* chorus girl went on for Tammy Grimes.

Ms. Grimes was none too happy with the idea until it was arranged for her to go on as the Elephant Man, John Merrick.

Merrick (David, not John) has gone even further, however, by occasionally moving the hit musical to another theater at the last minute. Thus, people who turn up at *42nd Street* often find they have tickets instead to *Mourning Becomes Electra* (or, in some cases, *Morning's at Seven*).

This so incensed one playgoer that he leaped up on stage and took over the part usually played by actor Hurd Hatfield, who threw off his shroud, ran down into the audience and watched his role being played by Lyle Stark, a Patchogue, L.I., milkman.

The star, in return, agreed to drive Stark's milk truck the next day, and seasoned customers along his route agreed it was inspired recasting.

TRADE SECRETS

FOR PEOPLE WHO wonder how a professional critic chooses which movies to see, here is my private set of criteria:

1. The most important single factor is, of course, a *Reasonable Starting Time*. That is: Does it neatly dovetail with my own dinner hour? Is it a nice, even, easy-to-remember time, like 6, 8 and 10, so I don't have to carry a movie page around all day in my pocket? Does the film begin at an hour when I'm likely to be in the mood?

In practice, it works like this: If I'm considering an 8:12 movie, and it's 7:20 but I still haven't eaten, I must skip the picture in lieu of supper, a rather more significant cultural event. Due to this, I have to miss some fine films, but that's one of the hardships of this job. In brief, the movie times must coincide perfectly with my biological clock (a Timex).

2. Is there likely to be *Decent Parking?* "Decent," in this context, means anything within fifteen blocks, which can be determined only by driving past the theater and "checking out the parking situation," an evening in itself. You line up four or five movie houses in a row, with staggered starting times, and then simply go to the picture with the best parking place.

This, incidentally, is why many great films fail to win major awards—they have superb acting, directing and writing, but lousy parking. I still wouldn't have seen *The Europeans* had there not been a parking space right in front of the theater itself, an incredible moviegoing experience!

3. A third criterion for selecting a film is the *Line Outside the Place.* I know somebody who set out to see *The Electric Horseman* and ended up going to *The Goodbye Girl,* which bears almost no resemblance to *The Electric Horseman.* This person had seen *The Goodbye Girl* but there were no lines.

I approach the cinema in much the same manner. If I should see a long line (*and* no place to park), I feel the film probably is of little lasting interest. Often, it takes me months to catch up with a movie. At long last, the coast looks clear for *Starting Over,* although it's in Union City. If there's parking, and no lines, I'm not averse to driving to Reno to catch an old Jacques Tati movie.

There's also the subsidiary factor of the sociological makeup of the crowd waiting in line. If the people standing out on the sidewalk are screaming, stamping their feet and eating hero sandwiches, or contain more than 45 percent of what is termed Motley Individuals, I'm forced to turn on my wheels and flee the area.

4. Another thing to consider in choosing a movie is, obviously, the *Stills Outside the Theater.* I discount quotes, realizing it's easy enough to make *Mandingo* sound like *Gone With the Wind,* but you can't fake those stills, which I examine carefully before making up my mind. It's a crucial moment, for a really dumb-looking still will send me home at the last instant, in time to catch Bob Newhart.

5. Speaking of which, there's the final critical factor of *What's on TV Tonight?* Even a mediocre movie, if it's on TV at 9 P.M., can edge out an Oscar contender. As it happens, all the best old movies are not on TV until 2:30 A.M., and on Channel 27.

A little-known FCC regulation stipulates that "no really great movie can run on a major local station in prime time." The FCC, of course, is in cahoots with the motion picture industry, which pays TV stations to keep all movies off the air between 8 and 11 P.M., starring James Cagney, Margaret Sullavan, Cary Grant, Jean Arthur, Gary Cooper and Katharine Hepburn. Only movies featuring Yvette Mimieux, George Maharis, Silvana Mangano, John Saxon and Horst Buchholz are permitted to be seen in prime time.

RULES OF THE GAME

TO PUT ON your shelf alongside Parkinson's Laws, Peter's Principles and Plutarch's Lives, I offer Nachman's Axioms, an anthology of show-biz truisms:

—A bad show never gets better; it only gets worse.

—If, at 8:35 P.M., the only two empty seats left in the theater are in front of you, one will be filled promptly at 8:40 by a person no shorter than 6′3″.

—Almost anyone can imitate a robot.

—Beware of singers who open with "I Write the Songs the Whole World Sings" unless their names are Irving Berlin or Cole Porter.

—The funnier dressed a comic, the less funny the comic.

—Any singer with three or more amplifiers on stage is in major trouble.

—A singer who begins with "This Could Be the Start of Something Big" is finished right away.

—Try not to sit right next to moviegoers with backpacks, balletomanes in tanktops or playgoers wearing parkas.

—Avoid movies that "introduce" anyone, feature former Playmates or that suggest you read the Warner Paperback.

—Almost anyone can impersonate Johnny Mathis.

—Never date a person who doesn't understand why Bob and Ray are funny.

—God did not intend for bass players to solo.

—When you read over a program at a comedy and see that one of the characters is named "Zeke" or "Myrtle," keep your overcoat on.

—The better the singer, the fewer glasses of water visible on stage.

—People who buy buckets of popcorn always laugh in the wrong places.

—People who laugh in the wrong places always applaud the credits.

—People who applaud the credits always giggle at the rating code.

—People who giggle at the rating code always go to movies with Dolby Stereo.

—People who go to movies with Dolby Stereo always buy buckets of popcorn.

—Never order seafood at any place named "The Captain's Galley"; never eat steak at a restaurant with *'n'* in the title; never try a hot pastrami sandwich where they serve sprouts; never order spareribs at a "bar-b-q-style" place; never eat anything serious in a restaurant where teenage girls in long dresses announce your name on a PA system.

—Almost anyone can tell a Polish joke.

—Two out of three gorgeous blondes don't find Woody Allen amusing.

—The one time in your life that you arrive at a show four minutes late, the curtain will rise precisely at 8:30 P.M.

—Don't discuss theater with people who call musicals "plays" and refer to an intermission as "halftime."

—Any movie in which Bo Derek or Brooke Shields tells Johnny Carson that certain scenes are "only dirty to people with dirty minds," is dirty.

—Avoid all films that involve monkeys, dogs, midgets and Chevy Chase in any combination.

—Warmup acts may be dodged by arriving two days after the published show time. Allow twenty minutes for a late start, thirty minutes for intermission and forty-eight hours for the opening comic.

—Supper club singers are good in inverse proportion to the number of hands grabbed in the audience during their opening number.

–Nine out of ten improv routines fail, and the one that works is part of the act.

–Cartoons from Eastern Europe are not "funny." The correct word is "droll."

–Almost anyone can sing "Sing."

–Entertainers who take drum solos are less versatile than they think.

FESTIVAL SECONDS

UNBEKNOWNST TO SOME, not every work entered in the New York Film Festival is accepted. Here are a few worthy films that just missed making this year's program:

Eci Nannu Quiav ("My Arm Is Long"): A brilliant first film by Pakistani director Ahztjl Brignyii, whose work is an allegorical satire on the class system in his native homeland, as seen through the eyes of a twelve-year-old blind boy, Nhyuiol, and his dog Tige.

Du Poto Peelif ("The Potato Peelers"): A brilliant first film by Lapland's only working director, Tshalj Yngiinb, who sets his story during the final days of the Lapp Revolution, when the country was forced to exist on baked potato skins for sixty-seven days and nights. The film, though harsh, has its wry comic moments, though not many.

Island of the Damned ("Isle of Damnation"): This brilliant first film from Micronesia depicts the rise of a poor family of sugar-cane workers after winning the Irish Sweepstakes. It stars emerging Micronesian actress Flinq Tyruko, formerly a factory worker, as the wise earthmother who brings her family to Chicago, where they are destroyed.

Wutthin Cruleg? ("Where's Charley?"): A brilliant new comedy from Sri Lanka about the coming of age of a young man at a British boarding school not unlike those found in director Ghrywui Pliobi's native country. Pliobi calls this film "a denunciation of English colonialism." The movie begins a commercial release at the Bete Noir Cinema on Tuesday.

My Soul Is Stained!: This brilliant German-Argentinian coproduction by director Adolf Valdez is about the little-known 1886 uprising in Buenos Aires when the bolo-throwers went on strike. This no-holds-barred film, a serious indictment of South American bolo-makers, won the Serious Indictment Cup at the 1979 Pampas Film Festival.

Grifmerz Da Skivski ("Give Them Our Skivski"): This brilliant parable by Nolli Drikniziki, the so-called Father of Latvian Neo-Nihilism, deals with the decadence of the Romanian upper class during Christmas week, 1975, when forty-six bureaucrats failed to report for work the next day. Tragedy followed with it—and with it, this film.

There Is Nobody in Finland ("Jjkllo hui na Muguuvikk Finni"): Undoubtedly the finest—some say the only—film ever to come out of Finland, this brilliant look at twenty-seven generations of a typical Finnish family finally taps the potential of the Finnish film industry, so long dormant.

Bas Esymoo Vattin? ("Didn't We Come in Here?"): A bitter, lengthy antiwar film, this brilliant twenty-four-hour-long documentary of the Crimean War (originally made for Dutch TV) is movingly recalled by some of the remaining participants.

Francine et Francoise ("Fran and Francis"): The most controversial entry in last year's Pan Am Games, this film depicts the seduction of a lovely French schoolteacher by one of her female pupils and subsequent dalliance in the lesbian world during finals week. The film was denounced and censored when it was first shown but has since found an appreciative following. Director Denise Vendome calls it "an honest, brilliant, up-to-the-minute appraisal of lesbianism around the world."

The Pelican Is Rising . . . the Bear Flies High (originally titled "The Bird and the Beast Soar Together"): This film, which caused bloody and brilliant riots in Albania when it was first shown, is an unflinching look at the power struggle taking place in Albania, told in the form of a fable well known to every Soviet schoolchild, though less known to Americans. It marks the return to the screen of director Blini Vorskjnov, last represented by the first part of his trilogy, *The Bear Stumbles, the Pelican Awakes.*

Makin' Out: The only U.S. film entered in the festival (it opens Friday in a nationwide release), this is an amusing glimpse at campus life in the 1950s by director Joel Goldfarb, making his directorial debut–and a brilliant one it is, too. The film co-stars Chevy Chase and Susan Anton as a pair of typical college students at Screw Loose University. (Although *Makin' Out* arrived too late for showing at the festival, Miss Anton will appear at a Wednesday afternoon retrospective, replacing the previously scheduled King Vidor.)

JAZZIER THAN THOU

I'VE ALWAYS BEEN afraid of jazz, which I think of as a secret society that only certain people are allowed into when they've become certifiably hip. Stan Getz sends you a letter.

Listening to Count Basie's band the other night, I was more convinced of this than ever. I was doing fine, until the place began filling up with what looked like *true* jazz fans. Suddenly, I felt inadequate.

Much of jazz's popularity, I suspect, has to do with this sort of hip pecking order. When you're in a roomful of hardcore jazz fans, you sense (unless you're a hardcore jazz fan) that you really don't belong there and may be thrown out at any time for impersonating a cool person.

You can always tell a jazz buff from a phony, like myself, by the way they conduct themselves. Whereas I merely sit there and listen, the jazz buff greets the opening bars of every tune with cries of "Oh, *yeahh!*" and "Swing it!"

They also applaud the beginning of every solo, and at the end of it, plus any fast parts in between–riffs. I mean, Basie himself hardly moves all evening. Nobody's ever told Count Basie about proper jazz-listening behavior.

Your legit jazz buff knows all the names of the guys in the band, so that when Basie introduces his guitarist, Freddy Green, there are fond little swoons. Everyone knows Freddy, and probably Booty Wood, too. Booty's on trombone.

One thing in jazz I do appreciate is the names of the players. For some reason, jazz musicians have the best names in show business. Where else do you find people called Zoot Sims, Cootie Williams, Cat Anderson, Cannonball Adderley and—well, Count Basie?

These guys have worked on those names. If classical musicians were smart, they'd assume nicknames to warm up the public more. Itzhak Perlman is popular enough, but he could work twice as many concerts if he were known as Fats Perlman. Vladimir Horowitz might have widened his audience as "Moody" Horowitz. Even Jean-Pierre Rampal missed out by not billing himself as Pete ("Fingers") Rampal.

You know a man is a jazz aficionado if, as it happened the night I heard Basie, he yells out "Bird!" during a sax solo. Shouts of "Aw-*ri-i-ight!*" further persuade those nearby that you know your stuff and aren't just idly listening.

A good way to make one's fellow onlookers feel square is to bounce up and down in your seat, grinning throughout the entire set. When it's over, you turn to a friend and say, "They sound *real* tight." Or, "They sound *real* loose." It means the same thing. Just to be safe, you add, "They're hot!" (or, "They're cool!")

The big-time jazz buff is sure to shout "One more time!" several times, and is among the first to wildly applaud tunes nobody ever heard of, nodding numbly, eyes shut, shoulders hunching, when the sax player bends in half, blowing notes that sound like dustballs.

I just realized that, in fact, Basie is considered more swing than jazz, which only proves what I've been saying all along—that I'm not qualified to discuss this subject.

QUOTE HOOKS

IF YOU READ enough interviews with celebrities, pretty soon you can write them from memory. In each of these all-too-familiar quotations, circle the unthinkable phrase:

"Sure it's a violent film, but . . ."

(a) "Life is violent."

(b) "Shakespeare and the Greek tragedies are full of violence, too."

(c) "How else are we going to attract drooling idiots off the streets?"

"I won't do a nude scene unless . . ."

(a) "It's inherent to the story."

(b) "I get another twenty grand up front."

(c) "My husband is present on the set."

"We got a few bad reviews, sure, but what matters most is that . . ."

(a) "The public seems to love the movie."

(b) "The Modesto *Bee* called it 'brilliant.'"

(c) "I signed a multifilm deal before this piece of schlock was finished, so who cares?"

"I won't do commercials, but this beer ad is different, because . . ."

(a) "I haven't worked since 1974."

(b) "It's very tastefully done."

(c) "TV exposure is vital in our business."

"What's 'obscene,' anyway? After all . . ."

(a) "Not even the Supreme Court can agree on a definition. To me, war is obscene."

(b) "Everybody loves filth."
(c) "This isn't Victorian England."

"We didn't cancel our birth control documentary because of pressure from religious groups, we merely . . ."

(a) "Delayed it until next spring."
(b) "Couldn't get any stations to carry it."
(c) "Decided to make it more hard-hitting."

"I believe network loyalty comes before financial considerations, except . . ."

(a) "I have my family to think of."
(b) "I need to expand my career and move into nightclubs."
(c) "When you're a star."

"The only reason I'm telling everything about my love life in this autobiography is . . ."

(a) "To set the record straight at last."
(b) "People expect me to be candid."
(c) "Nothing else I've done in twenty-five years is worth reading about."

"Mr. Euripides has left the show as director, because he has . . ."

(a) "Difficulty showing up sober at two consecutive rehearsals."
(b) "Philosophical differences."
(c) "A prior commitment."

"I decided to do a Disney movie over everyone's objections for one simple reason . . ."

(a) "My kids asked me to."
(b) "It's the biggest part I've had in years."
(c) "I've always dug Benji movies."

"All I'd heard about Barbra's/Bette's/Brando's demands is plain nonsense. In fact . . ."

(a) "I've never worked with such a pro. She's/he's on the set promptly at 6 A.M., knew all the lines the very first day and is an absolute dream to work with."

(b) "We've become great friends off the set."
(c) "The SOB hasn't even said boo to me yet."

"We decided on Miss Decolletage for the part of Golda Meir for one reason only . . ."

(a) "She was the best qualified of all the actresses we auditioned in our talent search."
(b) "I've got a silly schoolboy crush on her."
(c) "She impressed everyone here at Universal Fox Bros. with her thorough knowledge of Israel's troubled history."

NOT ENOUGH COOKES

THERE'S NOTHING WRONG with American TV that a few civilized introductions by Alistair Cooke can't help. It's just plain British snobbery, that's what it is. In England, they probably think of Cooke as a sort of Ed McMahon. If the networks were smart, they'd hire Cooke to lead off *their* shows, as follows:

"Good evening. I'm Alistair Cooke for 'Love Boat.' Tonight we join the crew of one of the republic's finest sailing vessels as it plows toward Mazatlan on what, we shall see, turns into a rather perplexing and, to be sure, romantic interlude at sea.

"A brief word about the class system that prevailed aboard these ships. It was considered quite unthinkable, you know, for a crew member to fraternize in any way with one of the passengers. Thus, when aristocratic Purser Andrews sets his cap for the fetching Miss Gratz, the young manicurist from the upper stratas of Burbank society, all of those in the first-class section are, I should say, somewhat alarmed . . ."

The usual complaint against BBC series is that they're "just highbrow soap operas." If so, it might lend American soaps more class if they were politely introduced by Cooke:

"Hello, again. This is Alistair Cooke for 'Guiding Light.' If you've been following our dramatization, you know that young Dr. Pfeiffer has been seeing quite a good deal of the Widow Slattern, causing bewilderment throughout the town of Apple Center, especially in the local hospital, where Nurse Crinoline is having a rather trying time with former Mayor Hoxiter, who has been somewhat out of sorts since being run down by Jill Crinoline's former husband.

"This afternoon, there is a hint of scandal when Dr. Pfeiffer encounters Judge Henry Crinoline in the corridor and they discuss Henry's daughter's girlfriend's abortion. I might add that when 'Guiding Light' was first seen in the States, in 1967, it caused quite a little stir.

"As today's chapter opens, Dr. Pfeiffer has just come out of surgery—but before we begin our episode, it may be helpful and perhaps enlightening to examine for just a moment the state of American medicine in the early 1980s, with a footnote on Clara Barton and the worldwide nursing movement . . ."

Even an ordinary third-rate movie on TV could be given a semblance of respectability with the right intro:

"Good evening. Alistair Cooke here for 'Monday Night at the Cinema Theater.' Before this evening's viewing, permit me to make some observations on the penal system. But, first, I hope you'll further indulge me if I add a few personal remarks on behalf of Putnam Buick . . ."

APPLAUSE, APPLAUSE

APPLAUSE ENGINEERING IS a relatively recent concept in show business—the technique of slyly manipulating audiences in such a way that, often much to their astonishment, they find themselves clapping wildly.

Formerly, people simply applauded at the end of a show and

that was that. Then the encore was invented (first introduced in America in 1914 by Maurice Encore, a French music hall performer and shameless milker of applause), and things haven't been the same since.

Later (circa 1964) Sammy Davis, Jr., devised the second encore; and now third and even fourth encores are *de rigeur* for piano bar singers at Hyatt Hotel cocktail lounges.

The standing ovation has begun to fill the void once occupied by encores. In place of a standing ovation at the close of a show, we now have the *opening* ovation.

Recently, performers have started moving the encore higher up in their acts, running offstage midway through the show, returning and starting over again, then dashing off and coming back for a finale and real encore.

Now there's a stunt I term *pre*-applause, where a singer is applauded prior to every tune as soon as he announces the title. It doesn't matter that nobody's ever heard of the song, if the singer pauses shrewdly:

"Now I'd like to do a number that each time I sing it, seems even more beautiful . . ." Here the band plays the opening bars of, say, "Maybe This Time," and the singer smiles to warm applause. Why, I don't quite know.

Congratulating the audience falls into the category of pre-applause. This is when a star emerges and, before doing a thing, tells us what a "great group" we are. Later, he may applaud *us*.

There's another phenomenon I call *post*-applause, which occurs after the main applause has died down and the entertainer says, "Hey, you were wonderful–really!" This triggers a renewed round of Secondary Applause, a sort of applause for the applause.

Comedians often encourage a hand by thanking the crowd for laughing at a joke even when nobody has made a sound. It's a reflex. After releasing the punch line, they'll fill in the gap where a laugh *should* go by muttering a fast *"Thankyouverymuch!"*

Magicians, acrobats and tap dancers are great applause milkers, since they don't speak and have to rely on body language to cadge applause.

One arm, outstretched, means Mild or Polite Applause. Two

arms held in front of the body, palms up (as though catching a pass), indicates Generous Applause. Both arms spread wide, feet together, with a low swooping bow signals Prolonged Applause.

Traditional applause getters include the mention of any city (state, township, etc.) or any relative in the audience (new wives, grown kids, long-time managers, etc.). Certain key phrases are sure ovations, such as, "Hey, how *'bout* that!" (said of virtually anything) or, "I just did a six-week tour of Europe and, boy, was I glad to set foot back in *this* country!"

Singers are squeezing more than the usual applause out of introductions. In the past, they'd introduce their pianist, but now the drummer gets a hand, too. It's all a ruse to get people applauding *some*body.

Singers will do anything to force a crowd to put its hands together. The old clap-along device is a cheap trick still popular with even the best entertainers. More subtle, but equally devious, is asking an audience to "clap in time," knowing very well that the rhythmic clapping will escalate into applause for *them*.

Last week, a singer thanked her light man who got a nice hand for throwing such great spots. Soon, I expect we'll be asked to applaud the maître d' and photographer ("Yessir, folks, Miss Rose Pingree on Graphlex!").

Each performer at any major room has his patter cleverly punctuated with little applause cues, like so: (1) "Boy, do I love this CITY!" (2) "Hey, isn't this a BEAUTIFUL ROOM?!" (3) "Ya know, I've been playing this hotel for . . . TWENTY-THREE YEARS!" and (4) "And how about this ERNIE HECKSCHER BAND, everybody!"

Well, thanks so very, very much! You've really been a marvelous bunch of readers today.

HARMLESS FICTIONS

THERE'S A MOMENT in *Absence of Malice* when Paul Newman taps someone on the chest with a newspaper to make a point—one of those things people only do in movies. In real life, I've never seen anybody jab anyone in the chest with a newspaper, not even in a city room.

I've made up a list of such Motion Picture Moments, fabled film phenomena that never occur in real life—mine, anyway.

Take, for instance, the famous scene when somebody hurls a drink in someone's face or chucks the entire glass into a fireplace. There always seems to be a fireplace handy. People in movies never throw drinks at hall closets or bookcases. Always a fireplace.

I suppose that people have thrown drinks in people's faces, but not nearly on the scale that it occurs in films and plays. You always sense when it's going to happen, too, and there's nothing you can do about it. It's got so that, as soon as I see a scene that includes a fireplace, I know there's going to be an argument and somebody's drink is going to wind up on the hearth.

Then there's the bedroom scene where the light switches off by itself. The scene always opens in a sort of half-light, but when things get torrid all the lights go off, as though connected to a timer in the man's shoe. In movie love scenes, nobody ever has to get up to turn off the light, put the magazines on the floor and move the pillows around.

I also observe that people in movie restaurants never order dessert. You always wonder what they're going to have, but by the time dessert arrives, they're ready to go, leaving me very unsatisfied. And it's always a ritzy place where you *know* they have great desserts.

I wish the camera would zoom in for a fast closeup of the entrée, which always looks like either hash or applesauce—whether the setting is Maxim's or a New Jersey diner. I spend the scene hunting for clues as to the food being consumed so unthinkingly by the characters.

In real life, people never order so casually ("Whatever's good tonight, Jules!"), and they always comment at some length on the food. In movies, people hardly notice what they're eating. No wonder they skip dessert.

Speaking of restaurant scenes, people in movies always get great tables—even minor characters. Nobody ever gets a table near a noisy crowd, under a ventilator or facing the men's room, the way you do in real life. They always have a quiet table, diners talking in hushed voices. This gives children an unrealistic view of the world.

In a film called *Richard's Things,* there was a terrific sequence when Liv Ullmann goes to a hospital to visit her injured husband and can't find the right ward. It's the first time I'd ever seen this on film. Usually, people zip into a hospital and magically turn up at the apt bedside.

In real-life hospitals, it takes thirty minutes to track down the right wing and the correct corridor, only to find that the person you came to see was moved that morning to a new floor.

Most irritating of all is the ease with which movie people get taxis, especially at waterfront bars at 2 A.M. or right after the theater lets out. The hero just steps to the curb, a cab pulls over and the driver opens the door. Some writing.

SHOWBIZ SPOKEN HERE

SO MUCH JARGON is thrown around talk shows and gossip columns that some sort of entertainment lexicon is needed to help the general public translate into basic English certain obscure terms and idioms from the original native Showbizese:

A singer's singer: Somebody who's never quite made it with The

People, or is slightly too good for them; often called a "song stylist." Mel Tormé and Bobby Short used to be "singer's singers" until they went public, playing big showrooms and doing "Charlie" commercials. Another "singer's singer" is Carmen McRae. There are also "actor's actors" (Kim Hunter and/or Kim Stanley, Shepperd Strudwick, Jo Van Fleet) and, by now, probably even a "car salesman's car salesman."

This cra-a-zy business: Slang endearment for the entertainment world generally; also referred to as "The Industry," especially by bearded screenwriters at awards ceremonies.

Films: Modern term for motion pictures used by people under fifty; those over fifty call them "pictures." Nobody calls them "movies" except moviegoers, or "civilians" (pejorative for paying customers).

An exciting project: Phrase bandied about by everyone in showbiz, meaning virtually anything. All movies are at first "projects"—or possibly "properties"—after they cease to be "deals" or "packages," the past tense of "project." All "projects" are, by definition, "exciting," as in: "Grant Tinker (or Hal Prince, or Francis Ford Coppola) is very excited about this project."

Extremely interested: Prior to Tinker, Prince or Coppola becoming "excited," they must first be "extremely interested," which means, essentially, that so far nobody has said no; used mainly as a plant in the trade papers to get Tinker's attention.

Everybody loved it but the critics: A disaster, bomb or stinkeroo.

Very close personal friend (VCPF): As opposed to impersonal, distant friend, this phrase is applicable to anyone in the Industry, a vast network of Very Close Personal Friends of Sammy who's a VCPF of Johnny, a VCPF of Dinah, a VCPF of Marlo, a VCPF of Barbara (Walters), a VCPF of Frank, a VCPF of Sammy.

Seen together a lot: Showbiz couple sleeping together; same as "constant companion" and "We've loved working together."

Business manager: Star's lover, often hard-core unemployable (ex-press agent, record company shipping clerk, etc.).

We give each other enough space to do our own thing: Married showbiz couple no longer sleeping or even dining together.

We have many separate interests, which makes us closer when we do see each other: Showbiz couple on verge of divorce.

The preview cards were very encouraging: The movie's being recut and now has a happy ending.

The notices in Boston and Toronto were quite encouraging: We have no second act.

Up for the role: Agent has just sent the actor's résumé and photo to the producer's office.

Being considered for the part: Actor has made appointment to audition.

It wasn't the right part for me: Richard Dreyfuss got it.

Taking time out to be with my family (same as, *Looking at a lot of scripts right now*): The phone hasn't rung in a month except for an offer to appear on the National Vertigo Foundation telethon.

Flying to New York next week to meet with some people in the business: Going East to see some Broadway shows and have lunch at Joe Allen's with other out-of-work actors.

I can't say any more about it at this point except that it still looks very, very good: Producer hasn't called back since October.

This show seems to appeal to people of all ages: Nobody likes it much, no matter how old they are.

Limited engagement: A show so great that it has to close right away, much too wonderful to be seen by a lot of people.

Five years in the making: Overbudget by a good $10 million; the director went bananas.

Mixed reviews: A show nobody much liked except Bernard Drew of Gannett Newspapers and a radio critic in Buffalo, N.Y.

You heard the hit song, you read the book, you saw the TV series—now experience the movie: One of the most dog-eared properties in Hollywood, on which the option hasn't quite run out.

A cute show: Your mother will love it; lots of parasols.

Entire production conceived by and under the supervision of . . .: A musical that almost closed out of town until a big enough director could be hired to put his name on it; see also, "Nichols, Mike"; "Robbins, Jerome"; "Bennett, Michael"; "Ross, Herb."

This year's Star Wars: Last year's ripoff.

Excellent word of mouth: A show that the cast's friends can't stop talking about.

A movie you'll want to see again and again: If perhaps not the first time.

Additional dialogue by . . .: The playwright got in a snit and walked off the set when asked to redo the second act.

Breathtaking cinematography: A $4 slide show.

Extended engagement: The composer's mother came up with another twenty grand; see also, "held over" and "positively last weeks."

Winner of seventeen international film awards, including the coveted Greased Palm: They loved it in Zagreb, but no American distributor would touch the thing.

A comedian's comedian: Very big at Friar's Club roasts.

World premiere prior to Broadway: Or Newark, if possible; see also "Zenda," "Kelly" and "1491."

The movie all America has taken to its heart: After a near-ruinous ten days in New York, Chicago and Los Angeles, it's breaking even in Nebraska.

"The Best Film of 1982!"—GLAMOUR: Great coifs.

A multimedia extravaganza: Contains numerous 1970s avant-garde techniques, such as blinking lights and echo chambers.

Marvelous dancing: A musical with plenty of jumping around to take your mind off the plot.

The show all the critics are raving about: If nobody else yet.

A star as demanding on herself as she is on others: Impossible to work with; a real bitch on wheels.

That little film everybody adores: May be spoken of quietly at wine and cheese parties.

Second record-breaking week: Broke the first week's box-office mark (23 percent of capacity) by a solid two percentage points.

An untiring worker for humanitarian causes the world over: Hasn't had a decent gig in twenty years.

Monumental special effects: A movie requiring no parental discretion whatever; may be enjoyed by a first trimester fetus.

This year's Carrie: Next month's HBO.

See this movie with someone you love: The little kid dies at the end.

YOU DESERVE A BREAK

AUDIENCES ARE DIVIDED on many things, but nothing raises more hackles than the sensitive issue of intermissions, which hard-nosed playgoers consider a nuisance.

I'm a rabid intermission-goer. Of course, for critics an intermission is more of a coffee break. You always can count on an intermission. No matter what's being let loose on stage, the intermission is a given, a calm island in the middle of the evening, something to cling to if all else fails.

I even crave an intermission when I'm enjoying myself, as simply a seventh-inning stretch (I could even do with a fourth-inning stretch). My feeling about intermissions is that they're too short and there should be more of them.

Shakespeare wasn't just a great playwright, he was a great intermissionwright. He stuck as many acts into a play as he could get by with, realizing, as a shrewd theater man, that people need several breathers to get through a play, no matter how brilliant it is. A tragedy demands at least two intermissions; a historical play, three; a comedy or musical, one. The heavier the show, the more rest periods.

An intermission is not only a pause in the night's occupation, but a happy hour, a time to trade quips with colleagues and check if all the husbands and wives match.

Best of all, there's no need to review the intermission—except today, but this is more of an homage to a dying art form. You can totally relax, turn off all critical faculties, put away your opinions and behave like a regular person.

Just as plays seem to demand an intermission, movies don't

seem to need one. It's the intermission, however, that adds a civilized one to playgoing. Movies would draw a better crowd if filmgoers knew that they'd be seen at intermission, unable to slink down in their seats all night. An intermission smokes out everyone.

I can't understand grouches who stay in their seats at intermission and won't get into the spirit of the thing. People who say, "Oh, I'll just sit here and read the program," are no fun at all.

Shows that drop the intermission are a shade suspect, as if they're trying to finish as fast as possible. What are they hiding? Are they afraid we'll all leave in the middle or huddle in packs and conspire that the play's awful?

At Yves Montand's show, I felt shortchanged with no intermission. It's like cutting the overture or forgetting programs. It put me out on the street at 10 P.M. with nowhere to go. I'd much prefer milling around the lobby a half hour, if only to avoid the eleven o'clock news.

The more intermissions, the tonier the evening. Many operagoers would prefer forty-five-minute interludes between fifteen-minute acts. Ballet has perfected the intermission and invented subintermissions, called "intervals," which often outnumber the ballets. This keeps me in a most receptive mood.

Intermissions are ruined by rude buzzers that send you back inside just as you've squirmed up the aisle and broken loose. I wonder who decreed that intermissions will be fifteen minutes, which often is pared to a cruel twelve minutes and, in some backward places, ten minutes.

It takes two minutes to push up the aisle, three minutes to shake off people who want to know what you think of the show (it's improper to discuss a play between acts and can put a real damper on the whole intermission), five minutes to order a drink, ten minutes to sip it and a final five minutes to stroll leisurely back inside.

The ideal intermission is thus thirty minutes. That extra five is for glove-hunting, babysitter-calling and a little freelance flirting.

True, this might extend the evening by ten minutes, but it would be a well-spent ten minutes. If need be, they can cut part of Act One, which is always long by *exactly* ten minutes.

SHYING AWAY

WHEN GLENN GOULD, the reclusive pianist, died last week, we lost one of our last great remaining recluses. Or reclusive "geniuses," as the phrase normally goes. I don't know why, but recluses tend to be geniuses or, at the very least, eccentric. Gould hit the jackpot in hermitry—he was a recluse, an eccentric and a genius.

I mourn his passing, not only as a great pianist but, perhaps more crucially, as a great classic recluse. With J. Paul Getty and Howard Hughes gone, with Garbo and J. D. Salinger growing older, about all we've got left is Bobby Fischer, still in his reclusive prime.

We need Fischer to emerge again, even if for only an hour or so, simply so he can go *back* into hiding. As any long-time celebrity recluse knows instinctively, you can't hide forever. Every five years or so, you have to let people know you're still in there, doing whatever recluses do.

So they make what is known as an Unheralded Appearance, often where they're least expected. They do this by letting a few people know, being sure to add coyly, "No heralding, please."

Georgia O'Keeffe was the grande dame of recluses until she came out of the desert a while ago for a show at the Museum of Modern Art. This is the *kind* of thing I'm talking about.

Her semiunheralded appearance was covered by the press, hot for a peek at the aging artist. The media pursues recluses with a passion.

To be frank, I was rather disappointed in old Georgia. She seems to be loosening up a bit in her middle nineties, definitely not the aloof girl she was at eighty. Her standards could be slipping. I'd hate to think she suddenly craves attention. Maybe a PR guy finally got hold of her and convinced her to let people see her, lest she be considered legally dead. You can overdo the hermit bit if you're not careful.

I've long been attracted to recluses, especially famous ones, though I guess it's impossible to be an *unknown* recluse, by definition. Famous recluses work hard to retain their standing in the world of celebrities, because they're both anticelebrity and above celebrity at the same time.

Anyone can be famous, but not everybody can make it as a recluse. Glenn Gould was one of the very few. He retired from the public eye eighteen years ago and, thereafter, was only glimpsed ducking in and out of recording studios.

As befits all great recluses, Gould was afraid of being touched and never shook hands. This is the first symptom that one is on his way to becoming a recluse. Howard Hughes had a thing about being touched, and I bet Garbo does too.

What grabs *us* is that we're dying to know what recluses do when they're reclusing. I envision Salinger gathering wood for his New England hideaway, where he hunches over a typewriter and very, *very* slowly pecks out a story, averaging twenty-five words a week.

Recluses must love all the fuss they create by not courting publicity. You've got to hand it to Bobby Fischer that he hasn't caved in. Yet every two years, Bobby cagily reveals that he's "considering" a comeback. This drives the media bananas.

There's a thin line between being a private person and a plain recluse. Joe DiMaggio is a private person; Irving Berlin is a recluse. If nobody's seen you since 1945, you're definitely recluse material.

Of course, should Bobby Fischer or Irving Berlin do Mr. Coffee commercials, they'd lose their standing overnight and get busted to private persons.